Praise for *An Island Apart*

"Too often discussions of the Brexit referendum dismiss it as an odd political aberration. Fortunately, Spangler provides readers with a witty journey through the years leading up to the surprise Leave victory and the mounting disillusionment with Brussels and the EU. *An Island Apart* is essential reading for anyone who wants to understand the causes and consequences of Brexit."

> —*Mark Field, Member of Parliament for the Cities of London and Westminster and Minister of State, Foreign & Commonwealth Office*

"This is an important new perspective on Britain, Brexit, and the European Union from one of the most insightful and sage commentators of his generation. With wit and rigor, Timothy Spangler's captivating and stirring book reveals how the lofty ideals of the EU at its formation have descended with a thump into a self-satisfied, complacent bureaucracy intent on self-preservation. It is a highly engaging book whose stinging message rings true."

> —*Tom Berger, Former Deputy Assistant Secretary of the US Treasury*

"Spangler writes with style and seriousness. Unlike so many other books on the same subject, this one is unburdened by agenda. Instead, we get an analytical but humorous take on the idiosyncrasies of European politics and society and Britain's relationship with both. This is a very fine work."

> —*Tom Rogan,* Washington Examiner *columnist and "The McLaughlin Group" panelist*

"To some, Britons voting for Brexit made as much sense as turkeys voting for Thanksgiving. But *An Island Apart* reveals the method behind the seeming madness—and what the decision means for the world. I don't know if we'll get a hard Brexit or a soft one, but what is certain is that we now have the definitive book on the subject."

—*Sandro Monetti, CNN International contributor*

"A timely exploration of soft power, realpolitik, and hard-nosed diplomacy during Britain's tumultuous withdrawal from the European Union. Spangler's insights shed much needed light on what will matter to not only Europe but indeed the world for years to come."

—*Stirling Larkin, global investor columnist,*
Australian Financial Review (AFR)

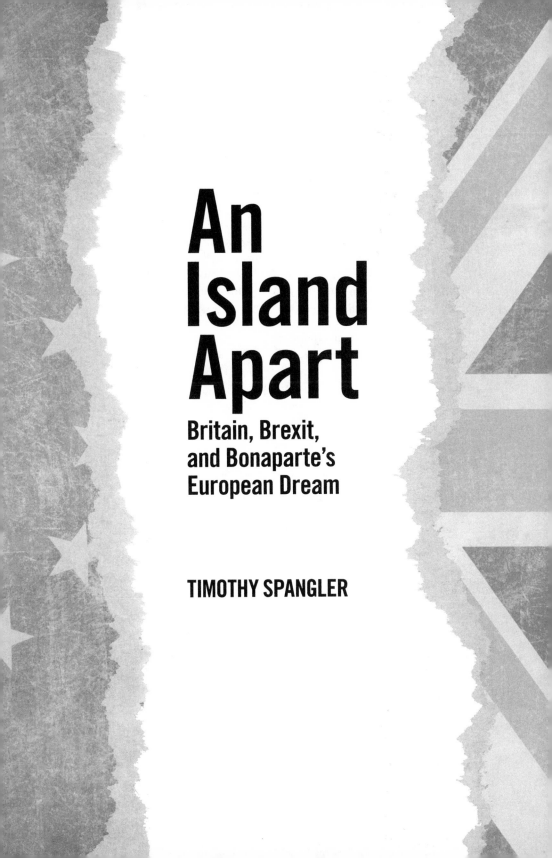

An Island Apart

Britain, Brexit, and Bonaparte's European Dream

TIMOTHY SPANGLER

Cover design by Elmarie Jara/ABA Design.
Interior design by Betsy Kulak/ABA Design.

Printed in the United States of America.

21 20 19 18 17   5 4 3 2 1

ISBN: 978-1-64105-012-8
e-ISBN: 978-1-64105-013-5

Discounts are available for books ordered in bulk. Special consideration is given to state bars, CLE programs, and other bar-related organizations. Inquire at Book Publishing, ABA Publishing, American Bar Association, 321 N. Clark Street, Chicago, Illinois 60654-7598.

www.ShopABA.org

For my three amazing children, who regularly remind me that no matter where in the world we travel, the most important things are to always have a sense of adventure, a willingness to try new things, and, most importantly, the password to the wifi.

Contents

Prologue

*The battle of Waterloo was won on
the playing fields of Eton.*

—Field Marshal Arthur Wellesley,
First Duke of Wellington

Simply put, the European Union is a nineteenth-century solution to a twentieth-century problem. Therefore, the question of whether it can ever be made fit-for-purpose in the twenty-first century is a perfectly valid one for us to ponder. Even the staunchest Remain voters who eagerly lined up starting in the early hours of June 23, 2016, to cast their vote—in Cardiff and Birmingham and Glasgow and Newcastle and Brighton and Richmond upon Thames—for Britain's historic Brexit referendum would have been hard-pressed to argue that the European Union was actually "democratic" in the way that it operates.

It is interesting to note that the most democratic nation in Europe—Switzerland, which possesses a thousand-year history of electoral democracy—has never been part of the European Union. The fact that Britain—with several hundred years of democratic experience under its belt—decided to part ways with the Brussels-based reenactment of the Holy Roman Empire should have come with less shock and surprise around the world than it did when the results of the referendum were becoming clear the following morning.

If we are being candid with ourselves for a moment, the democratic experience of much of the rest of the EU membership varies between "periodic" and "very recent." By contrast, more people voted for Brexit than have voted for anything else in the history of voting for things in Britain. These are important points to bear in mind when we consider the long road to Brexit in the years preceding the referendum.

Whether it's "breaking away" or "breaking up," countries regularly reconfigure themselves in response to important political imperatives of the day. The disintegration of the Soviet Union and Yugoslavia was a direct result of the collapse of Communism, with the former spinning out its constituent parts relatively peacefully and the latter somewhat less so. The creation of Eritrea from Ethiopia in 1991 and South Sudan from Sudan in 2011 are only two recent examples of citizens deciding that their best future lies outside their current political configuration.

Unsurprisingly, Brexit was quickly co-opted on the other side of the pond into the US presidential political brawl during the summer of 2016. For Donald Trump and his supporters, Brexit was an example of populist forces shifting the direction of a country while bypassing a distant political elite that was either unable or simply unwilling to make necessary decisions. For Hillary Clinton, Brexit demonstrated the uncertainties that can result from rash decisions that are motivated by anger and fear, rather than more measured and nuanced responses hammered out with due consideration.

For those seeing visions of secession in the Brexit vote, the most important question is probably when and how people should make decisions about the type of democratic structures they do—and do not—want to be a part of. People making decisions and then changing their minds is one of the key aspects of democracy—as well as such other noble human activities such as buying clothes and dating. These various choices are then woven into a definition of ourselves. This definition will inevitably change over time.

Of course, it was somewhat odd that so many international commentators—including countless American talking heads—reflexively came out as such strong champions of the European Union after the Leave camp's unexpected victory. It was especially odd given how few Americans are able to describe the European Union's structure and operation in even the most general terms.

There exists a significant disconnect between the idealist expectations that observers outside of Europe have developed in recent decades for this supranational behemoth and the mundane contradictions and shortcomings of its various pronouncements—often arriving in a style and manner not easily distinguishable from Franz Kafka's *The Castle*. I decided in the days that followed the Brexit result to sit down and attempt my own portrait of a continent in transition in part to bridge this gulf in understanding.

At its heart, this book is a portrait of the failure of leadership across Europe. The campaign for Brexit put a Remain camp backed by the great and the good of British political leaders across the ideological spectrum against a ragtag Leave team almost completely devoid of establishment players. The primary exception was former London mayor (and eventual British foreign minister) Boris Johnson, who was able to reposition his buffoonish persona, replete with frequent A-Level Latin references, to successfully attack Brussels and advocate effectively for Britain's departure from the European Union and the Bonapartist dream of a reunified continental empire that it had come to represent in the minds of many Britons.

This, however, is not a book about Brexit. It is a book that tells a series of stories about events across the European continent in recent years that laid the groundwork for a growing popular dislike and distrust of Europe's political classes. It is about a vision of European harmonization and integration championed by the great French military and political leader Napoleon Bonaparte, who brought radical changes to the continent, sweeping away the lingering vestiges of feudalism in all of its various guises. Although Bonaparte is celebrated in the popular imagination as an unparalleled general, one of his great regrets as he lived out his last few years in exile on St. Helena was that he fell short of his dream of a "European association" that would have shared a harmonized system of governance, law, and even currency and measurements. He would have looked upon the Brussels' bureaucracy with a paternal fondness—and probably chuckled to himself that Brexit was ultimately for the best!

Although Theresa May quickly replaced David Cameron in Number 10 Downing Street after the votes were counted and declared, "Brexit means Brexit," almost all of the most important questions about what will follow the referendum result still remain unanswered. This book, therefore, will focus on the long road to Brexit. It will recount how sentiments in Britain and on the continent diverged more and more in recent years as neighbors faced common challenges but with significantly different perspectives. It will detail how Europe got to where it was that solemn day in June 2016 when British people decided to once again go their own way.

★ ★ ★

But first, before we begin our tour back and forth across the greater European continent—from the Atlantic Ocean to the Urals—we should pause briefly and prepare for our journey. We would benefit greatly from some context within which to analyze our large and weighty topic. Some experts would recommend a sojourn into the annals of European historical arcana, others a quick recap of economic theories underpinning today's globalized economy. Not here, though. Instead, I would beg your indulgence to spend a few minutes with me, casting a skeptical eye on a prestigious sporting institution.

Sports? Surely there must be a better way of orienting ourselves to the Brexit debacle than an excursion into sports, even if that sport is—unsurprisingly!—"football," or as Americans, Australians, and a few recalcitrant souls still refer to it, "soccer." But what better way to start to appreciate and understand Europeans than by studying their favorite competitive pastime?

Despite Britain's uncontested paternity in regard to the beautiful game, there is perhaps no more quintessentially European organization than Fédération Internationale de Football Association (FIFA), the sport's global governing body. The scandal that finally unfolded within FIFA in June 2015—after years of twists and turns—displayed many of Europe's current leadership shortcomings in vivid and gruesome detail. It can easily serve as a parable for us as we consider in more detail in the chapters to come the long road to Brexit and whether British and European leaders could have done more to avoid the rupture.

In this cautionary tale, we observe that just days after winning yet another term as soccer's untouchable and unaccountable Grand Pooh-bah, Sepp Blatter was forced to submit his resignation. Even with his multibillion-dollar organization in disarray and rumors circulating that he was himself the target of FBI investigations into corruption, the unexpected move still took many by surprise. Observers worried about how best to reform FIFA—a sprawling, opaque, multinational leviathan—to make it fit-for-purpose in the twenty-first century. Comparisons to the European Union almost make themselves!

Blatter's electoral success the prior week ended up being a Pyrrhic victory. He was able to demonstrate to his critics that he had command over his constituencies, but the pressure of simultaneous investigations by US and Swiss authorities provided too much for him. In his resignation speech, Blatter seemed a deflated man. Where was the bold figure who casually deflected and disregarded the mounting evidence that his organization was rife with bribery and dirty dealing? He defensively claimed that he would use the time left to him in office to start the process of far-reaching reforms that the footballing world demanded. After seventeen years as FIFA president, though, it was unclear how much reform Blatter would be able to push through in the final months at his disposal, having pushed through so remarkably little of it previously.

Response from within the world of international football was immediate. Key figures in the game as well as many fans and players expressed their relief that a post-Blatter world would soon be upon us. Not all voices were in unison about Blatter's demise, though. No less a soccer fan than Russian president Vladimir Putin dismissed the anti-Blatter witch hunt as a thinly veiled American attack on Russia's selection to host the 2018 World Cup!

There is, unfortunately, an awkward truth sitting at the heart of the FIFA scandal and FIFA itself. Many people today champion multilateralism and international organizations as far superior to arrangements where the United States wields disproportionate power on the international stage and only a handful of other countries have any effective say on important decisions. Such visions can be enticing. Surely everything would be better if every country had an equal vote!

Sadly, FIFA gives us a particularly vivid picture of what multilateral organizations such as the European Union are capable of when they are awash with cash and free from effective oversight and transparency. Just as we can ask who the ruling elites of FIFA actually serve, we can and should ask who do the ruling elites of the European Union actually serve? In addition, international soccer can also provide us with a particularly interesting window into the passions, prejudices, and privileges of Europeans and their leaders. Hopefully this quick sojourn into the beautiful game will place Brexit in a wider cultural and historical context, making it a little easier for non-Europeans to understand.

★ ★ ★

When Europeans think sport, they think football—the round variety rather than oval. Many Americans would name the New York Yankees, the Dallas Cowboys, and the Los Angeles Lakers as the towering brands of professional sport. But even added together, they fail to have the global media presence and mindshare of a Manchester United or a Real Madrid.

When walking down an American street today, passing teenagers and adults in an Arsenal, Bayern Munich, or Barcelona jersey is a common occurrence. This was not the case ten years ago and certainly not when I was a young boy growing up in Southern California in the 1970s. My memories of watching the 1982 and 1986 World Cup finals on Spanish language television at a friend's house in a barrio a short bicycle ride from my suburban tract home are unique ones and not widely shared. What a difference three decades makes!

One important feature of soccer outside the United States is the frequency of international matchups. Unique and powerful emotions are opened up when eleven men from one country line up on the same pitch across from eleven men from another country. In Europe especially, few cross-border matches can occur without some deep and harrowing reference to history or deep, lingering animosities. The various battles, with their victories and defeats, may be many miles (and years) away from the stadium, but on the night of the match, those memories can rise to the front of people's minds.

My own favorite soccer chant (which also benefits from being suitable for a family audience) is the one frequently heard whenever the Dutch play the Germans: "Can we have our bicycles back?" I am touched that when reflecting back on the brutal and bloody Nazi occupation of their country, the memory surging to the front of the Dutch minds is quite simply the fact that, on their ultimate retreat, the German armies stole all the bicycles of Amsterdam.

"Can we have our bicycles back?"

Nationalism at a very basic level requires comparisons to be made between countries—and their cultural traits, stereotypes, histories, and faults—in order for a particular country to come up as the better of the two. Regular soccer matches between the rivals' national teams provide ample opportunities for such comparisons to be made on the playing fields and in the tabloid newspapers.

Until recently, soccer in Britain and across much of Europe was also very closely tied to class. As the working man's sport, soccer served as a regular focus around which individual and family loyalties could be developed and passed on from one generation to the next, father to son, standing side by side in the terraces. But recent years have seen players rewarded with ever greater sums of money, their teams become the gaudy baubles of billionaires, and the impact of "celebrity status" have a larger and larger impact on the modern game. David Beckham's brief "summer holiday" in the Los Angeles suburb of Carson was perhaps as good an indication as any of the celebrity lifestyle that features so prominently in soccer today.

Regardless of the recent flood of money into soccer and the distorting impact that this has had, the sport's prominence in twenty-first-century daily life is still undeniable. As the founders and codifiers of the game, the British have much to be proud about when reflecting on their legacy here. However great is the reach of the English language, the reach of soccer is greater—even if the United States remains largely excluded from this conversation.

★ ★ ★

The debacle surrounding FIFA's selection of the host countries for the 2018 and 2022 World Cup paints a very disappointing portrait of both international decision-making and European leadership styles. The "secret report" prepared by former US prosecutor Michael Garcia was finally released in July 2017. Investigating the decision-making process for those two tournaments paints a shameful portrait of expectation, entitlement, and disregard of ethical standards.

Allegations of rampant corruption and vote-selling had very quickly surfaced in the days immediately following the controversial decision to award Russia the right to hold the games in 2018, to be followed four years later by the tiny Middle Eastern country of Qatar. In effect, the two bidders with the weakest technical infrastructure won out over the stronger contenders. The clearly articulated standards for evaluating the bids were simply ignored. The three countries that were judged by FIFA to have the strongest technical qualifications—England, the United States, and Australia—received the fewest numbers of votes.

In the vast mountain of WikiLeaks material that was eventually released, Russia was described as a mafia state and Russian fans as notoriously racist. Qatar is a tiny country with a summer temperature exceeding 120 degrees Fahrenheit, where Amnesty International continues to identify serious human rights issues. Rumors quickly began circulating that China was FIFA's preferred bidder for 2026. If true, this would mean that we must look out twenty years for the mere possibility of a potentially fair and transparent World Cup selection process.

The presence of a culture of bribery at FIFA put the credibility of the world's most popular sport at risk. Widespread outrage erupted at the shadowy, politburo-style operation of the twenty-two-member FIFA executive committee. Appeals for root-and-branch reform of the FIFA oligarchy were being loudly made. Unfortunately, there was little clear indication that the current regime would be replaced with a more transparent and accountable one. The line between inducements and bribes cannot always be clear. When intense lobbying meets opaque decision-making, the risk of crossing that line increases exponentially.

Although the direct quantifiable economic benefits of hosting a World Cup or an Olympics are fleeting (if not illusory), the prestige and prominence that comes with being in the global media spotlight is the ultimate prize. Of course, these exercises in national self-promotion are motivated in large part by vanity. The powerful desire of a country to demonstrate its place at the top table of modern life is both completely understandable and totally irrational. Unsurprisingly, individuals in positions of influence often seek to profit from insecurities such as these.

Fortunately, FIFA may provide us with some useful insights of another type of world order and its practical consequences. Decision-making in a truly multipolar world, where no single country is able to play a disproportionate role, may not be as inclined to moralism or legality as many of its champions would have us believe. Perhaps in such circumstances, where no effective referee can be seen to consistently oversee and enforce agreed codes of behavior, we will see instead an environment clouded by corruption and collusion, where secret side deals and pay-offs between nations (and individuals) who enjoy intense, yet brief, periods of importance become the norm.

Such a world may, in fact, not be an improvement on the world we live in now.

* * *

There is a frustrating tendency among many American commentators to see the issue of race in the United States as a template for all racial debates and discussions around the world, as if we possess some moral monopoly on the subject. Many others are almost entirely ignorant of the role that racism plays in other countries, whether in ways similar to or different from the American experience. It is difficult at times to know which perspective is worse.

In the spring of 2011, France found itself in the midst of a sporting scandal that called into question the country's most cherished notions of "equality" and "fraternity." A transcript had surfaced of a meeting between top French soccer officials. These coaches and administrators openly discussed imposing quotas at leading national sports academies for young players with dual nationalities. Although a number of French citizens also have passports from countries such as Spain, Hungary, Germany, and Italy, the officials' concerns centered very specifically on young boys whose parents or grandparents came from North Africa and sub-Saharan Africa. France has a rich colonial history in these regions, and in recent years a steady stream of immigrants had moved from these countries back to France.

The French sports minister, Chantal Jouanno, quickly and controversially cleared the national team coach, Laurent Blanc, of any legal charges under the antidiscrimination laws. Even though racial quotas were clearly and unambiguously discussed, they were not actually implemented. Regardless of this legal contortion, she soundly criticized the remarks made during the meeting, judging them "racist."

France famously won the 1998 World Cup with a multiracial team, which actually included Blanc himself. Apparently, such personal experiences were not sufficient for him, in his current role of soccer supremo, to dismiss out of hand suggestions of racial quotas. Under FIFA rules, once a player has represented his country at the highest level, he is prohibited in the future from playing for any other country. By contrast, a player who represents a country (e.g., France) at "age group" levels (e.g., under eighteen) could go on to represent another country (e.g., Senegal) and play for their national team at the World Cup.

Perhaps Blanc was simply naive and not actually racist. His focus could have been that French money should only be used to benefit players who would eventually play for the French national team. Unfortunately, for a country such as France that still seethes with violence in many ghettos where generations of recent immigrants remain isolated and unassimilated, such allegations can prove incendiary.

In an attempt to address these issues, the French sports minister announced that a committee would be established to fight discrimination in French sport. This committee followed on from a similar panel established the previous year that targeted homophobia. However, wider criticisms were made in the French press that their national team and its management were adrift and out of touch with the realities of the twenty-first century, especially after the high-profile embarrassment of a first-round elimination at the previous World Cup.

Soccer, as the world's game, can be a useful prism for breaking down the issues and challenges that a country faces and making these comparable between countries. In France, the controversy focused on race, but across the English Channel, British soccer bore witness at the same time to a reprise of religious-based violence in Glasgow.

In Scotland, the beautiful game has for the past century sat tenuously atop long-standing Catholic-Protestant resentment and aggression. Recently, this has been expressed only in terms of songs and chants. A longer tradition of actual violence had been fading from public view. However, the line was again crossed in spring 2011 when parcel bombs were sent to the manager of the Celtic Football Club, the historically Catholic team in Glasgow, and other high-profile fans.

Clearly, the stereotypical Islamic extremist bomber has no monopoly on bomb-related violence!

* * *

The summer of 2011 saw the world's game submerging deeper into crisis. FIFA was wrestling with a corruption scandal that threatened its continued stability and success. Sepp Blatter ran unopposed for reelection to yet another four-year term. His only competitor, Mohammed bin Hammam, withdrew after he was drawn into ongoing investigations of bribery allegations. Bin Hammam was suspended after accusations were made that he paid $1 million in bribes to help secure the 2022 World Cup for Qatar.

Many accused Qatar of using illicit means to "buy" their way to host-country status, after a number of other candidate countries, which were better prepared to coordinate and host a large international sporting event, were defeated in the early rounds of voting. Bin Hamman denied any wrongdoing.

Compared to the civil war that was breaking out at the time in Yemen and the uncertainties about whether Islamist extremists would be the ultimate beneficiaries of the Arab Spring uprisings, the question of Qatari bribery and foul play seemed at the time almost quaint. But those passionately idealistic supporters of multilateral bodies like the European Union should examine the FIFA debacle very closely. Unfortunately, the realities of day-to-day diplomacy, with its base motivations and petty rivalries, often bear little comparison to the abstract beauty of academic theory or the morally superior "warm fuzzy feeling" preferred by the shrill critics of unilateral action.

"Presidents for life," who run unopposed for reelection time after time after time, are an uncomfortable feature of institutions not subject to adequate oversight. The standards of transparency and accountability that we have become accustomed to in our domestic political lives often have no direct comparable in the international arena, where far too often idealistic musings, divorced from real-life consequences and responsibilities, serve merely to obscure a variety of sharp practices.

Blatter, who promised to hand out $1 billion in "development funds" upon his reelection, frustrated many of his critics who sought to delay the FIFA election. English, Scottish, and American officials were highly vocal in their concern over these corruption allegations and their desire to see meaningful and effective governance brought to the sport. Ultimately, though, such criticisms often have too little effect in the face of entrenched bureaucrats who are immune to effective oversight. As Blatter flippantly remarked once to reporters, "What is a crisis? Football is not in crisis."

Soccer is not just a multibillion-dollar industry that involves multimillionaires kicking a round ball around a huge stadium to a television audience of hundreds of millions. It is also a game played by men and women, boys and girls, played in fields and schools and humble sporting grounds.

It is the sport played by Bollington United, the Cheshire, England, club. In 2013, its Under 9 team decided that, in order to thank their sponsor—a local Indian restaurant—the players would have their favorite Indian curry printed on the backs of their shirt, instead of their surname. As result, "Tikka" was in goal, and their backfield was made up of "Madras" and "Jalfrezi." Their "on fire" striker was unsurprisingly "Vindaloo."

It is the sport loved and followed by Ander Ung, the Swedish soccer fan who in May 2013 found himself the *only* fan of his beloved team Brommapojkarna to travel to watch the time play away at Mjällby. One of the Brommapojkarna players saw him in the stands, singing and proudly wearing the team jersey, and was so touched by the devotion that he offered to send Ung to the away game of his choice.

Perhaps it is unsurprising that in the money-driven upper echelons of the modern game, the only voices that FIFA too often listens to are those of the multibillion-dollar conglomerates that serve as high-priced sponsors for the World Cup. Adidas, Coca-Cola, and Emirates Airlines eventually expressed concern about the scandal. In the modern game, like in so much of modern life, money talks. Die-hard fans of multilateralism, however, should find this sole potential check on FIFA impropriety cold comfort. But in the absence of real accountability, how else can these international leviathans be kept in line?

★ ★ ★

The best soccer-playing nations in Europe met in the summer of 2012 in Poland and Ukraine for the European Championships staged by the Union of European Football Associations (UEFA).

As always, die-hard soccer fans across the continent and the world followed the fates of some of the world's best teams. A soccer tournament of this size brought with it many risks, such as fraudulent tickets, drunken escapades, and even a bit of "argy-bargy" from the handfuls of hooligans who still travel in search of a fight.

However, potential travelers to host countries Poland and Ukraine faced a further risk—racist violence. The British Foreign Office specifically warned Asian and black Britons to be careful when in Ukraine. A widely watched British news program broadcast a special report on the dangers of racist attacks there. Families of black players on the England team refused to travel to the tournament over concerns about the risk of violence. Former English great Sol Campbell went so far as to recommend to his fellow black Britons to "stay at home. Watch it on TV. Don't risk it, because you could find yourself coming back in a coffin."

Critics complained that UEFA, the governing body of European soccer and in effect a FIFA subsidiary, had not done enough to address the threat racism posed both to players on the pitch and fans in and out of the stadium. Apparently, UEFA bureaucrats failed to see the harm in a few monkey chants or the occasional Nazi flag! Michel Platini, UEFA supremo, even suggested that players would be punished if they left the field as protest against racist remarks or actions. It is difficult to see what such a one-sided disciplinary action accomplishes, other than reinforce the supremacy of the men in blue blazers who purport to run the sport and the lucrative commercial sponsorships that come with it.

Instead of denying the situation on the ground, UEFA should have issued a clear and unequivocal statement to the people of Poland and Ukraine that racism has no place in modern soccer and would not be tolerated. If a player feels that he needs to take a stand against racist abuse, then he should not be red carded. He should be supported.

In the days leading up to the start of the tournament, the Holland training camp in Kraków, Poland, was subject to racist abuse. By this time, even the most diplomatic of the game's administrators could not say that these concerns were imaginary. The Dutch players made clear their anger and frustration at these taunts. In addition, the sole black player on the Czech team reported that he received racist abuse during his first match against Russia. Regardless, Oleg Blokhin, the manager of the Ukraine national team, dismissed concerns over racist chanting at matches and stated categorically that "there is no racism in Ukraine."

Of course, racism is an issue in many countries around the world. To simply assume that any one country has "got it right" and then focus solely on criticizing the shortcoming of other countries runs the risk of sounding as out of touch and unreliable as Mr. Blokhin or Mr. Platini. Fortunately, the overwhelming majority of Poles and Ukrainians proved themselves during the tournament to be admirable and welcoming hosts.

During the summer of 2012, England itself was still wrestling with the consequences of an allegation of racist abuse between two players that cast a shadow over the chemistry and effectiveness of their national squad. John Terry, who has served as captain of England, was charged with racially abusing an opposing player when his club, Chelsea, was playing fellow West London team Queens Park Rangers earlier that season. What made these allegations all the more concerning is that the brother of the allegedly abused player was dropped from the national team, ostensibly for "football reasons," while Terry retained his place.

While training in Poland for the European Championships, the England team took part in a much-reported visit to Auschwitz. The reactions of many of the multimillionaire players who visited the concentration camp were genuinely moving. Hopefully, this visit left these individuals with a more concrete image of the results of dehumanizing racism when carried to its ultimate end.

With the next World Cup in Russia in 2018 rapidly approaching, concerns over the threat posed by well-coordinated racist gangs are still being raised by observers. Perhaps FIFA will use this as an opportunity to demonstrate how much their organization has changed post-Blatter. Or perhaps not.

Prologue

In late December 2015, just days before Christmas, Blatter and Platini each received a block of coal in their stocking, courtesy of the remaining FIFA hierarchy—namely, eight-year bans from the sport. Despite the widespread chorus of "I told you so" emanating from sports pages and social media around the world, the ouster of Blatter and his cronies still came as a shock to many. The surprise was not in that it should have happened but rather that it *actually* happened—much like the Brexit vote that would come just six months later!

As the world's biggest sport stumbled awkwardly forward in the aftermath of these scandals, we can rightly remain more-than-slightly perplexed by the high-handed leadership style and blatant disregard for legal norms that FIFA embodied for so many years. Does an organization so European in its strengths and weaknesses provide an example of the challenges facing the rest of the continent in the twenty-first century?

In the course of this book, I will be exploring many of the conundrums, contradictions, and absurdities facing Europe today, with special attention on the forces that contributed to the seismic shift unleashed by the Brexit vote in June 2016. In doing so, I will attempt to address both serious issues with an ample amount of humor and the more ridiculous aspects with a touch of somber reflection.

There is a tendency by many observers—especially on the other side of the Atlantic—to view Europe through rose-tinted glasses, imagining it as a highly idealized version of liberal thought and progressive values. The reality is of course more nuanced and—at times—much more disappointing.

Much of the populist rhetoric across Britain and Europe today makes reference to a vision of Europe as having declined from great heights of achievement and aspirations. This fails to make room for the far-less-flattering realization that, for several hundred years, China and the Muslim empires were the driving forces of global history. During these centuries, Europe was an uninteresting backwater forced to head west and south in search of empire out of necessity, not idealism or ambition. They were simply denied the ability to go east in search of lucrative trade by stronger, wealthier, and more successful powers.

Europe before Christopher Columbus's explorations was a place of poverty, disease, and subjugation. For example, the active market in Europeans kidnapped and sold into slavery by Muslim traders during the previous centuries has been estimated at approximately one million. When Cortés, Pizarro, Benalcázar, and de Valdivia landed their boats on the coasts of Mexico, Peru, Colombia, and Chile, they were simply fortunate to find locals against whom they had a chance to conquer, rather than be routed if they had instead landed at Quanzhou, China, or Áydhab on the border of modern-day Egypt and Sudan.

As a result of centuries of relative isolation and penury, the history of Europe is a history of a succession of competitive states still managing to construct a common culture based on common values and aspirations. However, the great wars of the twentieth century managed to eventually bring these bickering peoples together and lay the groundwork for continental peace and prosperity.

In navigating the challenges currently facing Europe, we obtain not a gilt-edged road map to a more humane and politically correct future, but rather example after example of the mundane and the squalid, the offensive and the embittered that remain a recurring feature of daily life in the cities, towns, and villages of France, Britain, Germany, Russia, and the rest of the continent. We will explore the Bonapartist tendency that lives on in the hearts of many European officials in Brussels, as well as Paris, Berlin, Ankara, Moscow—and even still some in London!

In short, the purpose of this book is simply to take Europe off its four-point Corinthian white marble pedestal. The breathless way in which an American journalist describes the "magic" of their first Eurostar train trip from London to Paris does frankly become tiring when heard repeatedly over the years. Rather than indulge in lazy exercises in wish fulfillment, we should instead view the continent with a critical (and at times admittedly cynical) eye to see what practical and pragmatic lessons it can teach us. The global financial crisis, which rose to the forefront of public consciousness in the autumn of 2008, is where this particular telling of the Brexit story will begin. A better understanding of the anxieties and concerns that gained momentum in the years that followed this near-collapse will help frame the motivations of many Leave voters who so surprised the world several years later.

1

Human Traffic Jams

*Victory belongs to the
most persevering.*

—Napoleon Bonaparte

Migration has always been a crucial aspect of human history from its very earliest days. Surprisingly few ethnic groups can claim—with any degree of certainty or sincerity—to have inhabited the same location since time immemorial. Movement and exploration are our natural tendencies. The rising and falling tides of prosperity and despair have always pushed individuals—and their extended families and tribal groups—to undertake the risks of migration. The certainties of their known life in their current location are exchanged for the uncertainties (and therefore hope) of an unknown life elsewhere.

In October 2009, Europe again witnessed the inevitable clash between people in motion and the communities and countries that they seek to move across. In a shantytown known locally as "the Jungle," located near the port city of Calais, French riot police conducted a highly publicized "dawn raid" on asylum seekers who were camped in squalid conditions in the often-vain hope of eventually reaching the nearby shores of Britain.

The operation was efficient and effective. Despite protests from sympathizers and activists, French authorities did their assigned job in a matter of hours. Migrants were arrested, and their makeshift tents and dugouts were emptied and ultimately cleared. Heavy machinery was brought in to dismantle all structures and raze the camp to the ground.

Many of the Jungle's inhabitants at this time were Afghans, a visible side-effect of the instability and military activity in their home country. Overall, just under 300 migrants were detained, approximately half being under eighteen years of age. For the French police, battle-hardened from their concurrent efforts to patrol and keep peace in the impoverished and incendiary *banlieues* surrounding Paris, razing the Jungle was a simple and straightforward task.

The French immigration minister, Éric Besson, made clear that his government was serious about its agreements with the British to control the flow of illegal immigrants through Calais—the closest point between France and Britain—and to combat the continuing epidemic of people-smuggling. But how successfully can one-off photo opportunities ever be in resisting the larger forces at work that push people out of their countries of birth and toward the "promised lands" of opportunity thousands of miles away?

It is worth noting here that immigration cannot be viewed as a uniquely American experience. A discussion of immigration (like a discussion of racism) cannot be monopolized by the American experience. As the United States has become increasingly self-absorbed in its own immigration debate in recent decades, the fundamental forces of migration around the world continued grinding relentlessly forward as they have for millennia. The ultimate destinations of the residents of the Jungle were London, Birmingham, and Manchester, not Los Angeles, Denver, or Atlanta.

Of course, no single raid—whether at the Jungle or elsewhere—can ever simply stop the human tide of refugees across the English Channel or any border or frontier. The underlying realities of current events—political, economic, and military—mean large-scale migrations will continue. After the 2009 raid, Jungle detainees were released once their maximum thirty-two-day detention was served. Many (if not most) of these determined individuals returned to rebuild the Jungle again and would rebuild again and again as subsequent Jungles were razed. There they would be joined daily by new arrivals, and together they would all wait for the opportunity to finish their journey to the "promised land" just a few miles away.

* * *

A spiral of violence broke out in the streets of France in October 2010. What began with a series of strikes and industrial actions seeking to paralyze the country and draw the French government back to the negotiating table steadily declined into the widespread destruction of cars, shops, bus stops, and even schools. The cause of these protests was not an unpopular war or an attempt to privatize a vast, national industry. Instead, protesters flooded the streets to oppose the slightly mundane government decision to raise the retirement age in France from sixty to sixty-two.

Then-president Nicolas Sarkozy claimed that pension reform was necessary in order to begin the process of reducing the country's vast public debt. Unions responded by flexing their muscles and filling the streets with their members and sympathizers. One critical element of these protests was their impact on gasoline supplies in France. As a result of blockades and strikes strangling the distribution chain, a third of French gas stations ran dry. Tankers sat in the port of Marseille unable to unload their liquid cargos. French refineries were also effectively cut off. Riot police were deployed to break through these blockades in an attempt to get the country moving again.

France was now at a near standstill. In addition to gasoline shortages, many train and airport services were canceled across the country. Even where flights were not directly impacted by strikes, such as at Charles de Gaulle Airport in Paris, strikers blockaded the access roads, forcing passengers to walk, luggage in hand, to gain access to the terminals and their flights. In a further blow, France reverted to importing electricity in order to keep the lights on, as strikes had eventually hit their energy sector as well.

Students and radicals also lent their voices and support to the unions. Some turned violent, progressing from throwing bottles and stones to tossing Molotov cocktails and burning cars, a favorite pastime in recent years for disenfranchised French youth in the grim suburbs that encircle Paris and other major cities. In one case, an elementary school was burned to the ground by an incendiary device.

Despite this paralysis and surge in violence, opinion polls in France reported that a majority of French supported the strikes and almost 80 percent wanted the government to sit down with these unions and reopen negotiations.

Perhaps many of the violent acts that occurred could be attributed to troublemakers who attached themselves to legitimate, peaceful protests. Similar explanations were offered in Berkeley, California, in February 2017, when the purportedly peaceful protests meant to prevent the controversial Trump-supporting blogger Milo Yiannopoulos from speaking on the university campus was superseded by violent rioting. So much for Berkeley's proud tradition as a bastion of free speech!

However, the scale and scope of the 2010 popular uprising in France was still noteworthy in its own right. Most sensible people would agree that the right to protest is not the right to cause damage or set fires. And the French have been known to overindulge their history of "street theater" over the years. But the vexing question of how to rein in spiraling national debts and balance national budgets is one that many countries around the world are having to address in these years of financial crisis and fiscal constraints.

Britain, the United States, and many other countries will eventually need to also directly confront the effects of their rapidly expanding debt. The primary question at that time will be how effectively the government can put into action the changes necessary to bring their public finances out of the red. But an essential related question will be whether the growing number of unions and special-interest groups that have benefited from years of generosity and overspending will be able to block lawmakers from making the tough decisions that may be needed.

Unfortunately, riots such as these in France demonstrate how easy it is for a short-sighted and self-interested few to take an entire country, and its economy, hostage.

* * *

How does an enlightened, civilized, liberal European country deal with an unforeseen surge in immigration that causes social disruption and public concern? If you were President Sarkozy in September 2010, the answer was simple—you rounded these foreigners up, put them on a chartered airplane, and flew them back to the country they came from.

After a honeymoon period that followed his election, Sarkozy quickly faced mounting dissatisfaction from French voters. In order to reinvigorate support from his traditional political base, Sarkozy set his sights on immigrants and proceeded to take steps that were Trumpian in both conception and execution. First, he ordered the deportation of Gypsies (known more formally across Europe as *Roma*) back to Bulgaria and Romania, where they previously resided. Unfortunately, Roma have traditionally faced widespread discrimination and violence in Eastern Europe, which has increased significantly since the fall of Communism. Roma communities in these countries are not well integrated, and as a result, they have been migrating westward in search of better opportunities.

The stated reason for these deportations was the belief that Roma were responsible for as much as one in five thefts that occurred in Paris—a line of reasoning that candidate Donald Trump would echo five years later on the campaign trail. Many French saw Roma as a nuisance, responsible for trespassing on property and illicit dumping and polluting around their illegal campsites. Since many Roma have no demonstrable means of supporting themselves, these expulsions would be permissible under international law. In a period of great economic upheaval, rounding them up for expulsion was popular in many quarters of France. Sarkozy's popularity even enjoyed a slight bump up in the polls as a result.

Second, the French president also suggested that if foreign-born French nationals are convicted of a crime, they would potentially be stripped of their citizenship. It is hard to imagine what the backlash would be in the United States if an American president suggested the same thing in a 3:00 A.M. tweet (even though the British government actually succeeded in doing just that in 2017, with little public outcry).

Sarkozy was not without some vocal critics. The Roma cause was taken up by many groups, and public protests erupted on the streets of Paris and other cities across France, calling these policies "inhumane" and "poisonous."

In the catacombs of Brussels, well-intentioned European Union officials took a stand against Sarkozy's policies. The European parliament in Strasbourg quickly passed a resolution condemning the deportations and asking that they be stopped immediately. However, the resolution was not legally binding. Pressure was also added by EU Justice Commissioner Viviane Reding, who stated that she was appalled by the actions of the French government and was considering launching legal proceedings against France to stop these expulsions, as they violated EU guaranteed rights of free movement, which are held as sacred and inviolable by all believers in the European enterprise.

Such criticism of a national leader was unusual in the otherwise circumspect and deferential European political circles, especially when directed at a founding member state of the European Union. However, images of police raiding Roma camps and escorting families, belongings in hand, off to buses raised uncomfortable memories for many of Nazis loading Jewish families into train cars.

During this same week in September 2010, the French parliament adopted an outright ban on wearing the burka in public, which passed almost unanimously in their Senate, an action that even President Trump has not yet advocated. Many Americans could question whether the enlightened, civilized, liberal policies of the French government matched up to their recurring, condescending criticisms of US actions over the years.

France began enforcing its strict prohibition on wearing full-face veils (known as a *niqab*) in public in April 2011 and quickly attracted significant attention around the world. The "burka ban" proved very popular among French voters and elicited an enormous amount of hand-wringing and self-critical mumblings among the well-read and well-informed sets across the Europe.

Importantly, the text of the law, adopted by the French parliament after a six-month inquiry that heard testimony from more than 200 witnesses, makes no explicit mention of Islam or Muslims. However, President Sarkozy and his government campaigned for the law's adoption on the grounds that Muslim women needed protection from being forced, against their will and contrary to their personal religious beliefs, to wear a full-face veil. Sarkozy went so far as to call the niqab "a sign of debasement and subservience."

The practical implications of the law, however, were questionable. Estimates placed the number of women in France who wear the niqab at fewer than 2,000. The punishment levied against a lawbreaker was 150 euros and a "citizenship class." Far harsher penalties were reserved for a man who forces a woman to wear a full-face veil. He could be fined up to 30,000 euros and be given a custodial jail sentence. Within hours of the law taking effect, two women in niqabs were arrested outside the Notre Dame cathedral in Paris, where they were engaged in an unauthorized protest.

Critics included both Muslims, seeking to protect their distinct cultural practices, and libertarians, who bristled at the thought of the state mandating what people should and should not wear. Some even suggested that a country that has suffered so much internal disquiet and animosity surrounding its ever-growing Muslim population should have focused on other, higher priorities.

Clearly the law, like most French military engagements over the last century, was almost entirely symbolic. France does symbolism quite well. It is perhaps their last national product that they are able to export in volume.

Police leaders quickly conceded that French police would not engage in high-profile mass sweeps in predominately Muslim neighborhoods, such as Trappes and Vénissieux, where violence has made French authorities reluctant to provoke further unrests. Also, police would not accost high-spending Gulf tourists standing in line to purchase couture fashion, accessories, or jewelry at a trendy Parisian boutique.

What, then, was the purpose of the law? Did police stand in front of mosques after Friday prayers to issue citations? No, they did not. Were citizens empowered to enforce the law themselves by "de-veiling" lawbreakers when they see them? No, they were not. Detailed instructions from the Interior Ministry clearly stated that none of the above was permissible. Regardless, the symbolic gesture was made.

With only one niqabi woman given the opportunity to testify to the French parliamentary commission, little attention seems to have been paid the motivations behind those women who voluntarily wear a niqab. The Quran does not mention the veil, and many theological interpretations of the Quran fail to establish a consensus that it is mandatory. However, several Muslim groups continue to define veil wearing as an element of required religious practice, thereby making any attempt to argue against it a potential apostasy.

Is a niqabi woman necessarily an Islamic extremist? Is the niqab a political gesture, a cultural gesture, or a religious gesture? Is that determination to be made by the woman wearing the niqab, her imam, or her elected representatives in the local or national government?

Many Western nations—including Britain and the United States—pride themselves on their tolerance and their support of religious freedoms. However, a decision to wear a veil is not a simple lifestyle choice of the kind that the mass media and consumer society flippantly champion. Cultural and religious identity is more powerful, and more resilient, than most of the decisions that we make about what we might wear today. A "burka ban" may be too simplistic a solution to the complex and mounting disconnection that has formed between those who look forward with fear and those who look backward with nostalgia. The threat by Islamist extremism is complex and multifaceted and therefore requires an equally complex and multifaceted solution.

*　*　*

Mohamed Merah, the twenty-four-year-old man responsible for killing seven people in the French city of Toulouse in March 2012, was eventually shot and killed by an elite French police unit after a bloody thirty-two-hour standoff at his apartment on Rue du Sergent Vigne. In the end, Merah sought martyrdom by ending his life in a blaze of gunfire, jumping out of his bathroom window to his death with his Colt .45 still firing. He boasted to advancing police that he had succeeded in bringing France to its knees and that his only regret was not being able to inflict more carnage and death.

Merah recorded his murder spree, including the deaths of three young Jewish children whom he chased down and killed at their school, on a video camera strapped around his neck. As one of his victims, a seven-year-old girl, tried to run away, he grabbed her by the hair and shot her callously in the head, before speeding away on his Yamaha motorcycle. Al Jazeera, the Qatar-based news channel, had announced plans to broadcast the gruesome video but soon changed its mind after receiving a wave of protests.

In the aftermath of Merah's death, the French police were accused of bungling the siege and failing to capture him alive. They were particularly criticized for not using sleeping gas to incapacitate him. President Sarkozy stated numerous times that he wanted Merah taken into custody so he could face trial. An autopsy ultimately revealed that Merah died of a bullet wound to the temple from the gun of a police sharpshooter, although he was hit more than twenty times across his body. He had been wearing a bulletproof jacket under his djellabah.

Merah grew up on an impoverished French housing estate and spent time in jails for various petty crimes. After becoming radicalized at Salafist mosques and inspired by horrific videos downloaded off the Internet, he was trained in Pakistan and Afghanistan as an Islamist terrorist. Previously, he had tried to enlist in the French Army but was rejected due to his criminal record. When he subsequently attempted to join the French Foreign Legion, he resigned after one day.

Operating independently, outside an established network or chain of command, Merah was labeled a "lone wolf" and a "do-it-yourself jihadi." The French domestic intelligence service, the Direction Centrale du Renseignement Intérieur (DCRI), was periodically tracking Merah and had interviewed him only a few months before the attacks. During one of his trips to Afghanistan, Merah was actually captured at a roadblock and handed over to US soldiers, who eventually returned him to France. When questioned by DCRI officers, Merah claimed to have visited Pakistan and Afghanistan simply as a tourist. Surprisingly, even though US authorities had already gone so far as to place Merah on its no-fly list, he was still able to avoid being put on official surveillance by the French police.

Unfortunately, lone-wolf terrorists have demonstrated repeatedly in recent years the ability to avoid the surveillance tools and methodologies that have been so successful recently at undermining Al-Qaeda cells and other terrorist organizations such as Islamic State. For all intents and purposes, Merah emerged from nowhere to launch his campaign of terror in Toulouse.

France has prided itself over the years for being a secular country, based on a bedrock of universal values—a concept known as *laïcité*. The traditional expectation had been that newly arrived immigrants would ultimately assimilate these values and take their places as citizens in the French Republic. In recent years, however, France has seen its social fabric stretched and torn, causing many to question how best to address these new challenges.

The hunt for Merah so captivated France in 2012 that even the presidential campaign between Sarkozy and his Socialist opponent François Hollande was ultimately suspended for four days. With Merah dead, however, the fight for the Élysée Palace resumed again in earnest. Sarkozy built his career on campaigns centered on reducing crime and better integrating non-European immigrants into French society and culture. He quickly tapped the vein of lingering concern over future Merahs by proposing new antiterror laws that would make it a crime to view websites that glorified terrorism. Traveling abroad to receive terrorist training would also be outlawed.

Terrorist experts must eventually come to terms with the growing threat posed by individuals, operating without external direction, who decide to launch low-cost attacks with readily available weapons. The horrific events in Toulouse demonstrated the risks posed by unpredictable individual militants, who cannot be traced or tracked through e-mail trails or other interpersonal connections.

President Sarkozy made clear his view that "terrorism will not be able to fracture our national community," but France remained a nation shocked and confounded by the damage inflicted by a solitary fanatic. With Merah's death, his victims and the French nation were denied his trial, conviction, and ultimate punishment. Instead, Merah became a *shahid*, a martyr, which was probably his goal all along. In obtaining his martyrdom on Rue du Sergent Vigne, Merah became an example for attacks that would follow in Paris, Brussels, Nice, Berlin, and London.

* * *

When thinking about Bonaparte and his legacy in Europe, it is important to acknowledge how much the demographics of the continent have shifted in the past two centuries. The emperor had a positive view of Islam and the men and women who practiced the religion, but he could not have foreseen what a large portion of France they have become today.

Even with those changes, it is hard to deny that Bonaparte had an extensive and lasting influence on Europe. Unsurprisingly, Brussels reflects many of the former emperor's priorities, such as an emphasis on bureaucracy and administration, a fascination with legal documentation, and a uniformity and confidence that what they are doing is in the best interest of those they govern.

Some critics may reprimand me for my comparisons of Bonaparte's regime and the efforts by the European Union to bring prosperity and security to its members. Brussels may not have conquered the continent using the force of arms, but the ambition driving the EU project forward is Bonapartist in scope and intensity. It is also an ambition that from the beginning has looked down upon the peoples of Europe in search of an effective way to govern them efficiently and effectively.

Given Bonaparte's ultimate defeat at Waterloo, there is a strong argument to be made that although his military victories were impressive, Bonaparte's true legacy for Europe lies elsewhere. He recognized at the end of his life that his most lasting legacy would be his codification of laws that would eventually become known as the Napoleonic Code, which is still in use today across the continent and around the world. Every new directive issued by Brussels is a tacit recognition of the importance of laws in maintaining and expanding power, regardless of how that power was originally won.

With the launch of his "Continental System"—Bonaparte's attempt to exclude his British adversaries from trading in his dominions—an early step toward the European Union was taken. His approach was in the same vein of protectionism as each subsequent attempt by Brussels to construct a "Fortress Europe" for its member states' benefit. Of course, it is useful to point out here that many historians argue that Bonaparte's Continental System did much more harm to his own French citizens than was suffered by British interests.

Also like Bonaparte, Brussels tends to favor democratic forms more so than the actual roller-coaster ride of democratic accountability. The Corsican general's rise to power has been called "dictatorship by plebiscite." He was generally not opposed to going to his subjects from time to time to get their enthusiastic approval for further consolidation of power in his hands. His elevation to emperor received the blessing of millions of French voters.

But contested elections in which the results are unknown or unpredictable, where the results would radically shift the direction of the ship of state? Neither Bonaparte nor Brussels would have much time for that!

2

Social Distortions

Men are moved by two levers only:
fear and self-interest.

—Napoleon Bonaparte

Pessimism takes many different forms, and the British excel at several of them. Over the past millennium, Britons have learned to embrace a stoic, "stiff upper lip" attitude when faced with a crisis, such as the loss of their global empire and the cancellation of *The Benny Hill Show*. The global financial crisis that kicked off in the autumn of 2008 was no exception. While in America the meltdown of the international economic system led to a historic change in the occupancy of the White House and a far-ranging self-examination over the nature of our recent prosperity and its likely future prospects, in Britain the views being expressed at this time were noticeably more circumspect.

There was no lack of fevered forensic discussions among British "experts" on the possible responses to financial crisis. The details of newly elected US president Barack Obama's stimulus plan—and how it compared to the more modest one adopted by Prime Minister Gordon Brown—were outlined and debated in great detail in the British media. There was noticeable concern and fear and dread about what the future would hold for this small trading nation attached somewhat awkwardly to the continent-sprawling European Union. Britons had much to be pessimistic about.

Americans, by contrast, are optimists when given half a chance. Driven by their optimism—by the sense that things will get better, that they must continue to get better—Americans see prosperity as their birthright. Or at the very least, the promise of prosperity. They are accustomed to believing that as a general rule their children's lives will be better than theirs, that hard work and diligent effort will be rewarded. Clearly, there are many cases where this does not seem to have actually happened (at least not in the near term), but these exceptions often drive Americans to believe in those prospects of prosperity even more fervently.

Is an America without this powerful and pervasive optimism still "American"? To a Briton, this question appears odd, in both its construction and assumptions. Britain's "Britishness" is not based on 401k account balances or the ability to get a "Super-JUMBO" nonconforming loan on a house well above your price range.

When I first moved to London in the 1990s, my British coworkers engaged me in a long, drawn-out debate at a pub near Notting Hill. The question before us was how best to sum up the fundamental difference between these two countries. The conversations lurched from one well-worn set of stereotypes to another, with the expected digressions in the areas of class, race, sports, and cuisine, including, of course, the acceptable range of flavors for potato chips. The existence of "prawn-flavored crisps" always seems to come as a shock to visiting Americans!

Ultimately, and almost by accident, we stumbled upon a quite profound observation that has stuck with me to this day: the difference between Britons and Americans is the difference between "greed" and "envy." In short, perspective. What is the basis of the comparisons I make to my current situation? Do I look at what my life was like some time in the past and then perhaps look forward and form a best guess on what life will be like at a point in the future? Or do I look at the people around me and assess my circumstances in the light of those individuals I encounter as I go about my day?

As I saw, several years later, my British friends and neighbors effortlessly adopt their "keep calm and carry on" attitudes in the early months of the 2008 global financial crisis, I was reminded once again of this insight. Pessimism can be much easier to carry if shouldered quite widely and without singling oneself out disproportionately from the crowd.

* * *

As 2009 wore on, however, it became increasingly hard to resist the notion that Britain was a country once again in noticeable decline. Prime Minister Brown eventually unveiled plans to dispose of $25 billion of government-owned assets in an attempt to make a meaningful dent in the country's spiraling national debt. Dubbed "selling off the family silver" by critics, assets potentially on the auction block included the Channel Tunnel underground rail link (affectionately called the "Chunnel"), the nuclear energy and technology group Urenco, the national gambling franchise Tote, and numerous central government and local government properties ranging from central London–based landmarks to sports centers and parks in the distant provinces.

Unfortunately, much of the high-value assets that Britain once owned were already privatized in the 1980s and early 1990s as part of former Prime Minister Margaret Thatcher's attempt to move the country toward a more market-oriented economy. As a result, little of significant value remained up in the attic to be peddled off in a distinctly gloomy 2009, when markets were soft and demand was low.

With the 2010 general election only months away, British political parties were jockeying to come up with brave new proposals for addressing the country's financial problems. The economic challenges that Britain faced—like those of America and numerous other countries—were still growing and demanded immediate attention. But at a time when British voters should have been looking up to their political representatives for leadership and bold thinking, their members of parliament were mired in a highly embarrassing scandal over their personal expense claims.

High-ranking MPs, including Prime Minister Brown, were accused of violating either the spirit or the letter of the rules concerning the reimbursements of expenses. The fact that the sums involved have been small—what is a few thousand dollars either way?—actually propelled the media furor even further along, giving these salacious stories a particularly petty and demeaning scent.

As history has repeatedly demonstrated, there is nothing that the tabloid-reading British public love more than a healthy portion of voyeurism and the inevitable shock and dismay that follows!

Brown eventually received a letter from the auditors demanding a repayment of almost $20,000. The items covered? Claims made in relation to cleaning, gardening, and related decorations for his own home. Other claims by wayward MPs included items that ranged from the mundane, such as a canvas shopping bag or a candy bar, to the more unique, such as a floating "duck island" for a small pond and "moat cleaning" services.

All three major British parties—Brown's Labour Party, which he took over from his highly charismatic predecessor Tony Blair almost two years earlier, the opposition Conservative Party, and the independent Liberal Democrats—were hit by the 2009 expenses scandal. As a result, a tangible sense of gloom and melancholy emanated from the historic Palace of Westminster, where the British parliament has sat for several hundred years. Given the challenges and hurdles and sundry inconveniences of serving as an MP at the best of times, especially in light of the steady erosion of sovereignty and responsibilities to Brussels with each passing year, it was difficult to see where the next generation of leaders would come from. As former London mayor and wayward Labour MP Ken Livingstone once remarked, "Anyone who enjoys being in the House of Commons probably needs psychiatric help."

Some observers hoped that the 2010 election would lead to an infusion of new blood—of new vision and new ideas—that would reenergize parliament and the government and give Britain the momentum that it required to confront its current challenges head-on. The alternative—simply managing a stately and dignified decline, while maintaining some sense of decorum and propriety—has been tried by Britain before, of course.

The results then were mixed at best.

★　★　★

In addition to political scandal at the heart of British government, as 2009 headed to a close, youth crime and antisocial behavior in Britain appeared to be reaching epidemic proportions. Or so many newspapers and television news programs might have led you to believe. Britons were unsure of how to protect their communities and families in the face of this amorphous threat, leaving the Labour government open to the accusation that it had not done enough over its past decade in power to confront the problem.

Whether in the large urban centers or the quiet edges of towns and villages, many quarters of British society were adopting a "siege mentality" in response to a deluge of brutal, senseless violence by their own children. The sight of groups of teenagers, idly lingering in parks or shopping centers or council estates, was increasingly a worry for nearby residents and passersby.

Whether it was the trend of "happy slapping"—recording assaults of helpless victims on cell phone cameras—or the stark rise in fatal stabbings among teenagers, the effectiveness of the British criminal justice system was being questioned. Of course, it is worth bearing in mind that under British law it is not a crime to kill a Scotsman found in the city of York if he is carrying a bow and arrow. And it is still a crime to wear a suit of armor in parliament. And you could be convicted of treason if you place a stamp featuring the head of Queen Elizabeth upside down on the letter you are posting. So overall pretty strict!

However, to jaded American eyes, which have witnessed decades of gun-wielding, drug-related gang violence, many of the crimes being reported in Britain seemed unfortunate but not unusual or even noteworthy. But among this steady flow of news reports of so-called yobs wreaking havoc on a Saturday night or engaging in minor acts of mischief, increasingly shocking stories were appearing with more and more frequency.

In one particularly chilling case, a mother and her mentally handicapped daughter committed suicide by setting their car on fire alongside a road. They had been subjected to years of sustained and escalating abuse from neighborhood children. Despite numerous attempts to seek protection from police, the criminal campaign against the pair continued unabated. In another case, two young brothers were attacked, abused, and horrifically tortured by two local boys, only slightly older than their victims, despite being known within the community as repeated lawbreakers. Such stories would not have been out of place in Anthony Burgess's dystopian novel *A Clockwork Orange*.

Brown and his Labour Party pledged to address these issues. However, this call to action came two years after Brown downgraded youth crime as a priority, as a reaction to perceived "fearmongering" by his predecessor Tony Blair's previous government. It is a natural, compassionate response to look at young offenders and want to provide them with an opportunity to redeem themselves and another chance at a law-abiding life. On the other hand, victims of crimes and the community at large need to see that justice has been done in each particular situation. The fundamental need to balance these two concerns is just as relevant in Birmingham and Brixton as in Corpus Christi and Cleveland.

In the past, the British actually had a much simpler solution to their youth problem. They exported it! For four decades ending in the late 1960s, the Child Migrant Program operated to transport and resettle overseas—that is, to Canada and other countries in the British Commonwealth—the children of poor families and unmarried mothers. Overall, 150,000 boys and girls were exiled, in some cases under the misinformation that their parents had died. Many arrived in their new country to find conditions of near-servitude and sustained abuse, rather than a fresh start in a new land of opportunity. The British government finally announced in 2009 that it would be issuing a formal apology for its actions and the suffering that resulted.

Hopefully, lawmakers in Britain, the United States, and elsewhere will eventually realize that the problems posed by an underclass of children that are underparented, undersupervised, and underdisciplined are among the most pressing and urgent challenges that they face. Solving these problems would be a good step forward in addressing many other challenges as well.

* * *

The realities of class in modern British life remain a divisive topic, in spite of the word's near-total absence from public debate and discourse in the decade prior to the global financial crisis. The Labour Party, under its "New Labour" rebranding by Blair, studiously avoided referring to "class" in its policies and political manifestos. A senior minister even went on record in the very early days of Blair's time in Number 10 Downing Street to make clear that they were quite comfortable with people getting very rich. "We are all middle class now," was a common refrain in the heady days when "New Labour" dramatically took power from the Conservative Party in 1997.

In the United States, our problems with the concept of "class" are even more profound because of our deep-seated reluctance to engage with it as a causal factor in modern life. The awkward academic-sounding term "socioeconomic" is added instinctively as a reflexive qualifier whenever the word "class" is used. In American minds, the two concepts—social class and economic class—are synonymous and for all intents and purposes are overlapping and interlinked. Few Britons would make such a careless mistake!

The American view of the British class system is one still subtly transformed by the rose-tinted glasses of various Masterpiece Theater costume dramas on television, such as *Downton Abbey*, *Brideshead Revisited*, and *Pride and Prejudice*. The day-to-day realities of class in Britain, however, weave themselves through a range of mundane decisions made each day, including a person's choice of sport, supermarkets, holiday destinations, or simple vocabulary. After the last thousand years of cohabitation in the blessed isolation of their tiny island nation, Britons feel each such distinction has come to mark an important difference. "We" do this, and "they" do that. In fact, the "islandness" of Britain and the self-containment of its citizens are not often fully grasped by the casual American viewer of public television. The two farthest spots in the country are Land's End in Cornwall and John o' Groats in Caithness. From the southwestern edge to the northern top is a mere 870 miles, but Britain has more than 11,000 miles of coastline. Its frontiers are so clearly defined that there is ample opportunity to turn one's attention inward and parse the numerous distinctions to be found among one's fellow countrymen.

When social classes represent a tangible accumulation of real differences in shared language and shared values between groups, attempts to move from one group to another can mean changes on a scale comparable to emigrating from one country to another. The challenge facing Britons is, in part, deciding whether it is better to acknowledge the barriers that still exist and address them or continue to pretend that they don't exist and deal solely with their consequences in individual lives. The battleground where this "class war" is most noticeably being fought is education. The language, however, is frequently coded, with the distinction between private schools and state schools used as a convenient proxy for complexities and nuances of social class in contemporary Britain.

So much of modern life—whether in Britain or in America or in many other developed countries—is based on the assumption that economic mobility is something that all citizens can reasonably and fairly aspire toward. Built into this assumption is the implied presumption that social barriers will not unduly impede true talent from "rising to the top." Education is supposedly the engine for personal transformation, to the benefit of both the individual and the country as a whole. Without this belief in the fluid nature of society, promises of personal-transformation-through-prosperity become empty and meaningless.

Wealth has always found a place in the most desirable and pedigreed English neighborhoods. A Russian billionaire oligarch can have his multimillion dollar Georgian townhouse in Chester Square in Central London. The star player and captain of the soccer team, purchased by this billionaire as a plaything, can have his mansion along the village lanes of Oxshott, Surrey. But the question of when class becomes caste is more pernicious. A few examples of sudden, windfall wealth do not fully address the underlying concerns. Britain is, of course, a country where approximately 70 percent of the people play the state-sponsored National Lottery. A change in your economic circumstances, however temporary, may be just one winning ticket away, but your social class is not so easily discarded.

When social class is believed to grant advantages to some and provide impediments to others, it becomes more important than knowing the difference between mushy peas and guacamole. The "class war" in Britain was, in fact, not over in 2010, as many commentators and politicians had claimed during the Blair years. The decade-long armistice would eventually break down as the results of the 2010 general election raised once again concerns over an upper-class social elite dominating the highest echelons of British life. However, as difficult as the problem of class is to wrestle with in contemporary Britain, it is still a problem that can be acknowledged as existing and in need of solution. The situation in America is, in that regard, much more pernicious.

How can you solve a problem that you are unwilling to even acknowledge that you have? One key element of the American sense of exceptionalism has been that America is a classless society—or the very least, it is where social class has no real meaning anymore. Class can only ever be conceived as economic classifications that change automatically as your wealth and income changes. Would the promise of prosperity and the optimism that propels Americans forward unravel if there were actually barriers and impediments that exclude hundreds of thousands of young people each year from achieving their full potential? In such a world, prosperity might not be enough. And in a world where prosperity was harder and harder to come by, those barriers and impediments might become more substantial and noticeable—perhaps so substantial and so noticeable that an outsider candidate for the US presidency might be able one day to launch a campaign based on a populist uprising promising to throw out the out-of-touch elites.

When Britons voted for Brexit in June 2016, some observers parsing the polling data began to decipher class patterns in the results. Four months later, it would be argued that similar patterns were evident in how Americans cast their vote for Donald Trump or Hillary Clinton. Should America continue trying to imagine itself as a "classless society" when, at least when it comes to voting for president, class is increasingly hard to ignore?

★ ★ ★

By the time the British general election kicked off in earnest during April 2010, a dark cloud of hot air and blinding dust had settled over Britain. The country was at a standstill. The volcanic ash plumes spreading high across the British sky served as an apt metaphor for the recently launched political campaign. With a polling date set for May 6, many British voters felt that although the election may indeed be the most important in a generation, the choices available to them were ones about which they remained stubbornly ambivalent.

The disruption caused by the unexpected eruption of Icelandic volcano Eyjafjallajökull was felt up and down the British Isles. As many as 150,000 Britons were stranded abroad, unable to get home. Plans to assemble a Dunkirk-style, ragtag fleet of privately owned fishing boats and cabin cruisers to rescue British holiday-makers stranded in Spain were even proposed. The plume of ash, caused by the rapid cooling of lava by the ice cap that sits on top of Eyjafjallajökull, was invisible to the radar equipment on board commercial aircraft and posed the risk that jet engines flying through the dust clouds might stall.

Election campaigns, so often imbued with the fiery rhetoric of "greatness" and "destiny," are much more ponderous affairs when the voters must instead make their decisions against a wider backdrop of powerlessness and irrelevance. One result of this national introspection was that the election campaign quickly became a "three-man race." The left-leaning Labour Party, championed by unpopular incumbent Prime Minister Gordon Brown, and the right-leaning Conservative Party, led by Eton graduate David Cameron, were being forced to make room for a third party, the Liberal Democrats, attempting to return to national government for the first time in more than six decades.

The first televised election debate in British history occurred during the 2010 election, only five long decades after the United States originally included them in the campaigning calendar. Largely a bland affair, the debate's only real success was to give the Liberal Democratic leader, Nick Clegg, a surprising boost in the polls, placing him in the lead against Brown and Cameron. Some newspapers went so far as to report poll results that put Clegg's popularity ratings at the level of wartime leader and British icon Winston Churchill.

The human costs of any recovery in the British economy were going to be just as real as the human costs of the financial crisis. The choice among the three major parties—Labour, Conservative, and Liberal Democrat—was simply a choice of how those costs would be allocated among British society and how quickly and intensely the pain would be felt. Voters were asked, in effect, to decide when these essential government spending cuts would occur, either immediately or at some later date when the recovery was further along. Each party, therefore, jockeyed to portray itself as the safest to entrust with Britain's economic future.

The risk of a "hung parliament," where no party has an outright majority of seats, led many observers to fear that a prolonged period of indecision and inertia would descend on Britain just when bold policy choices are required. The "elected dictatorship" approach of successive British governments meant that, under normal circumstances, a party that can wield an effective majority faces little in the way of meaningful impediments from the opposition parties. This would fundamentally change with an electoral deadlock. A hung parliament might be satisfying to disgruntled voters as a sardonic "none of the above" option, but Britain had little experience with such a volatile electoral outcome.

The future can be a very scary thing. When it comes to the political and economic future of an entire country, the fear is magnified and distorted, like in a series of fun-house mirrors. In 2010, change seemed inevitable for Britain, although it remained frustratingly unclear what form such change would take or whether in the short term it would be change for the better or change for the worse.

★ ★ ★

When the ballots were counted in the days that followed the 2010 election, the message from the British people was clear—change. But the questions of direction and priorities remained frustratingly unclear.

As violent rioting continued in Greece and further economic malaise descended on Europe, Britain had a "hung parliament," with no party having an overall majority. Elections around the world routinely threw up odd and ineffective results. The memory of the 2000 US presidential election is still painfully vivid to this day in many Americans' memories. Until the 2010 general election, however, the British voters had routinely given the victorious party enough of a clear mandate to govern effectively.

Brown was given a humiliating rejection by the voters, with his Labour Party losing a third of its seats in the House of Commons. At the same time, Cameron and his opposition Conservatives saw their seats increase by almost half, leaving them as the largest party and, comfortingly, also the party that received the largest share of the vote. The insurgent third party, the Liberal Democrats, failed to capitalize on its media successes in recent weeks and finished down a few seats. But in a hung parliament, the Liberal Democrats held the keys to Number 10 Downing Street, the prime minister's residence. Whether Cameron or Brown would successfully claim them depended in part on how well they were able to reach an effective compromise with the idealistic, and mercurial, Liberals. Both Cameron and Brown made clear that they were willing to "do a deal."

While the British people awaited the outcome of these "backroom negotiations" and the Liberals enjoyed their new role as "king-maker," the currency markets punished the pound. Investors crave certainty. Weak leadership in government leads to nervous investors selling off their British assets and voting with their financial feet.

The fear shared by many at this time was that the British public finances were in such bad shape that a Greece-like debacle was possible. Surprisingly, after sixteen years of growth, Britain found itself almost entirely unprepared for the global financial crisis. Public spending skyrocketed during the Labour years and little was set aside for the proverbial "rainy day." In a great example of the black humor of which Britons are so fond, Labour's outgoing chief secretary of the treasury, Liam Byrne, was kind enough to leave a short personal note for his successor, the Liberal Democrat David Laws:

Dear Chief Secretary,
I'm afraid to tell there's no money left.
Kind regards and good luck!

Liam

How thoughtful!

Despite increased voter turnout for this election and widespread coverage of the televised prime minister debates in the weeks prior to voting, a malaise remained in many sections of the British electorate. A growing number of Britons were voicing their distaste with their country's entire political structure, from the Victorian era polling booths, with the pen-and-ink "X" in the box ballots, to the lopsided constituencies, which vary significantly in the number of voters, to the lingering anger that was unleashed by the expenses scandal described earlier, where their national representatives were filing expense claims for plasma screen TVs and "duck islands."

The coming years would prove challenging for all the British political parties, as they attempted to establish a solid government that could calm the worries of the financial markets, while at the same time galvanizing the British people to accept and undertake the great sacrifices that lay ahead for them. The smug comfort of the first two-and-a-half terms of the incumbent Labour's government now seemed a very, very long way away.

And in one of those small ironies that can often go by unnoticed, this British election was held on the birthday of the former Labour prime minister, Tony Blair. After his three resounding election victories, the poor results for his Labour Party in the 2010 election must have made for a bitter birthday present.

3

Go Along, Get Along

*History is a set of lies
agreed upon.*

—Napoleon Bonaparte

Europeans have become over the years used to looking to California—the Golden State!—for inspiration and guidance. In the past, perhaps, this has been more often in the areas of entertainment choices or fashion icons or lifestyle options. In May 2009, however, it was the economic crisis that engulfed the California state budget process and the setback at the polls suffered by Governor Arnold Schwarzenegger that had attracted attention. The drama of controversial referendums and the monumental tasks that lay unresolved in Sacramento struck a chord across many member states of the European Union.

If the question on some Americans' lips at this time was when the solution to California's problems ultimately becomes one emanating from the federal capital of Washington rather than the state capital of Sacramento, then Brussels, the home of the European Commission and the governing organs of the European Union, was taking notes. Just as taxpayers and their duly elected representatives in Virginia, Idaho, and New Hampshire may be reluctant to put the full faith and credit of the federal purse behind profligate California, how difficult will it be to corral the Dutch, French, Germans, Britons, and others—who (at least relatively!) can claim some measure of fiscal self-restraint in recent years—when the need arises to reduce the financial pressure building up at this time on Ireland, Italy, and Greece?

The United States benefits from more than 230 years of experience in how best to negotiate the limits of state sovereignty (and responsibility) in the face of overarching national concerns. When is it right to bring the weight of an entire nation to address the shortcomings and challenges of an individual state? Given the porous borders between each individual state and the single economic engine of interstate commerce (for which the federal government has responsibility under our Constitution to police and maintain), at some point a purely local difficulty (such as California's eye-watering $21 billion deficit) becomes an issue of national policy.

From Europe's perspective, with the training wheels only recently removed from their shiny new single currency—the eponymous euro—and only a few decades of experience in their proto-federalist experiment under their belt, the challenges they would face in addressing a wayward member state were just as dramatic as posed by California's situation in 2009. However, the European Union lacked the depth of collective experience—and perhaps affinity and affection between their citizens—to shoulder the tough decisions ahead that the United States possessed.

If Spain were unable to pay interest on its sovereign debt, when would the other European member states step in? To "sit out" that round would almost certainly force the abandonment of the euro and set back perhaps permanently the dreams of a "United States of Europe."

Would old enmities raise their woolly heads? The purpose of the European Union has been to put the prospect of war within Europe, waged by Europeans, beyond the realm of possibility. But when does a fiscal bailout become simply war by another means? As anyone who has attended an international soccer match between the national teams of any two European countries can easily attest, beneath a thin coat of EU paint lies the unvarnished soul of patriotic sentiment for one's country.

Fortunately, some might argue, Europeans do not suffer from the "excess of democracy" that California does, courtesy of its generous referendum system. Equally true, though, is that the decades' old criticism of the EU's highly decentralized and collectivist governance structure—"Who do I call when I want to speak to Europe?"—remains valid. While referendums, for example, have a very particular role to play under the California Constitution, its role in Europe has been limited and vague, at least until the results of the Brexit vote were announced in June 2016.

An attempt to intervene and resolve a crisis of Californian magnitude that erupted along the Mediterranean or North Sea coasts would not be based on a relative small number of decisions made in Brussels. Instead, political machinations of a much vaster scale would be required. In the grandest European traditions, the convoluted path would necessarily veer between the Hobbesian and the Machiavellian, before ultimately being resolved in a last-minute deal brokered by a cabal of French dairy farmers.

But that is the European way!

* * *

As the global financial crisis continued to drag on into 2010, Europe found itself under siege, but from a very unlikely source.

The most potent symbol of European unity in the modern era—the euro—was under mounting threat in February 2010. The engine of European integration has historically been the French-German nexus, and the perennial stumbling block to these federal dreams has typically been their common foe, the British. However, by this time, attention was turning to the outer periphery of the European Union. The small country of Greece, rich in history but unfortunately very highly indebted by most other measures, was at the brink of breaking the euro and putting an end to the currency union that has been decades in the making. As every schoolchild knows, a chain is only as strong as its weakest link.

For many Europeans in 2010, the euro now meant Europe—it had come to represent, tangibly in their day-to-day lives, the accumulative reality of decades of integration with their neighbors. But the benefits of the euro did not come for free. The price of maintaining it has been for many European countries a stubborn willingness to forgo the eye-watering stimulus packages that were seen in the United States, Britain, and elsewhere during the first several months of the global financial crisis.

However, the budget discipline being demonstrated in other countries within the euro-zone was conspicuously absent in Greece. Huge national debt, and huge annual budget deficits, led Greece to the point of crisis. Greek civil servants of various stripes and grades were on the streets protesting the implementation of proposed austerity measures. Meanwhile, the sixteen euro-zone finance ministers were attempting to launch a coordinated, multifront defensive maneuver to prop up their languishing ally.

The euro was originally meant to be simply a monetary union, not a fiscal union. The ability to tax remained intentionally and unambiguously with each individual member state. Unfortunately, in the face of mounting crisis and uncertainty, by 2010 swift political action was required by the euro-zone governments. The fear of "contagion" was rapidly spreading across the continent. The other so-called PIGS (the headline-friendly acronym that groups together Portugal, Italy, Greece, and Spain) countries feared that any one of them could fall quickly and ingloriously if the markets moved against them. Since much of their debt was provided by French and German banks, the fate of these wealthy, well-behaved countries was inextricable intertwined with the overall financial health of their profligate southern neighbors.

Questions were also being raised at this time about whether more Greek debt had been hidden within complex financial derivatives and currency swap contracts. In the absence of clear and definitive answers, fear grows and concern spreads. Currency speculators, whether based in the tall glass towers of investment banks or the discreet offices of hedge funds, were increasing their bets against Greece and against the euro. As this pressure was building, Greece faced increasing challenges to deal with the massive debt they had accumulated over recent years.

Their problems did not arrive suddenly but had been steadily growing over recent years. Ultimately, the "debt problem" they faced was probably better seen as a "growth problem"—the Greeks had not been able to grow their economy (and their tax base) at a rate to match the amount they would otherwise wish to spend on the patronage possibilities provided by government jobs and generous pensions.

Like California, Greece suffered from structural problems that went to the very heart of the government's ability to raise adequate revenue through taxation to fund the increasing commitments that have been made toward expenditures. Both could be seen in 2010 as having succumbed to a similar crisis of confidence in the ability of elected officials to face down persistent long-term problems.

Unfortunately, like patients awaiting treatment in a crowded emergency room, problems often need to become proper catastrophes in order to be dealt with on a priority basis. Although Greece was certainly not "too big to fail" on its own, the euro itself (and the other European member states who back it) might be. Through concerted effort and generous cross-subsidies, European finance ministers were able to keep disaster at bay in 2010, at least for a time, but more fundamental questions about the continued viability of European institutions remained frustratingly unanswered.

* * *

The award for Most Overused Metaphor of the Decade (Europe) easily goes to the *Costa Concordia*, the 1,000-foot-long cruise ship with more than 4,000 passengers and crew on board that in 2012 hit a rocky reef off the coast of Italy and quickly foundered in water fifty feet deep. Like the *Titanic* sinking a hundred years earlier, horrible scenes of fear and desperation were reported, as individuals tried to reach safety and protect their loved ones while the ship capsized.

Captain Francesco Schettino was quickly charged with manslaughter, as a result of his inaction and delay, having allegedly given the evacuation order seventy minutes after the ship first suffered the 160-foot gash in its hull. As the casualty lists from the *Costa Concordia* were being compiled, Europe itself was struggling to keep its head above water. Several European countries faced huge debt problems, and despite renewed efforts by the European Central Bank (ECB) to intervene in the financial markets and uphold the euro, fears were still mounting across the continent and around the world.

The rating agency Standard & Poor's had just recently stripped France of its prized AAA rating, which it had held since 1975. This was a significant blow to a famously proud country that was at the center of rescue efforts for the euro. But France was not singled out maliciously. Eight other euro-zone countries were also downgraded at the same time, with Italy facing a precipitous drop of two notches to BBB+. S&P then went on to downgrade the euro-zone's rescue fund, the European Financial Stability Facility, for which France is responsible for 20 percent of the funding.

Not all euro-zone countries, however, were tarnished with the same brush. Frugal countries such as Germany and the Netherlands survived with their AAA ratings intact. Britain also maintained its credit rating under the deficit-cutting "austerity policies" put in place by the center-right Coalition government that took over from the discredited Labour government of Gordon Brown.

The euro-zone works as a monetary union only if members feel, first, that there are valid reasons to stay within the union long-term, and, second, that members who do not play by the rules will be brought into line, whether by way of the stick or the carrot. Unfortunately, in 2012, European countries needed to raise approximately $1 trillion in order to refinance their existing debt and address their lingering budget deficits. Without the money to pay off their debts as they come due, these governments would have no choice but to keep issuing more bonds, and more bonds, and more bonds.

Week by week, month by month, EU governments had to go back into the financial markets and raise billions in new debt financing. Should investors become spooked, the interest rates they demanded could spike up dramatically. With each rise in borrowing costs, the likelihood of default rose. In the case of Greece and Portugal, the situation became so difficult that the European Financial Stability Facility was established in order to provide a "co-signer" for them!

Despite over $600 billion in loans made by the ECB to provide liquidity to the banking system, surprisingly little money flowed into European government bonds. Investors turned their backs on what, at least on paper, were easy profits to be made by borrowing at 1 percent from the ECB and then lending that same money to Spain or Italy, thereby collecting 4 to 6 percent as the middleman. Instead, banks preferred to sit on the money, uncertain what the perfidious future would ultimately bring.

Interestingly, although a legion of valid criticisms could be made about the operation of the European Union and the anti-democratic effect of the faceless bureaucrats who reside in Brussels and pursue their managerial Bonapartism far away from voters' eyes, the debt problem faced by European countries was largely of their own making. The example set by the fiscally prudent states, such as Germany and the Netherlands, demonstrated that austerity and a balanced budget were not impossible in the European Union. They were simply a policy choice that political leaders must have the courage to pursue. Voters can and will back them if the benefits of prudence are clearly explained.

Meanwhile, reports quickly surfaced that Captain Schettino manually overrode the preprogrammed course of the *Costa Concordia* in order to conduct an unauthorized "sail by" of his head waiter's family home. The consequence of this decision was devastating and humiliating, regardless of the sentimentality and good wishes that originally motivated it.

The owners of the vessel quickly blamed the accident on the "significant human error" of Schettino. As European political leaders continued to live outside their means and indulged in the vanity of propping up excessive government spending with costly public borrowings, their own "significant human error" would soon have its own devastating and humiliating consequences.

* * *

The awarding of the Nobel Peace Prize each year is a curious affair. Sometimes the announcement incites bemusement, other times anger and dissent, and on rare occasions something like general consensus.

The 2012 recipient—the European Union—proved to be a controversial one, both at the time and in the years that followed. At the ceremony in Oslo, the capital of Norway, representatives of the Brussels bureaucracy, together with designated guests from member states, accepted the award for the European Union's services in bringing peace to the world. The Nobel committee recognized the efforts of the Brussels-based institution over five decades to promote democracy and human rights among nations that had previously fought bitter wars against each other.

Interestingly, although apparently worthy of international recognition and plaudits, the European Union is not particularly popular with actual Norwegian voters. Twice Norway has voted to stay out of Europe, preferring instead an arm's-length relationship that ensures Norwegians enjoys all the economic benefits, without sacrificing its own sovereignty when it comes to other areas, such as international peacekeeping efforts.

There were no doubt several "Eurocrats" attending the award ceremony who were busy contemplating how exactly the prestige of winning a Nobel could be most effectively turned into more money, more power, and more patronage for Brussels. One recommendation that quickly made the rounds, courtesy of the EU's foreign affairs department, was that the European Union should form yet another "institute." Pithily titled the European Institute of Peace, this new organization would spread the word about the benefits of conflict resolution. The Nobel Peace Prize comes with a generous $1 million cash prize, which could be used to jump-start new projects such as this. Many EU champions felt that the Nobel Prize brought with it an obligation to expand European peacemaking efforts even further. Estimates for an Institute of Peace envisioned a budget of over $3 million a year and a staff of a dozen or more.

Such an institute, however, would follow in the well-trod footsteps of both the United States and the United Nations. Legitimate questions were eventually asked about whether yet another institute was actually necessary, especially in light of the budget difficulty facing European countries, as well as the European Union itself. The United States Institute of Peace has been up and running for almost thirty years and has a budget of more than $40 million. Critics quickly pointed out that Brussels's copycat institute could be duplicative and unnecessary.

Unfortunately, protests in Oslo the day before the award was handed out demonstrated that anti-EU sentiment was still intense, at least in some quarters. Even former Nobel Peace Prize winners such as Archbishop Desmond Tutu of South Africa came out against the European Union as a worthy recipient. Two past laureates, Mairead Maguire (1976) and Adolfo Pérez Esquivel (1980), attended the protests in person to voice their concerns.

The bloody war in Bosnia during the 1990s, which raged as the European Union stood idly by, is just one example of Brussels' inadequacy on the international stage. Closer to home, the economic collapses that have engulfed the continent in recent years threatened the continued viability of the euro, the single currency at the heart of EU consolidation, while revealing significant gaps in the European Union's effectiveness.

Champions of European integration, however, stressed that Brussels will ultimately emerge even stronger from the economic crisis. This is perhaps what most concerns its critics—both in Britain and elsewhere. No matter what the challenges and shortcomings facing the Brussels bureaucracy, the answer that comes back from Brussels always appears to be "more integration, more harmonization." The benefits of such goals are always self-evident to the political and economic elites across the continent, as represented every year by the self-satisfied collection of corporate chief executive officers, tech-guru billionaires, central banking chairpersons, media superstars, and sundry other fellow travelers who descend on the Swiss ski resort of Davos every January for the World Economic Forum. For those outside this "party of Davos," the benefits of Brussels' ceaseless hunger for integration and appetite are less obvious.

The backlash against Brussels at the time of the Nobel was shown most strongly in Britain. Prime Minister David Cameron staked out a position for his government early on in his time in office that attempted to address the anti-European sentiment building up inside and outside his party, while at the same time trying to reassure others that the future of Britain was within Europe. Cameron pushed for significant reforms in how decisions were made and how money was spent within the Brussels bureaucracy, while angry voices condemned the European experiment as an antidemocratic failure that undermined Britain's own political institutions and its long history of liberty and civil rights. Unfortunately, the results of the June 2016 Brexit referendum would demonstrate to Cameron, his party, his country, and the rest of the world how far short he ultimately fell in maintaining this balance and, ultimately, Britain's place in the European Union.

An arm's-length relationship with the European Union, such as Norway enjoys, was an appealing option to many of the disgruntled Britons who would eventually vote Leave, although the state of early Brexit negotiations did not appear to be headed in this direction.

On the other side of the Atlantic, a number of patriotic Americans loudly cleared their throats and quietly pointed out that the role of the North Atlantic Treaty Organization (an alliance largely subsidized by US taxpayers), and the extended commitment of US troops to Europe for many years after the end of World War II, had much more to do with bringing peace and stability to a war-torn continent than developing a common agricultural policy or uniform regulations on arcane topics like the acceptable curvature of a banana. The Nobel selectors obviously disagreed.

The Nobel Peace Prize has always been more a means to make political statements than a rigorous assessment of the actual contributions made toward limiting the casualties of war and violence. We need only look back to the most recent American winner. Barack Obama's receipt of the award in 2009 did little to prevent him from overseeing the expansion of his controversial drone bombing campaigns without any sustained public backlash.

Perhaps the European Union will eventually produce a better legacy from its Nobel win. It was clearly insufficient to prevent 17 million Britons from voting for Brexit. If Brussels isn't able to reestablish a meaningful mandate after Britain's tortuous departure, the prize itself risks a further marked decline in both its prestige and its effectiveness in promoting the value of peace to the world.

* * *

Apparently, Swiss neutrality—like my ability to sit through old episodes of the 1990s American television show *Designing Women* and any movie directed by Michael Bay—has its limits. To the shock of many observers, the Swiss voted in February 2014 to significantly limit the level of migration from the European Union into their small country. Despite the vocal opposition of the federal government, the controversial cap was adopted by a small but decisive margin.

Business groups quickly proclaimed that the Swiss economy would suffer dramatically if the free flow of migrants was in any way curtailed. The vote required the Swiss government to reinstate quotas on the numbers of EU migrants who enter the country within the next three years, returning to the policy that had been in place before a treaty was entered into during 2002. Although not formally an EU member, the Swiss are highly dependent on their giant European neighbors for trade and, as a result, have entered into several treaties with the European Union to obtain access to the single market and mimic many aspects of full membership.

Brussels was not amused by this inconvenient and embarrassing poll result. Switzerland, a country of just 8 million, is the most prosperous country on the continent and has been a beacon of light to many neighboring Europeans. Many Swiss soon expressed concern over retaliatory steps that could be taken by the EU bureaucracy in response to their referendum. Switzerland participates in a large number of EU programs that result in significant financial benefits for the tiny, landlocked federation.

At the time of the vote, approximately one-fourth of the population consisted of foreigners, alarming many Swiss who were concerned about the future integrity of their country. Taking advantage of the direct democracy tradition that still plays an important role in modern Swiss life, the right-wing Swiss People's Party launched its Stop Mass Immigration campaign to give voice to these concerns and again exert some level of control of the quantity and quality of immigration.

The debate in Switzerland over the real benefits of unlimited migration echoed similar discussions occurring across Europe at this time, including in Britain, where many Conservative politicians, as well as the single-issue UK Independence Party, were challenging the merits of EU membership. The leader of the Dutch Party for Freedom, Geert Wilders, indicated that he saw the Swiss move as a precedent that even full EU members could follow.

When a country's economy is humming along nicely, questions about immigration policy are often not pressing ones. Both politicians and voters are content to shrug off such difficult and divisive questions and instead enjoy the benefits that derive from increased labor supplies and declining wages—a simple example of the laws of supply and demand that can be quickly explained to a fifth grader. However, when the economy turns, critics of unrestricted immigration are often able to gain wider and wider appeal.

Academics make a great effort to argue that large-scale migration does not negatively impact unemployment numbers—although when pressed many may acknowledge short-term impacts that are worked through in only a few years. Studies covering the *pieds noir* (French settlers returning home after Algerian independence in 1962), *retornados* (refugees from Angola and Mozambique moving to Portugal after independence granted in the 1970s), and Jews moving to Israel after the collapse of the Soviet Union in the early 1990s all discount concerns over sudden mass migration. It would seem then that labor markets are an area uniquely impervious to the forces of supply and demand.

What is the proper function of an immigration policy? At least in theory it should be about determining the optimal population growth rate for your country, subtracting out the natural demographic trends that are already occurring, and settling on a policy that allows for migrants to make up the difference, while keeping an eye on the skill sets and industry sectors most in needed of further workers.

However, modern immigration policies are frequently set for a variety of reasons other than the straightforward calculations above. Too often, though, these reasons are never fully explained and publically acknowledged. For example, more immigrants can be admitted in order to fulfill a sense of public duty to the poor and disenfranchised from other less prosperous countries. This charitable sentiment can operate as some sort of redistributive tax that must be paid in order to morally justify the wealthier country's good fortune. Also, excessive immigration could be useful to either accelerate or undermine domestic electoral trends, where one political party feels it would disproportionally benefit from the influx of new voters.

Today, unfortunately, it seems that to the self-appointed champions of unrestricted migration, any attempt to approach immigration policy objectively reeks of racism and prejudice. In their eyes, the long-term subjective benefits far outweigh any short-term tensions or distortions or even the impact of supply and demand on wage levels.

What made the Swiss vote particularly noteworthy at the time was that, when compared to the migration flows occurring on a global basis, one might have expected that the movement of a few thousand Czechs, Estonians, and Portuguese from their developed-but-sluggish economies into Switzerland would be relatively unproblematic, given the cultural and linguistic commonalities across Europe. But clearly the Swiss were beginning to believe that the minuses of mass migration outweigh the pluses, even in this relatively contained situation.

The Swiss referendum in 2014 was an important example of a country deciding to take control of its borders and ownership of a key contributor to its population growth and demographics. By refusing to abdicate their responsibility here, Swiss voters recognized that these are issues far too important to be left to mere chance and circumstance. Many British voters would remember this two years later when it was their turn to go to the polls and vote to either Leave or Remain.

4

Red Dawns

A soldier will fight long and hard
for a bit of colored ribbon.

—Napoleon Bonaparte

Russian president Vladimir Putin had put his personal reputation behind staging the 2014 Winter Olympics in the Black Sea resort of Sochi. Unfortunately, it proved to be an arduous task. The issue was not a reluctance to spend money. On the contrary, these games ended up being the most expensive ever staged, whether in the summer or the winter. Some estimates had Russia spending almost $50 billion. By comparison, the 2008 Beijing Games cost approximately $40 billion. Britain got away with hosting its "Austerity Games" in London four years later with a mere $12 billion. The most expensive Winter Games prior to Sochi were Nagano in 1998, which cost about $17 billion.

The problems lay elsewhere. To begin with, there was the weather. Surprisingly, it doesn't actually get that cold in Sochi during the winter. With an average temperature of about 50 degrees Fahrenheit during the colder months, Sochi was connected to nearby ski resorts by high-speed trains. However, organizers still deployed more than 400 snow machines in order to coat surfaces with the powdery white stuff so essential for most of the sports on display.

Then there was Sochi's inconvenient location. It is, unfortunately, near "hot spots" like Chechnya. Much work was done on the security side to ensure that Islamist extremists based nearby did not see the Sochi games as an appealing target for terrorist acts.

Of course, the typical drama of unmet deadlines, accusations of corruption, and the uncalculated risks of environmental damages that accompany any grand project, like hosting an Olympics, also circled around Sochi. The transformation contemplated for this region was massive, and Putin spared no expense to make this vision a reality, regardless of either the immediate or long-term consequences.

If Russia's first Winter Games was a failure, the backlash against Putin could have been severe. Now the pressing question has become exactly what sort of legacy the Sochi Olympics will bring to Russia. In part, the legacy will be driven by what use (if any) will be made of the many new facilities and transit links going forward. Interestingly, Sochi's future may lie not as a winter sports hub but as the location for other sporting endeavors. The 2018 World Cup will also bring soccer fans from around the world to Russia, and Sochi will play an important role in making this tournament a success, despite the controversy that surrounded Russia's original appointment as host by a now-disgraced FIFA leadership.

Even if Sochi does not ever become the Russian skiing destination of choice, Putin has demonstrated a willingness to sell it as an ideal location for international political summits and other high-profile gatherings. With good transport links, loads of international hotels, and plenty of fine dining and after-hours night spots, Sochi is slowly gaining all of the necessary ingredients for success as a twenty-first-century conference destination.

Recent Olympics have not been particularly kind to Russia, especially in light of the long tradition of Soviet sporting success that preceded Putin. Unfortunately, the medal tally in both London and Vancouver did not flatter Russia. Expectations, therefore, were high that Russia would be able to return to its historical form in Sochi, adding even more pressure on Putin to deliver a successful Games.

To Putin, sporting success is a key element of Russian national identity. He has stressed the need to expand sports funding and sports institutions that focus on young children. The Soviets stressed the redemptive and curative value of sports for a weary, but striving, proletariat. Putin, a product of that era, has clearly internalized this view. His own personal success in judo was almost certainly a key element in his personal development—as are his late-night pickup ice hockey games!

The Cold War is long over (at least in its initial configuration between Washington and Moscow), but the demonstration of sporting prowess is still an important element in projecting national prestige on a global scale. Austerity Britain would come out of the London Games with a tremendous boost to its "brand." Brazil's success at soccer, New Zealand's accomplishments in rugby, and Canada's prowess in ice hockey infuse the image of these countries held by neutral observers.

Putin understands that national pride is a very important asset that must be maintained and nurtured over time. Like Bonaparte before him, the Russian president was not content with only military victories and diplomatic success. He knew he would need civil triumphs and legacies to secure his reputation and place in history. By putting so much of his personal reputation behind Russia's hosting of the 2014 Winter Games, Putin needed Sochi to be a clear success, not only in the eyes of his countrymen, but also in the eyes of the world.

Unfortunately, events in Crimea would quickly overshadow the pageantry that had just concluded in Sochi.

★ ＊ ★

In February 2012, Putin announced he intended to spend more than $700 billion on upgrading and modernizing the Russian military over the next ten years. The "Christmas list" of projects was comprehensive, including new nuclear missiles as well as more submarines and warships, more tanks and aircraft.

Putin, who was serving as prime minister at the time, faced a presidential election on March 4, 2012, that would mark his return to the Kremlin for a third term after being prevented from running for reelection due to constitutional term limits. Clearly, Putin believed that there was a limit to what diplomatic endeavors and economic engagement can accomplish (and developments in Crimea only two years later would allow him to put certain military assets to productive use)!

Concerns over potential holes in Russia's defenses fed on long-standing fears in the country. Memories still linger over six decades later of the ease in which Nazi forces were able to take Russians by surprise and bring the country to its knees. Notably, Putin did not feel the need to distance himself from the legacy of Soviet military achievements during the conflict that the Russians refer to as the "Great Patriotic War." In addition to ensuring that celebrations of VE Day were staged with sufficient pomp and sense of grandeur, Putin has made sure that wartime veterans have received a significant bump in their pension benefits.

Putin clearly knows the benefit of when to side with history and when to distance himself. He took significant steps away from the ruling party at this time, known as United Russia, to affect his 2012 reelection. Once reelected, he opened the door to potentially another twelve years at Russia's helm. But despite the significant popular support for Putin, there remained highly vocal opponents to his regime. Anti-Putin demonstrations in the lead-up to that election were the largest public protests against the government since the fall of Communism two decades earlier. One protest in Moscow even featured drivers sporting white ribbons and balloons on the vehicles to voice their displeasure with Putin's seemingly unimpeded progress toward regaining the presidency.

Some argued at this time that the seeds of a "Moscow spring" had been sown and that soon these protests would have the same effect of the 2011 protests across the Middle East and North Africa. Mikhail Gorbachev, the last leader of the Soviet Union who is still romanticized by many European and American elites, went on record to predict that Putin would ultimately lose his grip on power if he did not make room in the Russian political system for greater democratic participation. Gorbachev actually made an unfavorable comparison to the last days of British prime minister Margaret Thatcher, who, it has been argued, stayed in power too long and was ultimately shown the door. Clearly someone had been watching Meryl Streep's attention-grabbing performance of Lady Thatcher in the critically acclaimed film *The Iron Lady*!

Importantly, though, in 2012 Gorbachev no longer enjoyed anything like the adoration in his homeland that he still received abroad. The rise of anti-Putin protests may have burnished Gorbachev's historical legacy somewhat, but for many Russians he is still the doomed figure who allowed the Soviet Union's place in the world to be lost, with little benefit for such sacrifice coming to former Soviet citizens.

The "new Russia" under Putin's guidance was not reluctant to use tough diplomacy on Syria and Iran to support its long-term aims. Putin repeatedly demonstrated a willingness to draw a clear line around the interests of his country, together with a willingness to fund his military in a manner and to an extent that supports his foreign policy agenda. This line would soon be drawn around the Crimean Peninsula, and the Obama administration would come away from that experience with its reputation in foreign affairs noticeably scuffed.

* * *

Christmas 2013 witnessed the passing of a Russian man whose impact on the second half of the twentieth century is hard to overestimate. Whenever fighting broke out over the past six decades, the weapon of choice for both jungle revolutionary and proletariat utopian defender alike was the AK-47, designed by Lieutenant General Mikhail Kalashnikov. He died in his home in Izhevsk, the capital of Udmurtia, about 800 miles east of Moscow.

According to President Putin, "the Kalashnikov rifle is a symbol of the creative genius of our people." In addition to the vast Soviet military and its various client states, such as the Warsaw Pact, the AK-47 also found many satisfied customers in terrorists and mercenaries around the world. At its peak, the automatic rifle was licensed for production in over a dozen countries, with a reputation for reliability in a wide variety of climates and battlefield environments. Its success was based in great measure on its simplicity in construction and operation, making it especially useful to insurgents and irregular fighters in the Third World. As perhaps the highest symbolic honor that can be granted to an inanimate object, an image of the gun has for years graced the flag of the African nation, Mozambique.

Although created by Kalashnikov to help defend his beloved motherland, Russia, Russian soldiers would ultimately suffer significant losses when they encountered these weapons in the hands of rebel fighters in Afghanistan and, later, in Chechnya.

After the Berlin Wall fell and Communism was consigned to the dustbin of history, Kalashnikovs were frequently associated in the public imagination with Islamist extremists and African child soldiers. Estimates have at least 70 million AK-47s produced since its creation by the self-taught gun maker. Firing 600 rounds a minute and with accuracy to 1,000 feet, the AK-47 was originally designed in 1947 based on a German gun from WWII, the Sturm-gewehr 44. It was a simple and effective weapon, which eventually became a symbol in its own right of the revolutionary causes in which it was used.

Given the Communist society in which the gun originated and the anticapitalist purpose to which it was so often put, the AK-47 earned Comrade Kalashnikov little during his life. He died having spent his years showered with fame and recognition, but enjoying only a modest lifestyle. Since the fall of the Soviet Union, he tried several times to capitalize on his recognizable name, including through a launch of his own vodka, but with only limited results. By contrast, Eugene Stoner, who designed the M16 assault rifle for the US military, earned substantial sums for his own invention.

The decades after WWII saw the immense utility in an inexpensive weapon that could easily arm a vast peasant army while withstanding the uses and abuses that such nonprofessional soldiers would subject them to. But even as the face of conflict changed during the War on Terror after the September 11, 2001, attacks, it is clear that asymmetrical warfare will remain a feature of military engagements for many years to come.

The AK-47 was a weapon for the villages and souks and remote, inaccessible locations. It found its greatest utility and fame a long distance from the multibillion-dollar nuclear weapons that were mass produced at a rate that ultimately bankrupted the wobbly Soviet economy and served as a significant drain on American resources. While the nuclear threat of "mutually assured destruction" remains to many people the defining military construct of the Cold War, the willingness to which both sides indulged in proxy wars between "allies" of various stripes is perhaps its more lasting legacy. The AK-47 fueled generations of violence in a way that a nuclear warhead design or an intercontinental ballistic missile system simply could not. While we wallowed in the existential crisis that a theoretical Armageddon might have brought, we largely ignored the proliferation of these "cheap-and-cheerful" weapons that delivered death with an inexpensive efficiency.

Widely advertised on the Internet today, the AK-47 will have a legacy that long outlasts its human creator. The democratization of warfare is a trend that first gained momentum in the trenches of WWI and continued with each wave of national independence that was unleashed in the aftermath of WWII. War as a populist endeavor, in which each citizen could be required to participate, rather than as a trade for a limited number of well-trained and specially equipped professionals, was a defining trait of the twentieth century.

Although the rhetoric of national liberation and Communist revolution has now been replaced in the twenty-first century by the cries of *jihad*, the Kalashnikov assault rifle continues to serve as the symbol of the effectiveness and lethality of a highly motivated revolutionary, especially when he is well armed.

⋆ ⋆ ⋆

Disregarding the threats of sanctions and international ignominy, in March 2014 Putin signed a treaty formally annexing the region of Crimea. In doing so, he reunited his country with a former province that was signed away sixty years ago to its neighbor, Ukraine, by the Soviet leader Nikita Khrushchev. As US and Western attempts to either stop or stall Putin clearly failed, the interim government in Kiev voiced their disapproval in very strong language.

For those fearing that Crimea was merely the first course of a long meal, the boldly Bonapartist Putin claimed he had no further aims on Ukrainian territory. Given the unique history of Crimea, neutral observers might argue that this action has all the makings of a one-off incident, rather than a radical repositioning of Russian foreign and military policy toward repeated "land grabs."

Putin's speech to parliament to defend the annexation made clear his view of the historical justifications for his actions. By referring to Crimea as an "inseparable part of Russia" in the hearts and minds of his people, he portrayed himself as someone merely resolving a historical anomaly. Putin drew parallels to the precedent set by Kosovo's separation from Serbia and suggested that it was inconsistent of the international community to permit Kosovars to choose their destiny but to deny Crimeans the same rights and prerogatives. He even threw in a reference to the reunification of Germany in 1990 for good measure!

To Putin, those claiming to be in charge on Kiev were illegitimate, having usurped the duly-elected president of their country by means of a coup. To make matters worse, they included among their numbers fascist neo-Nazis, an awkward fact not widely reported in the United States.

Despite the stern words of rebuke directed at Putin by President Obama and others, he refused to back down. The elaborate arguments regarding international law held little weight at the Kremlin, which saw a once-in-a-lifetime opportunity to correct what many Russians and Crimeans felt was a geopolitical aberration.

The "costs" to Russia of the ensuing diplomatic kerfuffle, including any eventual sanctions, were apparently ones that Putin was comfortable "amortizing" over many, many years to come. And he was not alone in his convictions. Members of the State Duma even went so far as to formally request that US and European authorities extend their flurry of visa bans and asset freezes to include all of them as well!

In short, the upheaval and instability in Ukraine provided a unique window through which Russia can act. It should not have come as a surprise that Putin ultimately decided to pursue his personal vision of his country's vital national interests.

The simple fact that Sevastopol serves as home to Russia's Black Sea Fleet cannot be downplayed or dismissed. Crimea isn't just any bit of land full of Russian speakers. Moscow was resistant to any significant realignment of Ukraine toward the West generally and the European Union specifically in large part due to concerns over the security of its tenure at Sevastopol. It will be interesting to see whether having now obtained that security, Putin will resist the ultimate, and perhaps inevitable, inclusion of Ukraine into NATO.

It would seem that, given the ineffectiveness of Western protests over Crimea, the least the United States and Europe would be willing and able to do in the years to come is grant Kiev the same courtesy they have to other former Communist countries. Importantly, not only is much of the old Warsaw Pact now full members of NATO, but also three full-blown former Soviet Republics—Latvia, Lithuania, and Estonia—each of which borders Russia.

The stock markets may have punished Russian companies in the weeks following the Crimean unrest as uncertainty grew over the risks of confrontation between Russia and Ukraine, but as certainty returned to the region, stock prices eventually responded accordingly. The ruble was quickly introduced as the official currency in Crimea. Crimean clocks were promptly switched to Moscow time. Although the back-and-forth of diplomatic retaliation will continue in the years to come, there was little ambiguity on the ground over the end result.

Perhaps the most important lesson of this crisis was how the impotency of the Obama administration in the area of foreign affairs had been demonstrated once again. Clearly, this was an important issue to both the White House and the State Department. Equally clearly, though, was how little regard the Kremlin had for the ability of the United States to extract any real consequences from Russia.

It is one thing to simply hope that the sound and fury of diplomacy will cause an errant country to pause and reflect. It is another thing entirely to actually have the influence and respect necessary to coerce and bend such a country to your will.

Crimea had put the relative diplomatic strengths and weaknesses of Putin and Obama on display once again, and the comparison was not flattering.

* * *

In the days following the tragic loss of Malaysia Airlines Flight 17 in July 2014, global indignation ignited against the Russian separatists in eastern Ukraine, who were believed to have launched the fatal SA-11 missile against the passenger aircraft. Separately, Moscow became a target of rhetorical attack and diplomatic backlash, based on its alleged role in sponsoring and supplying these separatists.

Despite the attempt by Kremlin critics to construct a narrative that included a prominent role for Putin in shooting down MH17, which resulted in the loss of 298 lives, US intelligence experts were not immediately able to establish a direct evidentiary link between the Russian government and the catastrophe. Despite the Obama administration's repeated claims that the Kremlin supported and trained the separatists' forces, crucial questions remain unanswered. First, who specifically shot the SA-11 missile in question? Second, were Russian officials present when that missile was launched?

No credible arguments were being made at this time that the downing of MH17 was intentional. Instead, many experts conceded that the attack was most likely a mistake by combatants within Ukraine. This, however, did not temper the efforts of international critics to punish Russia for its supposed involvement in the tragedy, by way of financial sanctions and blacklists for senior Kremlin officials.

For example, European politicians were arguing—yet again!— that Russia should be shown a "red card" and denied the ability to stage the 2018 World Cup. Meanwhile, attention turned to those wealthy Russians with ties to the Kremlin who were living successful, affluent lives in Austerity Britain, and whether British politicians were doing enough to actually hit them "where it hurt." In response, British prime minister Cameron criticized France for selling warships to Russia, thereby profiting from Putin's militarism. Protests were even brewing within the Netherlands to deport Putin's daughter, Maria Putina, who lived in the small village of Voorschoten with her Dutch boyfriend.

It is interesting how, even in the centennial year of the outbreak of World War I, so little attention was being given to the unfortunate precedent set one hundred years ago the same week. The assassination of Archduke Franz Ferdinand was conducted by a Bosnian Serb named Gavrilo Princip, who was a subject of the Austro-Hungarian Empire. Princip dreamed of a "greater Serbia" that would unify the Serbian population within the empire with the neighboring independent Kingdom of Serbia. In retribution for the attack and in the belief that Serbian government officials masterminded the scheme, Austria quickly declared war on Serbia, initiating a series of falling dominoes that would lead to a four-year continental bloodletting. Despite the obvious parallels with the Russian-speaking separatists in Ukraine, anti-Russian agitators seemed oblivious to the consequences of their actions.

Equally interesting was the near total silence on the culpability of Ukraine for these unnecessary deaths. Despite a special election meant to provide a measure of legitimacy to the coup leaders, Kiev still was not able to reach an accord with eastern separatists who remain doubtful over the central government's long-term intentions. Most troubling, though, was the refusal of Kiev to close Ukrainian airspace to foreign planes, thereby intentionally leaving the door open for disasters such as MH17. Kiev shouldn't have tried to have it both ways. Either it has the ability to exercise adequate control over its territories or it needed to be transparent to the rest of the world about its failure to secure its own skies. Simply put, if Kiev had closed its airspace, the MH17 tragedy would not have occurred. Yet the overwhelming majority of press attention was intent on establishing that Putin was legally and morally responsible for these deaths.

Clearly, the 298 lives lost on the flight from Amsterdam to Kuala Lumpur was tragic. To put the loss in context, the loss suffered by the Netherlands from the MH17 attack was proportionately greater (based on population) than the United States' loss on September 11, 2001. Consequently, it should come as little surprise that the countries whose citizens were on MH17 demanded that a full investigation be conducted and the responsible parties punished.

Many critics who championed a hard line against Moscow adamantly denied that they were motivated by politics. However, it is worth noting that the casualties from the Obama administration's drone program during his time in office were ten times greater than those who died on MH17. While Putin was being accused of war crimes, even though the missile launch was accidental, Obama was given a Nobel Peace Prize despite his drone attacks being intentional and subject to his personal supervision.

Obviously the "blame game" can be played very differently when the politics warrant.

5

Left Behind

Glory is fleeting,
but obscurity is forever.

—Napoleon Bonaparte

In May 2012, Socialist candidate and ample *bon vivant* François Hollande defeated the idiosyncratic incumbent Nicolas Sarkozy to become the next president of France. At a time of austerity, the defeat of staunch German ally Sarkozy demonstrated that some French voters were questioning the benefits of belt-tightening as the principal engine toward recovery. Hollande's narrow victory made him the first Socialist president of France in seventeen years.

Hollande promised a new direction for his country and for Europe. Instead of further budget cuts, growth would be his economic priority, although it was unclear where this growth would come from. He saw France as a nation worn down from the divisions and cuts inflicted during the Sarkozy years.

The German view on the financial crisis was markedly different from Hollande's. To German chancellor Angela Merkel, the best prescription available was balancing budgets and cutting future spending. Sarkozy was seen as so core to the success of Merkel's success in implementing this cure that the popular press awarded the two an honor normally received for celebrity couples. Their names were combined in a single honorific—"Merkozy."

But an important question was being whispered even in the early days that followed Hollande's victory—was the election actually more a rejection of the frenetic and America-phile Sarkozy rather than a choice for the bland and reassuring Hollande?

Sarkozy was clearly undone by his growing unpopularity. Many French had grown weary of his theatrics and clearly felt more comfortable with a traditional leadership style. His supporters argued that the global financial crisis largely prevented him from pursuing his plans to reinvigorate France. Fatigue over Sarkozy's "in your face" personal style seemed to be the deciding factor, rather than a comprehensive rejection of his policies.

Unlike Sarkozy, Hollande made clear that he would not micromanage the actions of his government. Instead, he would revert to the long-standing tradition of earlier French presidents, who maintained an Olympian detachment from the mundane details of day-to-day governance.

Importantly, Hollande was no ideologue. Many pundits predicted that Hollande would soon drift toward the political middle ground, like his Socialist predecessor François Mitterrand. Mitterrand's first years in office saw several attempts at radical change, but eventually the need for stability overrode the desire of the party faithful for dogmatic policies.

Hollande was expected to bring a more conciliatory, respectful, and deferential tone to the presidency, which is fundamentally a monarchical role created to suit the personal strengths and weaknesses of French war hero and icon General Charles de Gaulle.

Whether that is what France actually needed was not immediately clear. In Hollande, the French did not so much lurch to the left as they had selected the ordinary and the familiar. With his receding hairline and glasses, Hollande represented an image of respectfulness and dignity that his predecessor, nicknamed "President Bling," had lacked.

France faced massive deficits and stagnant growth. The stark reality of the global economy would limit any urge to experiment or dabble with unproven strategies and techniques. Sarkozy ultimately failed in his attempt to conduct a systematic reform of French institutions, so it was left to his successor to address these challenges through the tools currently available.

For so long as the euro survives, France will be unable to take the easy way out of its problems by simply devaluing its currency. Compare Iceland to Ireland for a simple demonstration of how the ability of the former to devalue has meant that it has avoided the pain and suffering that the latter must now live with. As a result, a French president must eventually look at cutting costs in order to regain French competitiveness. This will mean making unpopular choices, which—at least initially—a new French president would be reluctant to make.

* * *

When Hollande first took his place in the Élysée Palace, he arrived on a wave of widespread disenchantment in his predecessor. Instead of an in-your-face "bling-bling" leader, French voters had expressed their clear preference for modesty and tradition. With rioting breaking out in August 2012 in the streets of Amiens, in the north of France, it was soon clear that the honeymoon for Hollande would be a short one.

Unfortunately for Hollande, after the first hundred days in office, a different disenchantment had formed. This time, it was

Hollande himself who faced a country that was in need of a different style of leadership. Hollande promised his countrymen a "normal" presidency, in line with the aloofness that had traditionally surrounded French heads of state. Instead, the country witnessed a lack of leadership and an inability to articulate clear priorities. The return of large-scale street violence was an unhelpful reminder of the anger and desperation that lingers in French urban ghettos. With his approval ratings dropping, Hollande began hearing criticism even from left-wing newspapers such as *Liberation* and *Le Monde*.

France was lurching back into recession, and at such times people want their leaders talking about the problems they face, instead of avoiding them. The initial flurry of initiatives by Hollande, which were intended to distance the country from the more controversial aspects of the Sarkozy regime, were followed by little of note. In hindsight, Hollande overdelivered on his promise to be a "hands-off" president. He could be seen as the antithesis of a Bonaparte—reluctant, self-doubting, and indecisive. Perhaps the French had become more accustomed to the leadership initiative and overall pizzazz of Sarkozy than they would care to admit!

Hollande was also forced to keep his Socialist Party unified after he controversially reversed his position on the austerity measures being imposed across the euro-zone by Brussels. Hollande campaigned on the promise to resist austerity and to confront Chancellor Merkel, leader of the EU's pro-austerity camp. Instead, he quickly indicated after winning the election that he will still ratify the European Fiscal Compact, which required member states to commit themselves to a balanced budget. With unrest on the street, it was difficult for left-leaning Hollande to implement deep cuts in public spending without alienating many within his Socialist Party.

Regardless of these pressing issues, Hollande was not too timid to take a position on the most divisive question of the day—namely, where should the French go on their extended summer holidays?

Willing to brave dissent and derision, Hollande argued forcefully to his cabinet that in these difficult times, the country's leaders should not be seen traipsing around the globe to exotic locations. Instead, they should remain in France, spending their "holiday euros" at home, where it could help pump up the lagging economy. Interestingly, some German leaders also tried to make a political statement with their vacation destination. In their case, however, it was a vote of support for wavering Greece. A number of politicians publicized their plans to holiday in the Greek islands, despite fears by many Germans that if they went to Greece to enjoy the soothing whites and blues of the architecture and landscape, and a few stiff glasses of Ouzo along the way, they might be met with anger and violence!

Yet again, Hollande sought to distinguish himself from jet-setting Sarkozy, who created quite a stir when he spent his first presidential vacation at a palatial mansion in the Unites States. Rather than seeking out some high-end resort in a far-flung corner of the world, where he might rub shoulders with hedge fund managers, Hollywood megastars, or other members of the so-called party of Davos, Hollande and his then-partner Valérie Trierweiler spent their few weeks of holiday at Brégançon fortress, the official summer residence of French presidents. Like many other aspects of their lives, the French have turned their summer vacations into an art form. Whether lounging on a beach or lying contentedly in a hammock enjoying clear alpine air, France is a country where what you do when you are not at your desk sends a powerful picture to others about who you really are.

Hollande did interrupt his August vacation to address the Amiens rioting and promised a tough response. Images of burning cars and rioting raised awkward questions that could not be ignored, even when you are comfortably lying on a sun lounger by a pool. Style is hard to ignore in politics, regardless of country. But in time, substance inevitably triumphs, if only because style doesn't make the difficult choices any easier or the complex consequence of ignoring them any simpler.

In the aftermath of Hollande's electoral victory, both the far left and the far right began quickly repositioning themselves for the upcoming parliamentary elections. The confrontation between these two extremes soon played out most spectacularly in June 2012, in the poor mining town of Hénin-Beaumont, in the north of France. Hénin-Beaumont was wrestling with high unemployment and industrial decline, as the European economies continued to stall under clouds of uncertainty and fear. Unemployment here stood at 16 percent, well above the French national average of 10 percent, while life expectancy was also significantly less than the national average.

In what the French press has labeled "Le Duel," the leader of the far-right National Front, Marine Le Pen, squared off against the leader of the far-left, Jean-Luc Mélenchon, for the honor of representing the gritty, impoverished constituency in the National Assembly. Both candidates had previously participated in the recent national elections for the presidency, but each was eliminated in the early round of voting. As between the two, Le Pen outperformed Mélenchon by a margin of 18 percent to just 11 percent.

Le Pen had much to gain in these parliamentary elections, which could produce a National Front MP in the National Assembly for the first time in many years. Her eyes were not only on her own personal victory in recession-ravaged Hénin-Beaumont but were also on making significant gains among disgruntled center-right voters who had previously backed Sarkozy. Meanwhile, the "red devil" Mélenchon had much to prove. Hénin-Beaumont, reminiscent of the forlorn mining communities depicted in Émile Zola's bitter novel *Germinal*, had historically been a left-wing stronghold, represented by the Socialists. Mélenchon's relatively new, Communist-backed party sought to similarly displace Hollande's Socialist Party as the real party of leftist sentiment and action.

The extremes of European politics differ significantly from what purports to be the outer boundaries of respectable political discourse in the United States, despite what one hears on either right-leaning Fox News or left-leaning MSNBC. American partisan debates are significantly more constricted, even during these much-lambasted years of gridlock and lack of bipartisanship that have recently gripped Washington. Regardless, it can be insightful for Americans, usually engulfed by a media bubble that lets little unfiltered foreign news through, to see how their own domestic concerns are debated elsewhere around the world.

For example, at the heart of most European far-right parties, such as Le Pen's National Front, is a heightened concern over the impact of immigrants on their country and their social services. During these times of austerity, voters can become very afraid of how limited government resources will be spent. An "us versus them" mentality can easily develop, especially in those towns and villages that have historically been very homogeneous.

Interestingly, on economic policy issues such as stopping Brussels's austerity program and adopting protectionist measures, both the far left and the far right are often in broad agreement. Only on hot-button issues such as immigration do the two sides fall out.

Some French newspapers focused, with a certain amount of humor, on the potential obsession that Mélenchon may have developed with Le Pen after placing fourth to her in the presidential ballot. However, the threat posed by the National Front was a serious one for the far left. A Le Pen victory in Hénin-Beaumont, where 20 percent of residents were of Algerian descent, and there has been a long-standing pattern over the last century of immigrants coming to work in the mines, would have serious repercussions. Le Pen's message of "France first" resonated among many French voters who were put off by the failures of Sarkozy's traditional center-right party. Mélenchon's campaign was based on the countervailing belief that the Hénin-Beaumont voters were "furious but not fascists."

As much of Europe teetered on the brink of economic collapse, the tension between the far left and the far right was continuing to build. The causes of this collapse, and the unraveling of the social net that has bound the European working classes into the economic system for generations, will be questioned and argued over for years to come.

Clearly, President Hollande faced enormous challenges as his term began. Without a compelling case to French voters that they have the means and inclination to return France to economic growth, fingers will inevitably be pointed at scapegoats, of one type or another. Both the far right and the far left were showing all French voters that they are a ready alternative if current leaders proved inadequate to the task at hand.

* * *

When Hollande took over the French presidency, many French voters hoped that his new government would bring about a distinct change in direction from the "bling-bling" of the Sarkozy administration. By filling his cabinet with many fresh faces, Hollande seemed committed to looking at complex and contentious issues from new perspectives. In July 2012, one of the most awkward and inviolate elements of the French political foundation was explicitly called into question by one of Hollande's new ministers—the issue of race.

According to the philosophic orthodoxy that cuts across partisan politics in France, there is only one type of Frenchman. Everyone is equal in France because in France every Frenchman is equally French. As a result, the "hyphenated identities" that are so prevalent in the United States and are a key feature in contemporary Britain have not been officially sanctioned in France. Although there are "African Americans" and "black Britons," in France there is no such thing as a "French Algerian" or a "French African."

However, Yamina Benguigui, minister of the French language, made the radical proposal that the French government should recognize and accept that the concepts of ethnicity and race actually exist in the French Republic. Previously, no official statistics were compiled based on ethnic or racial backgrounds, so no formal attempt to analyze the French nation, or any problems it faces, from this perspective could take place.

Benguigui, a film producer whose father was from Algeria, argued that France should recognize the reality of how decades of immigration and the failure of assimilation have impacted many communities. Despite the importance of "equality" and "fraternity" to successive generations of French government officials, a lack of pragmatism has meant that abstract ideals about how the French state should be constructed have limited the government's ability to address important race-relation problems.

The television images of burning cars and nightly violence that regularly emerge from the dire suburbs that encircle Paris and other large French cities were a constant reminder that many men and women, born in France as the children or grandchildren of immigrants, still did not feel included in the Cartesian perfections of the French Republic. According to Benguigui, the time had come for the government to take off its blindfold and begin to recognize that communities based on ancestry have always existed in France and will continue to operate in the future. Only then could a pragmatic new approach be fashioned to address the challenges that France currently faces.

Unfortunately, for any French politician to stand up in front of television cameras and say that France should look to the United States or Britain for inspiration on how to solve its problems is either the very definition of "political bravery" or of "political suicide"—or both!

Hollande's honeymoon period was clearly over by the summer of 2012. He had just received a stark warning from the French government audit department, the Cour des Comptes, that he would need to cut over $40 billion from government spending in order to meet stringent deficit-reduction targets. Hollande had campaigned on a platform for shifting the country away from austerity, but the reality of France's spiraling debt and empty coffers was superseding his personal political priorities.

In the face of such negative economic prospects, Benguigui's radical rethinking of how French citizens should define themselves, and consequently how the French government should develop public policy to address the challenges that this diverse country faces, came at a less-than-optimal time politically. Like much abstract thought, there is something intellectually appealing about a government structured solely to deal with its citizens as philosophically undistinguished units devoid of any individual characteristics and "backstory." If such an approach could work in practice, it would satisfy the desire that many have for the highest level of equality before the law possible.

However, the reality of life in France shows that rather than facilitate assimilation and integration, France's inability to recognize or adapt to the ethnic and religious backgrounds of modern French citizens causes more harm than good. Discussion of these issues is coded and indirect and awkward, but these issues arise again and again regardless of the intoxicatingly abstract desire that they did not.

As France tried to climb its way out of the deep budgetary hole it had found itself in, millions of its citizens remained excluded from the economy and society. At times like these, a country needs all hands on the oars in order keep it moving forward as fast as possible. Eventually, the French will recognize that there are times when the direct results of pragmatism outweigh the aesthetic pleasures of abstract idealism.

★ ★ ★

By the fall of 2012, Hollande was facing significant criticism for his plans to hike taxes further on the so-called super-rich. In protest, a number of high-profile high earners announced that they would leave France and move abroad to avoid the new punitive rates.

As the French deficit ballooned in prior years, the question of how to balance the budget had once again taken center stage in French politics. Hollande's proposed budget for 2013 included a 75 percent tax rate for anyone earning more than 1 million euros ($1.6 million) a year. In addition, Hollande also planned to raise the annual wealth tax and the capital gains rate.

How attractive would these eye-watering tax hikes make the French economy? Were they more a reflection of a deeper hostility toward personal initiative and wealth creation than a viable solution for the deficit?

As the budget wound its way through the French parliament, high earners quickly began voting with their feet. Successful businesspeople, musicians, comedians, and athletes were giving up life in the City of Lights in favor of the fiscal stability of neighboring countries such as Switzerland. Even Austerity Britain got into the game, with Prime Minister David Cameron offering to roll out a red carpet for those departing French looking for a new home and London's idiosyncratic mayor, Boris Johnson, announcing that he was keen to welcome any talented French people who wanted to settle in his city.

Only in office for five months, Hollande was facing challenges on all sides. After campaigning on the platform of returning a "normal" presidency to France after the manic Sarkozy years, Hollande quickly began experimenting with far-left policies upon his arrival in the Élysée Palace. In 1981, François Mitterrand, the previous Socialist president, launched a campaign against the wealthy that drove many of them from the country. Hollande eagerly began to push France down the same path again.

Unfortunately, Hollande soon began to face a series of uncomfortable revelations about his personal life. It seems a distant memory now, but not so long ago the French press was once so accommodating and respectful that Mitterrand was able to maintain a mistress and a second family for years without the fear of exposure. However, in addition to the European financial crisis and the structural unemployment problems that France faces, Hollande was forced to contend with the ongoing saga of his current girlfriend, Valérie Trierweiler, and her open feud with his former partner, Ségolène Royal. Royal, in addition to being the mother of Hollande's four children, was also the unsuccessful Socialist candidate for president five years prior who lost against Sarkozy.

France is a very, very small place!

As a result, a comic melodrama involving Hollande's complicated personal life began playing out in parallel with his attempts to govern a country whose economy was in dire need of a reboot. As French magazines and satirical sketch programs showered him and Trierweiler with their relentless attentions, Hollande was forced to also navigate the treacherous economic waters that France, and Europe as a whole, had found itself in.

These difficulties were not distant and abstract, but rather pressing questions that demanded concrete answers. A gruesome side of modern French life has developed in recent years as a by-product of the economic stagnation that turned suburban neighborhoods into no-go areas where violence and rape were a far-too-common occurrence. Stories regularly appeared in the press of atrocities taking place in and around the tower blocks that house the poor and unemployed outside the bright lights of the leading French cities.

The fundamental problem facing Hollande's France was a lack of jobs. As a result, a generation of young people were finding it impossible to get themselves onto a meaningful career ladder. The children of immigrants whose parents had moved to France in search of a better life were unable to get a job when the economy was not rapidly expanding.

Socialist rhetoric supports the punitive taxation of high earners, and during his campaign, Hollande made clear his desire to further squeeze the country's financial elites. However, the realities of governing often trump the idealism of campaigning.

As more successful French men and women left their country and exchanged animosity and envy for the warm welcome of other more entrepreneurial countries, Hollande and his cabinet were forced to either reconcile their country's need for economic growth with the short-term populist sentimentality for "soak the rich" policies that deliver very little additional tax revenues or watch their country decline even further.

Notably, even within the left wing of French government and society, questions were being raised at this time about how effective Hollande's attack on high earners would actually be. If even France, with its historic distrust of wealth and ambivalence toward successful businesspeople, began to question these shortsighted policies, then observers around the world should have taken notice.

6

Mistakes We Knew
We Were Making

*Never interrupt your enemy
when he is making a mistake.*

—Napoleon Bonaparte

The debate over the impact of class on day-to-day life in Britain resurfaced again in the weeks following the 2010 general election. At a time when Britons were facing the most daunting challenges in decades, voters elected a government led by some of the most socially elite individuals in their country.

The new prime minister, David Cameron, was a graduate of Eton College, the hyper-elite private boarding school that has been the secondary school of choice for generation after generation of the British establishment. His chancellor of the exchequer, George Osborne, who was entrusted with safeguarding the nation's finances, went to the private academic powerhouse St. Paul's School. The deputy prime minister, Nick Clegg, was an alumnus of the equally prestigious Westminster School, a private school just a few hundred yards away from the Houses of Parliament. They were expected to lead the country out of its period of financial and economic crisis but could not be said to represent in any meaningful sense the diversity of modern British life.

The British press—and much dinner-party and pub conversation—often frames modern class issues in terms of education. The key distinction then becomes whether an individual was one of the handful of children in the country to be privately educated or instead attended state-funded schools. Since decades of financial and demographic trends have clouded so many other subtle distinctions in contemporary Britain, the state-versus-private dichotomy becomes a convenient shorthand.

Humorous discussions can always be had by Britons about what is or is not "posh," based on whether someone says "napkin" versus "serviette" or "supper" versus "dinner." Unfortunately, independent studies repeatedly highlighted the degree to which Britain suffers from the rigidity of its class systems. When attempts are made to calculate the net effects of the lost economic potential from children born into low-income and poorly educated families, the numbers come back in the tens of billions of dollars.

To what extent is the future of a young boy or girl just starting out in school predetermined by the educational or professional attainments of his or her father and mother? This conundrum is at the heart of arguments on both sides of the Atlantic over "social mobility," the belief that individuals can and should be permitted to rise and fall in accordance with their talents, and the efforts they expend to develop and use these talents in society.

American views of the class system in Britain can be blurred by our "Masterpiece Theatre" sentimentality, which relishes the period-drama qualities of *Downton Abbey* while passing quickly over the dreary lives of those who lived and worked "below the stairs." In reality, Britain faces less romantic, and incredibly daunting, problems from multigenerational poverty within families. The term *social exclusion* has come into use recently to describe this frustrating and persistent phenomenon.

When is the door to achievement finally closed to a person? How many second chances should an eleven-year-old, an eighteen-year-old, or a twenty-six-year-old expect? The British are able to discuss the impact of declining social mobility and the rise of social exclusion through the language of "class." This brings to the table several historic prejudices and a long list of unhelpful and inappropriate terminology, but at least it permits meaningful discussions to take place. In America, however, there is not a similar willingness to engage in a similar debate about the waste of human capital that occurs when children's prospects for success are curtailed before their talents are fully identified.

Historically, class is a slippery concept for Americans to deal with directly, and one that seems to be perennially obscured by larger and louder arguments about race. The election of President Barack Obama was historic. However, his educational background, which includes graduating from the expensive and exclusive private academy Punahou School, followed by obtaining Ivy League degrees from Columbia and Harvard, is much more traditional. And unfortunately it is also one that remains beyond the expectations of 99 percent (or more likely 99.99 percent) of Americans. Rather than confronting this issue head-on, Americans find comfort in a belief in a vaguely defined meritocracy that enables all who want to put in the work to achieve the "American dream."

We can easily become distracted from the hard and unforgiving realities of social class. We can laugh it away or define it out of existence with a linguistic sleight of hand. But to the extent that doors are closed to individuals from an earlier age and talent is left undiscovered, we waste the potential of our next generation before these children have had the opportunity to identify what their potential actually is.

And for that, we all suffer.

★ ★ ★

The violent scenes of rioting and looting and burning buildings that occurred across Britain in August 2011, less than a year before the Summer Olympics began in London, raised even more awkward questions about what type of country would emerge eventually from Austerity Britain. Armchair critics were keen not to let a social catastrophe of this scale pass them by without attempting to refashion the widespread horror and revulsion felt around Britain and around the world for their own rhetorical advantage.

From the right wing of British political discourse, the young perpetrators were labeled "wild beasts," illiterate and innumerate, who lack the moral compass necessary to allow them to feel either empathy for their victims or shame for their actions. In their eyes, Britain was no longer the country it was in the Victorian era, when morality was at the center of the national conversation. At the time of these riots, more Britons believed in ghosts than believed in God, and less than one-third of weddings were celebrated in a church or other religious establishment. However, even a casual examination of the individuals marched through the special twenty-four-hour-a-day courts that were rapidly established after the violence was initially contained revealed that children of millionaires and recent university graduates were among those being convicted of criminal activities.

Reflexively caricaturizing as "feral children" any youths who lack meaningful lives, or the potential to develop such lives, prematurely terminates any attempt at meaningfully analyzing the problem of long-term, multigenerational social exclusion. Talking heads who advocate such all-encompassing categorizations may be more interested in finding excuses not to act, rather than fully confronting the complexity of this problem and attempting to construct an effective response, one individual at a time.

The lack of skills and educational qualifications among many poor Britons, together with the collapse of family support structures, are real problems that inevitably contribute to the loss of values that support lifelong aspirations for individuals, their families, and their communities. There are many British youth who suffer under a culture of violence that brutalizes their day-to-day lives, while many British employers strongly prefer to fill their vacant positions with Eastern Europeans (readily available courtesy of the European Union's cornerstone principle of freedom of movement), who are widely believed to work harder and more reliably than young Britons.

From the left wing, however, some critics portrayed the burning and looting as a political uprising. They attempted to link this violence to wider discontent over policy decisions made at the highest level of government. However, smash-and-grab thievery and thoughtless destruction doesn't convey a meaningful critique of anything. Surely, "fighting for justice" must mean more than nicking high-end electronics and burning down a few kebab shops!

This rioting was not a British answer to the Arab Spring. This rioting was not a response to the austerity budget cuts adopted by the Conservative–Liberal Democrat coalition since it came to power in 2010. The crowds who assembled on the streets at night to firebomb stores and steal flat-screen TVs and expensive running shoes were not motivated by proposals to reduce library hours or reset the annuity rates of teachers' pensions.

These were criminal acts, committed by people of widely different backgrounds who succumbed to criminal impulses. With the rise of mobile phones and social networking, we witnessed the ability of localized crime to grow exponentially and spread with just a few keystrokes. Ultimately, the riots were a failure of policing on a grand scale. After a period of ineffective engagement, police eventually began to deploy in the numbers necessary to restore order. But those initial failures were very costly. Former Los Angeles and New York "top cop" William Bratton was quickly hired by Prime Minister Cameron to advise him on potential policing changes. However, even with the initial police mistakes, it is interesting to note that there were only two incidents of fatalities in Britain linked to the riots, one of which was a car crash.

Given the long-standing affection that Americans have for firearms, it is difficult to imagine a similar level of public unrest in the United States, where we enjoy the constitutional protections of the Second Amendment, without significantly higher casualty rates!

The British riots made clear yet again that society is not the same thing as government. Not every societal problem has a governmental solution. The government's responsibility on the first night of unrest was to effectively deploy police to the scenes of violence and arrest lawbreakers while restoring peace in those neighborhoods. We can also recognize that much must be done by Britons of every background to address the needs of the poorest in society. Unfortunately, this hard work must be done by individuals, volunteering their personal time and attention and support.

Some problems are too complicated and difficult to pass off to the government. Some problems we actually have to solve ourselves.

★ ★ ★

In the weeks that followed the August 2011 riots, order was reestablished on the streets of Britain, and the hard work to rebuild what had been destroyed was begun. To begin with, Britons familiarized themselves with the finer points of an arcane piece of Victorian legislation called the Riot (Damages) Act 1886. This century-old statute allows property owners to be reimbursed by the local police department for damages suffered as a result of rioting. Unfortunately, this produced yet another financial headache for a British government wrestling with deep and wide-ranging spending cuts necessary to address the enormous national debt accumulated under the prior Labour government.

Of course, much blame was passed out in the days immediately following the riots, whether to feral kids indulging in sick acts of wanton destruction or to successive left-wing governments that have created an underclass smothered by idleness and entitlement. Former prime minister Tony Blair, who first rose to national political prominence two decades ago with a stirring speech about the gruesome murder of toddler James Bulger by two small boys, strongly criticized this "muddleheaded analysis" over the rioting emerging from both the left and the right. Such political point-scoring only draws attention away from a very specific problem with an equally specific solution.

Crimes were committed during the riots on a scale that previously would have been hard for Britons to imagine. In London between August 6 and August 8, 2011, there were more than 3,000 crimes recorded, including 1,000 incidents of burglary and more than 100 assaults. The London police estimated that up to one-fourth of those arrested had links to gangs.

One unexpected hero that emerged in the riot's aftermath was the British judicial system. Through their speed and firm sentences, the courts restored credibility to the rule of law. Magistrates worked around the clock to process the unprecedented number of criminal cases in a matter of days, rather than the months such cases would take in the United States. Importantly, British magistrates are members of the local community, who live alongside both the perpetrators of crimes and their victims.

Some commentators noted that many rioting sentences were significantly harsher than normal. Ultimately, of course, this begs the question as to whether earlier sentences had been too lenient. Regardless, when sentences are handed down, rioting must be an aggravating factor. There is a real and fundamental difference between a crime committed against a backdrop of arson and looting and an isolated crime on a typical day in that community. During rioting, each criminal act feeds into the maelstrom of wider destruction, as observers become increasingly desensitized and their ability to make effective judgments and weigh the consequences of their actions is impaired.

Unsurprisingly, appeals courts were equally prompt in reviewing these convictions. In one noteworthy case, the conviction of a woman who received stolen clothing from a looter, but was not otherwise involved in the theft, was overturned. This is, of course, precisely the role of appeals courts. There must be a measure of consistency in sentencing to ensure that particular judgments are not disproportionate or unsound because of concerns over racism or other inappropriate considerations.

Prime Minister Cameron had long focused his political rhetoric on the need to fix a "broken Britain." Even his predecessor Tony Blair argued after the riots that the key problem was the growing subculture of alienated youths who were isolated from the social mainstream. Britons were beginning to look past oversimplifying arguments about the intersection of poverty and affluence, and instead address more awkward questions about families, parental involvement, and values in general.

A British public opinion poll in the weeks following the riots placed criminality, gang culture, and bad parenting as leading causes of the riot. Far below in the survey responses were unemployment, government cuts, or poverty. Where unemployment and idleness are passed down from one generation to another, a simple flurry of spending on job training or teacher overtime will accomplish little. Much more is needed to reverse the rise in selfishness and the decline in responsibility in these communities.

In the same survey, Britons displayed little confidence that government changes to education policy, welfare policy, or economic policy would fix "broken Britain." One-size-fits-all solutions dropped from above (whether from Westminster or Brussels), together with a flurry of check-writing, would do little to help. Instead, local leaders, both inside and outside of government, need to be enlisted to address these challenges. No one was advocating for a return to the dire days portrayed in Alan Clarke's 1979 film *Scum*, which cast an unblinking eye on the reprehensible state of British youth detention centers—known as borstals—at the time.

Importantly, a very large number of British youths, even among the poorest and most destitute, did not participate in the riots. Large numbers of citizens from various backgrounds, ethnicities, and generations actively engaged in the cleanup activities that sprouted up naturally in the worst affected communities following the riots.

Legal problems have legal solutions, and it was encouraging to see the British criminal justice system rise to the challenge it had been presented. However, the hard work of addressing parenting failures and the culture of criminality that festers at the margins of society will need to remain a priority for all Britons in the years to come—regardless of Britain's ongoing relationship with Brussels.

* * *

Unfortunately, the consequences of social exclusion and the collapse of families do not always exhibit themselves in the form of idle youth sitting around housing estates drinking cheap Belgian lager or even hoodie-wearing rioters smashing glass storefronts to grab a new flat-screen television. Sometimes it is seen in the faces of young girls who have been repeatedly raped and victimized by older men and largely ignored by those very government agencies and officials charged with ensuring their protection.

In May 2012, nine men of Pakistani heritage were convicted in a British court of the sexual abuse of seven young girls. The men preyed on girls between the ages of twelve and sixteen in the market town of Rochdale in Greater Manchester. They groomed them with gifts of food, clothes, alcohol, and drugs before forcing them to engage in sexual acts and prostitution.

These were local girls. These were not girls who shared the Pakistani heritage of the convicted sex offenders. Instead, these girls were white and working class. The groomers drove mini-cabs or worked in local fast-food restaurants. They focused on troubled children from at-risk backgrounds. They used empty apartments or cars as their venue for abusing and pimping out their young prey. They viewed their victims as fair game.

As a result of these uncomfortable attributes, the Rochdale case and similar incidents across Britain quickly became the subject of a highly politicized and emotional public debate over what was actually happening and why. The Rochdale convictions only came after unsuccessful attempts in 2008 to investigate claims made by young girls that they had been passed around for sex with much older men. The stories told by these girls were horrendous, but only after a second inquiry launched in 2010 was significant progress made.

Importantly, following these convictions, local police, prosecutors, and social services in Rochdale issued their own apology for not doing more to pursue these allegations sooner. One victim was supposedly under twenty-four-hour supervision by social workers but still managed to go missing for weeks at a time. It was clear that law enforcement and social services were both lacking in empathy and overly obsessed with political correctness.

Were hypersensitivity and fears of being branded "racist" enough to cause British police officers to turn their backs on these young victims? Police officials stressed that they saw the ethnicity of the perpetrators in the Rochdale case as secondary to the much more important element of adults preying on vulnerable children. However, days after the conviction, a further serious of arrests, involving nine other men, took place in Rochdale, regarding allegations of sexual abuse involving another young girl. The MP for Rochdale, Simon Danczuk, went on record with his view that there was a wider problem in his community and that this was not simply a one-off case.

In a separate conviction the same month, a Bangladeshi man in Carlisle was convicted of running a brothel from his kebab shop with girls as young as twelve. In his own defense, the man expressed contempt for the "white trash" girls he abused. They were not like his own children, who would never be caught out at night, after 11:00 pm, drinking in the middle of town.

The lead government prosecutor in the Rochdale grooming ring cases, Nazir Afzal, blamed "imported cultural baggage" for the prevalence of men of Pakistani origin being involved in these sex-grooming rings. Although some liberal voices stressed that these abuses occurred across all ethnic and religious groups, Afzal stated that these men viewed young white girls as "lesser beings." These were vile men who saw no reason not to take advantage of vulnerable young girls.

It is important for a society to protect its children. Recently, society has recognized honor crimes and female genital mutilation as unacceptable cultural practices that cannot be ignored under the rubric of multiculturalism. Similar steps must now be taken to identify and address those who indulge in the degrading and demeaning beliefs about modern, Western women that underlie many of these grooming cases. Notably, many of the defendants in the Rochdale case showed little shame or regret or empathy during their trial.

Is the threat of rape and sexual assault so ever-present in traditional communities in rural Pakistan that the only means to protect your sisters and daughters is to ensure that they are veiled and always accompanied by a male relative? Is the sight of a woman alone, in contemporary dress, a sure sign that she is, in fact, fair game?

More than 2 million Britons are of Pakistani, Bangladeshi, or Indian heritage, and more than 1 million Britons are Muslims. As a result, it is clearly wrong to oversimplify and overgeneralize the behavior of 9, 90, or even 900 men. However, a pattern has emerged involving a small subset of recent immigrants from rural communities who retain backward beliefs about women who are not members of their own insular communities.

Judge Gerald Clifton, who handed down the guilty verdicts against the Rochdale sex ring, stated that the sexual abuse of these white girls was acceptable to the perpetrators because they were not members of the same community and religion. The girls were something less valuable. They were fair game.

Although white men, acting alone, are responsible for most of the sexual offenses in Britain, these incidents of coordinated sexual grooming cannot be explained away as statistical anomalies or crude racist profiling by the far right. A blind eye cannot be turned to these cases—denial and delay have no place in circumstances such as these.

The difficult challenges facing Britons today—involving class, race, austerity, recovery—will need to be addressed with one eye on those institutions and traditions that have served the country so well over the centuries and another eye on the gulf that exists between the men and women who benefit fully from these institutions and traditions and those men and women who do not. The solution with not be an easy one, and Brexit itself doesn't provide a panacea. For example, in 2017, concerns were still being raised over similar grooming gangs operating across the country, including large cities such as Newcastle. Despite a series of prosecutions of British men of Pakistani background, a Labour shadow minister in August 2017 raised concerns that authorities were still reluctant to investigate such accusations due to concerns over being deemed racist.

7

Friends Indeed!

*There is no such thing as accident;
it is fate misnamed.*

—NAPOLEON BONAPARTE

A crowd of more than 10,000 angry Germans assembled in January 2015 to protest the detrimental impact that Muslim immigrants were having on their country, while denouncing the ruling political, economic, and social elites who had permitted this situation to become so intolerable. Meanwhile, a dozen people were killed in central Paris the same week when Islamist militants attacked the headquarters of the satirical magazine *Charlie Hebdo*, which published humorous cartoons featuring images of the Prophet Muhammad.

The organization behind the protests in Germany was Patriotic Europeans against the Islamisation of the West (known as

PEGIDA). Originally launched in the eastern city of Dresden in October 2014, the movement quickly spread across Germany, much to the dismay of the country's leaders. Despite the superficial similarities and easy comparisons that could be made with the Nazi party, swastikas and other fascist iconography were rare. Instead the group uses the slogan "We are the people," which was the motto of anti-Communist protesters who opposed the Soviet-backed regime.

Afraid that Islamist migrants will undermine both the German culture and, ultimately, the whole of German society, protesters believe that money being spent on asylum seekers should be spent for the benefit of all Germans. Despite the best efforts of Chancellor Angela Merkel to undermine PEGIDA, the march went ahead and received widespread coverage in the European media.

Given the impact that migration has had across Germany and Europe in recent years, it was perhaps surprising that such strong opposition had arisen in the state of Saxony, where the percentage of Muslims in the population is approximately 0.2 percent. However, historians pointed to the limited immigration in Communist East Germany. Men and women who grew up during this time would have had very limited direct experience with different cultures, particularly Islam. This did not explain, though, the number of young Germans rallying to PEGIDA's banner.

Concern of "Islamification" was not limited to Germany. Early that same week, beleaguered French president François Hollande took to the radio to encourage and cajole his country to not be afraid of the large Muslim community in France, which was estimated at 6 million. He identified this as one form of compulsive pessimism that continues to plague French men and women. One of the most popular books in France in 2014 was entitled *The French Suicide*, which argued that immigration and corruption had undermined France and brought the country to its knees.

Days later, Islamists conducted a brazen daylight attack on the offices of *Charlie Hebdo*. A number of France's most beloved cartoonists were among the victims. The attackers, shouting *"Allah Akbar"* and other religious sayings, were confronted by police as they exited the building but still managed to get away.

With a presidential election in France scheduled for 2017, many observers feared that support was gathering around the leader of the far-right National Front party, Marine Le Pen. Hollande was encouraging voters to have faith in French values and believe in France as a "great nation," but his approval ratings remained in the teens. It was unclear in the weeks that followed how the *Charlie Hebdo* attack would influence French voters.

Neither Merkel nor Hollande seemed able to guide their disgruntled citizens away from anti-Muslim and antimigrant movements. In her New Year's address, the German chancellor similarly argued to reject hatred and prejudice and instead embrace Muslims, including refugees from Syria who had been displaced by Islamic State fighting. As PEGIDA gained momentum in her country, German immigration was at its highest level in twenty years. Merkel argued that this was a benefit, since the German population was continuing to age, which would potentially drive down economic growth in decades to come.

Europe was wrestling with the question of how to best integrate Muslims into wider society while maintaining the best of its respective social, cultural, and political traditions. It was becoming increasingly clear that mainstream political parties across the continent had lost the upper hand in the discussion over migration generally and the impact of growing Muslim populations specifically. What would the results be?

At the same time as Islamic State was progressing steadily toward their oft-proclaimed caliphate, and foreign fighters continued to join the Islamist militants' ranks in Syria and Iraq in increasing numbers, Europeans were concerned that overly generous asylum benefits and unrestricted immigration policies were undermining their countries. The audacity of the Paris attack in January 2015 raised further questions about the ability of police and security services to protect their citizens, particularly as radicalized young fighters returned home with hands-on experience fighting in the Middle East.

Europe's governing elites needed to directly address these concerns, instead of languishing in platitudes while hoping that the crowds would disperse and their fears evaporate. In the absence of such "straight talking," worried Europeans would continue to be drawn to new political groupings and labels, which would make important elections in 2017—following the trend set by Brexit in Britain and Donald Trump's defeat of Hillary Clinton in the United States—particularly uncomfortable for mainstream politicians seeking a comfortable reelection.

* * *

With the arrival of spring in Europe comes the return of boats full of migrants making the perilous journey north across the Mediterranean Sea in pursuit of the prosperity of Europe. Sadly, April 2015 saw hundreds drown when a ship sank off the coast of Libya. Although the Italian coast guard was able to rescue 144 people, another 400 bodies remained unaccounted for.

After days of searching, Italian officials eventually declared that their efforts were at the end. Amnesty International promptly issued a scathing rebuke of the European Union for abdicating its responsibility to police the Mediterranean and prevent such tragedies from occurring.

As the weather improved and migration season began in earnest, European officials were wrestling with their appropriate response. A program run by the Italian government called "Mare Nostrum" had previously rescued 170,000 migrants, but concerns were raised that the program was in effect "pulling" more migrants across the Mediterranean.

Fearful that continuing to increase rescue resources was actually encouraging more migrants to make the trip over, Brussels made a point in 2014 of cutting back these operations. In the place of Mare Nostrum was a more limited surveillance program known as "Triton," which was operated by the EU migration agency Frontex. However, with several thousands of migrants already rescued this same week in April 2015, it did not appear that the point had been made clearly enough.

In 2014 alone, it was reported that 280,000 people illegally entered the European Union, with approximately 3,400 perishing en route. Pope Francis issued a stern warning that the Mediterranean was turning into a "vast cemetery."

Human traffickers profit from the lucrative trade of transporting migrants from the poverty and political instability of North Africa to the security of European shores. Demonstrating the brutal efficiency of market economics, smugglers are arguably in a "win-win" situation. Should EU governments close their borders and ratchet up aggressive antimigration measures, the smugglers will simply increase the prices that they charge.

Vast networks exist across North Africa and the Middle East that collect migrants along the southern coast of the Mediterranean. From there, they are packed on a variety of boats—not all particularly seaworthy—and sent across to various landing points in Spain, France, and Italy. After making landfall, the new arrivals try the best they can to integrate themselves in the underground economy as undocumented workers. The smugglers take advantage of the inability of European governments to work more closely with each other and with neighboring countries where criminal networks are able to operate beyond the reach of local authorities.

Interestingly, although the European Union currently has twenty-eight different member states, the majority of refugees put down their roots in only five countries. As a result, the challenge faced by Europe, and the burden to address it, is not shared evenly across the continent. One argument that has repeatedly been made in Brussels has been a pragmatic one—namely, that the best way to lower the number of migrants dying while trying to enter illegally may be to reform immigration laws and procedures so that these men and women and their families can move to Europe legally.

The question of how best to deter dangerous crossings is one that has perplexed policy makers around the world. For example, in the 1990s the US government sought to limit illegal immigration across its southern border by tightening security along the most popular crossing points. Arguably, this merely caused migrants to attempt their crossings at more dangerous parts of the border, leading to a significant increase in deaths.

Migration today is a global phenomenon. Economic, social, and political forces are operating around the world to push impoverished individuals from fractured, dysfunctional countries to more prosperous and law-abiding ones. The debates over "illegal immigration" that have been such a feature of American political discourse over the past thirty years are now being echoed in a growing number of countries, such as Britain, France, and Germany, as well as countries as far away as Australia.

The unrest in Syria, Iraq, and Afghanistan, together with the increasing instability across Africa, has created a growing pool of men and women desperate enough to undertake any risks to find a better home for themselves. The promise of prosperity in developed countries is too alluring for them, and like any human need, there are savvy intermediaries standing ready to profit.

What has allowed this problem to balloon in recent years is the growing number of ports that have become lawless and outside the reach of local authorities. See, for example, the collapse of Libya's central government. As a result, human traffickers can operate there with a free hand. In order to limit the number of ships arriving on their shores or capsizing in their territorial waters, the European Union will eventually need to figure out how best to prevent these ships from ever departing, overloaded with their human cargo.

Whether Brussels will have the courage to address these issues at their source remains to be seen.

★ ✳ ★

August 2015 saw further waves of migrants arriving illegally on European shores. On the Greek island of Kos, more than 2,000 Syrians and Afghans were rounded up from makeshift camps and relocated to a sports stadium, where questions about their treatment were soon raised by aid workers. In a single day, the Italian coast guard rescued approximately 1,500 migrants from unseaworthy boats attempting to cross the Mediterranean, although many were still lost at sea. Meanwhile, angry migrants in the Spanish seaside town of Salou clashed with local police after a Senegalese man jumped to his death as officers raided his apartment.

With each new illegal arrival on European soil, awkward questions were being raised about the ability of European politicians to address the migration crisis fully and effectively. Despite the cataclysmic Greek financial crisis, the near-bankrupt country still made an appealing destination for thousands of migrants. As police collected individuals from several camps strewn across the island into a stadium for processing, complaints of maltreatment were raised due to the excessive heat and lack of adequate food and water provided.

Kos sits just off the coast from Turkey, making it a prime target for illegal crossings. Greek prime minister Alexis Tsipras candidly admitted that while battling the financial crisis, his country lacked the financial resources to do more to address the migration crisis.

Farther west, the Mediterranean remained a deadly frontline between European authorities and waves of migrants in North Africa. More than 2,000 migrants died in the first half of 2015 attempting the sea crossing. Human traffickers in Libya profited from trafficking approximately 100,000 men, women, and children across the Mediterranean during the same period.

Members of the Italian military worked diligently to rescue as many migrants as possible, although their record of lifesaving is not perfect. Despite the widely reported casualty numbers, boats crammed to bursting continue to attempt the high-risk voyage.

Even when migrants make landfall in Europe, countries such as Spain, alongside Italy and Greece, must cope with undocumented migrants unable to work legally who must support themselves through illegal activities. In Salou, police targeted the homes of several people believed to be associated with the selling of fake luxury goods to tourists in the resort town south of Barcelona. When officers entered the apartment of a Senegalese suspect, he immediately jumped to his death to avoid arrest. Protests soon broke out on the streets of Salou, with one hundred migrants clashing with local officers, leading to injuries on both sides. With the holiday season along the Catalan coast in full swing, at least one tourist was also injured in these clashes.

Unfortunately, despite the mounting human costs of illegal migration into Europe, many European politicians, as well as countless learned observers in the mainstream media, continued to dismiss the crisis as scaremongering by far-right politicians with ulterior motives. To these generous souls, the surge in migrants arriving at Europe's borders was perfectly manageable and a moral duty of Europeans to embrace. The number of migrants reaching Europe was only a small fraction of the number of displaced individuals who remained in camps in countries throughout the Middle East, driven there by wars that were the creation of Western governments. Therefore, the answer was not stricter border controls and the enforcement of existing immigration law, but instead an increasingly generous international aid program and a general abdication of Western involvement in containing Islamic State and other extremist militant groups that were operating in legal vacuums around the world.

In hindsight, placing the blame for the increasing waves of migrants attempting to enter Europe on globalization and military adventurism was naive grandstanding. Asylum was already being provided in neighboring countries to families displaced by war and upheaval, in compliance with international law.

As horrific as it is to be driven from your home in fear of personal attack, this does not grant any individual a Willy Wonka golden ticket to relocate to the country of their choice in pursuit of economic gain. Refugees are a global responsibility, and in light of the need in the medium- and long-term to resettle these individuals back in their home country, the best answer in the short-term is to house and secure them as close as possible to the areas they are fleeing.

European leaders were tested in the months and years that followed as the number of illegal migrants continued to increase. Eventually, voters would be asked to judge whether their elected representatives had effectively addressed this challenge or simply avoided difficult decisions in favor of platitudes and political correctness. With numerous national elections scheduled across Europe in 2017, the wider impact of the Brexit vote was soon to be made a little clearer.

* * *

Migrants were entering Europe in record numbers during the summer of 2015, using whatever means of transport they had available and despite the mounting number of casualties being suffered along the way.

In August, an abandoned delivery truck was found on the side of a road in eastern Austria, filled with dozens of bodies of migrants who suffocated while locked in the back. Meanwhile, neighboring Hungary was seeing 2,000 migrants a day crossing the hundred-mile border it shares with Serbia, despite the use of razor wire as a deterrent.

In the face of the largest refugee crisis that Europe has seen since 1945, German chancellor Angela Merkel stated repeatedly and unequivocally that Germany and other EU member states must do more to address the humanitarian crisis that was unfolding before them. She was insistent that all Europeans must step up to the challenges being posed by the migrants, both in terms of processing and registering the new arrivals and shouldering the ongoing costs of housing and supporting them for the duration of their stay.

Merkel was sounding the alarm, arguing that without coordinated efforts by all EU governments, the situation would get much worse, leading to more suffering and more casualties. In order for the refugee burden to be shared evenly throughout the European Union, Merkel made the case for the imposition of mandatory quotas to ensure that each member state was admitting its fair share of migrants. However, attempts to adopt this as EU policy met stiff resistance among the more pragmatic European leaders, including a Britain preparing itself for its historic June 2016 vote on Brexit.

In addition to the perilous voyages across the Mediterranean departing from the shores of Libya in the hopes of reaching Italy, a well-trodden land route had emerged from Turkey into Greece, then north to Macedonia and Serbia, with the goal of entering Hungary and the wealthier EU countries. Attempts by government forces in Macedonia, for example, to stop the crowds of refugees from entering were ultimately abandoned. Instead, borders were opened and the migrants allowed to continue their trek to Germany and "Mama Merkel."

Domestic opposition to Merkel's migration policies varied at the time. Many Germans supported their chancellor's sentiments but were concerned that Germany was carrying an exceptionally large share of the asylum-seeker burden, while several other EU countries refused to accept any meaningful number. By contrast, a small number of Germans were taking their anger out on the growing numbers of refugees more directly, attacking migrants and burning down refugee centers.

Some critics suggested that Merkel should have done much more to directly address the rise in far-right violence and related rhetoric being directed at migrants on social media and in public demonstrations. Despite ten years in office, Merkel managed to visit a refugee center for the first time in 2015. Unfortunately, upon her arrival at the center near Dresden, she was met with jeers, insults, and claims that she was a "traitor" by protesters opposed to her "open door" policy toward migrants.

Of course, recent history leaves many Germans with a sense that they have a significant moral debt in need of repayment. In this light, generosity and hospitality toward asylum seekers were "good deeds" that could be seen as evidence of a meaningful change in German values and priorities since the Nazi era. There were, however, more pragmatic reasons for Berlin to be welcoming new arrivals with open arms—namely, an increasing demand for labor to boost domestic economic growth. A critical skills shortage existed in Germany, and skilled migrants who could play a contributing role in the German economy would find quick employment.

Merkel's challenge in 2015 was to establish a European consensus that the German model of "open door" asylum and equitable distribution of refugees was the best approach, while at the same time preventing the growing voices of fear and anger in her own country from gaining traction. Xenophobic attacks continued to increase in frequency within Germany and quickly gained media exposure as the images reinforced ugly ideas about Germany and Germans that have been cut deeply in our modern memory.

How Europeans ultimately react to these waves of migration will go a long way to demonstrate to themselves and the world what values Europe holds highest. Merkel's voice was perhaps the loudest among those working out the answer to this question, but she was still only one voice among many.

* * *

Much attention was focused in the fall of 2015 on the record number of asylum seekers making their way overland into the wealthier northern European countries from Syria, a country brought to its knees by prolonged conflict with the extremist group Islamic State. Unfortunately, the traffic between Syria and Europe was actually two-way. Reports circulated in September 2015 that another British family had been arrested in Turkey trying to reach Islamic State–controlled territory within Syria.

Zahera Tariq, of East London, had left Britain several days earlier with her four young children. Her husband, Ysair Mahmmood, was believed to have reported her surprise departure to authorities before being hospitalized due to the shock of the circumstances.

Approximately 700 British citizens had traveled to Syria by this time, although half were believed to have soon returned home. At least forty were women, including the widely reported academically gifted schoolgirls from East London—Shamima Begum, Amira Abase, and Kadiza Sultana—who received global media coverage when their clandestine trip from Bethnal Green to Syria was uncovered in February 2015. Within months, at least two of these girls had reportedly married Islamic State jihadists.

British police officers quickly developed very good relationships with their counterparts in Turkey, the most common point of entry into Syria, as well as other European police forces, in order to track individuals making their way to Turkey through more circuitous routes.

Although many attempts to reach Islamic State–controlled territory succeeded, many ultimately failed. Another couple from Slough, a commuter town near London, was arrested in Ankara, the Turkish capital, in May 2015 with their four children. Surprisingly, when given the choice of where to be sent, they chose to be deported to Moldova, only to be promptly arrested by the Moldovan authorities. In a near mirror image of the journey so many migrants have attempted, Asif Malik and Sara Kiran left England via ferry and headed to the French port city of Calais, made their way to Greece, and entered Turkey from the Greek city of Kirklareli.

Several weeks earlier, an unidentified British woman in her early twenties was also arrested in Turkey by local police, who believed she intended to enter Syria. A few days earlier, three teen-age boys from northwest London were arrested in Istanbul, Tur-key's largest city, and promptly sent back to Britain.

After the February 2015 departure of schoolgirls Begum, Abase, and Sultana, international pressure was placed on Ankara to increase the security at its border. Turkish authorities cracked down on foreigners seeking to use Turkey as a point of entry into Syria.

Clearly the view of the hundreds of thousands of Syrians try-ing desperately to reach the relative prosperity of northern Europe was not held by many of the Muslim individuals and families already settled there!

This raised the interesting possibility that at some bus stop or train station in Turkey or Serbia or Hungary men and women were brushing by each other headed intently to the same location where the other had only just left—each believing that their future salvation depends on getting to this ultimate destination.

Many arguments were aired in 2015 over the political, reli-gious, and ideological factors that drive some individuals into extremist terror groups, while others continue playing their tradi-tional roles in modern twenty-first-century life. Ultimately, these decisions are personal ones, made for all the same reasons—inse-curity, anxiety, ignorance, fear, anger—that drive, at least in part, every decision that we all make during the course of our lives.

Perhaps we all want at times to dress up our lifestyle choices with a higher purpose of some sort, to demonstrate to ourselves and our families, friends, and coworkers that we have "reasons" for taking a particular course of action and that we are not, by implication, just seeking change for change's sake.

Genuine fear of violence is part of the consideration for many Syrians trying desperately to reach the "promised land" of asy-lum declared by German chancellor Merkel in the fall of 2015. Unfortunately, many Syrians made the journey for more mundane reasons—such as short-term economic gains. What made Merkel's asylum free-for-all particularly unfortunate was that many of these

Syrian men and women will soon be needed back in their home country to help rebuild it, once Islamic State has been unwound and stability reestablished in Bashar Assad's war-torn Syria.

Instead, perhaps some day they—or their children or grandchildren born in the midst of Western decadence and bigotry—will eventually feel alienated by Western culture, frustrated by their lack of economic advancement, and make the decision to return to another "promised land."

Those decisions may be made for the same reasons that drove the initial journey west out of Syria during the summer and fall of 2015—or for the reasons driving so many east toward the divine promise of an Islamic caliphate.

8

Turkish Delights

*A man's palate can, in time,
become accustomed to anything.*

—Napoleon Bonaparte

The role of values in society is an important one, and questions over what constitutes "European values" have arisen with regularity over the years. Often it comes up when outsiders (such as Americans) are trying to reconcile the differences in responses and priorities between themselves and their putative European allies. One particularly useful perspective to frame a discussion of what being European actually means is the long-running saga of Turkey's attempt to join the European Union.

For example, in November 2012, Turkey's then prime minister Recep Tayyip Erdoğan dealt his country's prospects of EU membership a severe blow when he proposed reinstating the death penalty. Erdoğan pointed to the United States, China, and Russia as countries that regularly execute their citizens, and the death penalty remains broadly popular in Turkey today. Turkey banned capital punishment in 2002, since this is a nonnegotiable requirement for EU membership.

Unfortunately, Erdoğan continued to face armed resistance from the Kurdish minority in Turkey. The Kurdistan Workers' Party has been fighting for independence for almost three decades. Kurds in neighboring countries such as Iraq and Syria had taken significant steps toward autonomy in recent years.

European reaction was prompt and predictable. While encouraging its eastern neighbor to continue down the path of reform and liberalization, leaders in Brussels made clear that reinstatement of the death penalty would stall progress on membership. Recent years have seen increased criticism of Turkey from Europe over the decline in human rights protections, including the strict antiterror laws, which have resulted in thousands of Kurds ending up in prison.

The Kurdish problem in Turkey was not new and had been growing for many decades. Under Erdoğan, Turkey became deeply engaged in the campaign for regime change in Syria. However, many Turks feared the creation of a newly independent "Kurdistan," assembled from pieces of several different neighboring countries. Erdoğan was keen to portray himself as a strong leader, regardless of what shrill voices in distant Brussels might say. After many years of dutifully seeking a place at the European table, hostility toward EU membership was by this time growing significantly in Turkey. Given the catastrophic meltdown of the euro, this was perhaps of little surprise. Unlike the austerity and recession that had gripped the continent in recent years, Turkey at this time remained a vibrant picture of economic growth, while its western neighbors suffered mounting problems from the global financial crisis and its aftermath.

Despite Turkey's long-standing membership in NATO and other top-table international bodies, Europeans have always made a point of making their eastern neighbor feel like a second-class suitor. Since formal negotiations opened in 2005, Turkey had only managed to fulfill one of the thirty-five separate conditions that have been established by Brussels as prerequisites for joining the European Union. Ouch!

Turkey had its friends within Europe, such as Britain, and many neutral observers have supported cementing Turkey's position among the democratic and market-oriented club of nations. Unfortunately, the crackdown on internal dissent under Erdoğan made the case hard for even Turkey's staunchest friends and allies to progress. For many Americans, the 1978 movie *Midnight Express* still remains the only meaningful touchstone for any assessment of Turkish police and prisons.

As the security crackdown escalated during 2012 and concerns over police brutality spread within Turkish society, negative publicity was building against Erdoğan's government, although he remained a popular figure among his supporters within the Islamist Justice and Development Party. An important political dynamic underlined these issues concerning the domestic criminal justice system. Turkey, since its founding after World War I, was a secular nation, and the military served as the bulwark of those secularist beliefs. Erdoğan's Islamist movement came into power on a wave of popular support, but the military continued to resist efforts at desecularization. The police, therefore, proved to be an important group for Erdoğan and his ministers to support and defend.

At a time when many other countries in the Middle East and North Africa were shifting away from dictatorships and one-party rule, Turkey had the potential in 2012 to demonstrate how a Muslim democracy could operate, particularly one governed by an Islamist party. Negotiations for EU membership had put Turkey on a rigorous course for further liberalizations. Its economic growth in recent years clearly demonstrated the potential for spreading prosperity more widely within Muslim-majority countries.

The forces unleashed by the Arab Spring on the other side of the Mediterranean Sea could have looked to Turkey as a potential model for the types of institutions and processes that lead to stability, while allowing for greater popular participation in the machinery of government. Unfortunately, the government in Ankara was by this time the world's top jailer of journalists, a dubious honor that calls into question many of the achievements that have been gained in recent years during its unrequited pursuit of EU membership.

The growth of authoritarianism at home noticeably muted the potential influence that Turkey could exert as a champion for democracy in the wider Muslim world. At a time when the region was in particular need of a role model, Ankara let this historic opportunity to positively influence its neighbors simply pass it by. Turkish leaders had failed to maintain the standards of civil liberties and due process to which they had once so publicly committed themselves. Instead of possessing a Muslim member who could reinforce its goal for peace and stability eastward into the volatile Middle East, the European Union had allowed the opportunities presented by a democratic and liberal Turkey to be squandered—at least for the time being.

* * *

Not so long ago, Turkey was held up as a fine example of a secular Muslim-majority country, comfortable with modern life. In June 2013, the country's steady drift toward theocratic and authoritarian rule was highlighted by a series of violent protests targeting Erdoğan and his Islamist supporters in the Justice and Development Party. The unrest started when protesters in Istanbul, concerned over plans to turn a small park into a commercial development, clashed with police. Momentum quickly began to build. Soon half of the country's provinces were witnessing protests, fueled by Twitter and other social media. Back in Istanbul, a core of demonstrators established themselves in nearby Taksim

Square for the long haul. Observers across neighboring Europe and around the world looked on with grave concern.

Istanbul is the commercial and cultural heart of Turkey, but Erdoğan's drive to Islamify the country finds its support in rural areas across the Anatolian peninsula. Many in cosmopolitan Istanbul still favor the secular state that was a central feature of the Turkish republic, which rose from the ashes of the Ottoman Empire after World War I.

Turkey—a NATO member since 1952—has historically been an important US ally in this region. However, under Erdoğan, the country has become more unpredictable, as his government has focused its attentions on appeasing its Islamist base. With three election victories under Erdoğan's belt, his confidence has increased substantially, causing critics to claim that he is becoming increasingly autocratic. After ten years in office, with his popularity among his core supporters still very strong, Erdoğan was becoming more assertive in his Islamist beliefs, to the dismay of secular Turks. The fact that the Turkish economy has been booming under Erdoğan's watch has given him tremendous cover to develop plans that appeal to the many deeply religious Turks who are in favor of expanding the role of religion in their country.

Although it was relatively easy for Erdoğan to dismiss the protesters as simply looters and hooligans, the way forward for Turkey was not immediately clear. Simply put, there is a significant divide between rural and urban Turkey today, and Erdoğan has been very effective in navigating these conflicting viewpoints to maximum effect.

Class divisions are still very important in contemporary Turkey. Istanbul is a cosmopolitan city, the successor to Constantinople, seat of the Roman Empire. Life in the vast Anatolian hinterland, however, is quite different from the hurly-burly of a major city. Erdoğan has repeatedly marshaled regional envy to his advantage.

Many secular Turks now felt under attack by Erdoğan and his religious supporters. The 2014 protests over the redevelopment of a city park, which also included the building of yet another mosque, tapped into these frustrations. Perhaps more transparently than elsewhere in the region, Turkey allows us to see the great divergence of opinions and beliefs that rub up against each other in Muslim-majority countries today.

Interestingly, in response to a recently adopted law restricting the sale of alcohol, many demonstrators in Taksim Square made a point of publicly drinking beer while voicing their complaints about Erdoğan's regime.

Despite the friction that his ten years in office had generated, Erdoğan did not respond to these protesters like a leader on ropes. His hold on power remained firm. His political base lined up fervently behind him. The 2014 protests did not evolve into a "Turkish spring," which would eventually result in Erdoğan being driven unceremoniously from office.

Instead, Turkey continued to struggle with its identity. Is it a secular country, populated largely by Muslims, or a Muslim country that must make some minimal level of concessions to those who choose to live secularly? Is its future outside the European Union or within, potentially as an eastward Bonapartist expansion to counterbalance Britain's departure on the western flank?

Erdoğan clearly had his views on these subjects and on many, many more. He appeared set to continue consolidating power in such a way as to drive the country toward a more religiously oriented pattern of life. As a sign of his confidence in his own position and prospects, he actually left Turkey with these protests still under way to go on a diplomatic tour of neighboring countries.

The line between confidence and overconfidence, however, is always a fine one. The Taksim Square protestors were a clear sign that not all Turks believed in Erdoğan's shift away from secularism and toward more explicit Islamic policies. Erdoğan's deft handling of this domestic upheaval was an equally clear sign that he could survive such a speed bump without losing his grip on power.

★ ★ ★

Despite US efforts to turn the tide on Islamic State, in October 2014 the jihadist group appeared ready to potentially open a new front in the fighting. Rather than retreat from their positions in Syria and Iraq in response to airstrikes ordered by President Obama, Islamic State was eyeing yet another target country—namely, Turkey.

International news reports at the time revealed how strong Islamic State's connections were within neighboring Turkey. A high-ranking commander of the Free Syrian Army, Abu Issa, was brazenly kidnapped on the streets of the Turkish town of Şanlıurfa, near the Syrian border. Fortunately for him, when members of Islamic State came to collect him at the border, they stiffed the Turkish Mafiosi out of their agreed "fee." While being held in a safe house in Turkey as the local gangsters sought to "renegotiate" with the terrorists, Abu Issa escaped.

In his hospital bed, recovering from his wounds, Abu Issa warned reporters that Islamic State's influence within Turkey was growing, and they had access to enough money to enable them to do whatever they wanted.

In moments such as these, it is worth remembering that Turkey is a member of the NATO alliance. Under the treaty, all NATO members, including the United States, would be required to deal with an attack on Turkey by Islamic State as an attack on itself and respond accordingly. As a result, any expansion of foreign jihadist forces into Turkey would radically expand the nature and consequences of the terrorist threat.

Islamic State's growth as a threat to regional security during this time was predicated on two of the most important foreign policy decisions of President Obama's tenure—first, the desire to remove US troops from Iraq at all costs, and second, the White House's willingness to avoid any commitment of forces to Syria, even after the president's own "red line" on chemical weapons had been crossed.

Fighting in the nearby Syrian city of Kobanî gave Turks an up-close view of what a direct confrontation with Islamic State forces would look like. Comparisons to Stalingrad, the site of prolonged and bitter fighting during World War II, were soon being made. While the United States airdropped supplies to forces attempting to defend Kobanî from the jihadists, Turkish leaders in Ankara were wrestling with the consequences that would flow from any decision they made that would support the ethnic Kurds who made up a significant share of the ground forces resisting Islamic State at Kobanî.

Ankara has been fighting its own bloody battles against Turkish Kurds in recent decades, and a public show of support for Kurds elsewhere in the region could put the much-feared concept of a sovereign "Kurdistan" a step closer to realization, although political divisions between Kurds in the region could be enough to prevent them forming a united front in the foreseeable future.

Turkish officials had taken the hardline position of not allowing personnel or supplies en route to Kobanî be moved through its territory. Ankara argued that the Syrian Kurds were part of a terrorist organization in their own right. Obama was keen to see Turkey more involved in the fight against Islamic State. Fortunately for the White House, this same week Ankara announced that they would let foreign Kurdish fighters from Iraq willing to fight the jihadists cross its soil.

Turkish agnosticism toward the jihadists was never a long-term strategy. It was necessary that Ankara fully recognized the danger it faced should Islamic State ever be successful in establishing a caliphate in the region propounding its own extreme view of Islam.

Although Kobanî was not of any great strategic importance to Islamic State, the push to capture it highlighted the shortcomings inherent in President Obama's strategy in the region. The consequences of the fighting expanding to a third country—

Turkey—would have been a devastating blow to the White House. An attack by Islamic State on a NATO member will always be a game-changer.

* * *

A February 2016 car bombing in Ankara demonstrated to the world once again that Turkey existed on the front lines of sectarian violence. The attack was directed at a military convoy driving through the center of the city and resulted in at least twenty-eight deaths. The sound of the explosion was heard across the Turkish capital city for miles in each direction.

Erdoğan—now president of Turkey—wasted no time in condemning the attacks. He reiterated his steadfast resolve to bring to justice those responsible for this terrorist act. In preceding months, his country had faced escalating security threats. In addition to their campaign against Islamic State, Turks were witnessing a state of near civil war in the south of the country, where Turkish soldiers were fighting Kurdish rebels.

Early reports pointed the finger at the Kurdistan Workers' Party, or PKK, a separatist group that was banned in Turkey. However, other reports attributed the bombing to Islamic State. Unfortunately, due to a government-imposed media blackout within Turkey, coverage of the attacks and inquiries into its perpetrators by journalists was severely restricted.

The location of the attack was highly symbolic. The bomb was detonated near the parliament, as well as key defense and government buildings. Only four months earlier, Ankara had been the location of another suicide bombing, which resulted in 103 deaths. Attributed to Islamic State, the target was a Kurdish rally in the days leading up to an election.

Erdoğan's efforts to crack down on Kurdish separatists showed little sign of waning in the days following the bombing. Large numbers of security officers were deployed to contain dissent and pacify Kurdish-majority enclaves in Turkey. The PKK's long-running fight against Turkish authorities, which began in earnest four decades ago, had been renewed and expanded in the months leading up to the Ankara bombing, after a cease-fire broke down the prior summer.

Only one month earlier, the Turkish prime minister, Ahmet Davutoğlu, had claimed that Ankara's battle against PKK was almost over, although no formal agreement or cease-fire had been reached with PKK officials.

In addition to fighting Kurdish separatists at home, Erdoğan was also bombing Syrian Kurds across the border, in response to the success of the Kurdish Democratic Union in gaining territory in Syria at the expense of Islamic State. If Syrian Kurds were eventually linked to Ankara bombing, this would provide Erdoğan with the basis for sending Turkish ground forces into Syria to confront the Kurdish fighters there head-on.

For those dreaming of an independent Kurdish state, the facts on the ground in northern Syria at this time painted an encouraging picture. Benefiting from Russian air support, the People's Protection Units, the military arm of the Kurdish Democratic Union, were able to widen their presence toward the Turkish border. Vladimir Putin was targeting Turkish-supported rebels, who until recently had been battling forces loyal to Syrian president Bashar al-Assad, creating a vacuum that the Kurds exploited.

Cue alarm bells in Ankara, where Erdoğan's government had said repeatedly that Kurdish control over their Syrian border was an unacceptable threat. In many ways, the Turkish government viewed the Kurds as a bigger threat than Islamic State. As a result, they were accused by critics of tolerating the jihadi extremists as a way of keeping the Syrian Kurds in check.

Ankara's deep fear was that Kurds on either side of the Turkish–Syrian border would one day unite to declare an independent Kurdistan. Adding some substance to these fears was the willingness of the United States to coordinate its efforts in Syria with Kurdish forces, who were eager and resolute fighters of Islamic State. Lacking American troops on the ground, Washington was forced to turn to the Kurds as useful allies, even though this strained relations with fellow NATO member Turkey.

As Turkey looked east, it found its fears over Kurdish ambitions stoked by accommodating Russian and American military actions. In some ways, this was emblematic of the mixture of conflicting priorities and loyalties that were a feature of Syrian civil war over the preceding three years. Meanwhile, Assad showed little signs of packing up and moving on, especially since his friend in Moscow was exerting such great effort to secure his hold on power.

Half-hearted military engagement and ham-fisted diplomatic posturing did little to prevent Syria's slide into widespread violence. Islamic State initially took advantage of the chaos, but eventually the Syrian Kurds began to position themselves for peacetime opportunities, whenever peace eventually returns to the region.

As Erdoğan presented himself as resolute in the face of the suicide bombing in his capital, he still needed to establish a lasting settlement with his Kurdish citizens. Without that, he risked many more years of violence at home and unresolved threats abroad— and increasing indifference in the halls of Brussels to any lingering European aspirations he may still have.

9

Bad Fences, Bad Neighbors

*Nothing is more difficult, and therefore
more precious, than to be able to decide.*

—Napoleon Bonaparte

Ten Russian paratroopers were captured in August 2014 in eastern Ukraine, approximately fifteen miles from the border with Russia. The incident provided Kiev further evidence of Moscow's ongoing support of the separatist forces. The arrests occurred on the same day as Russian president Vladimir Putin and Ukrainian president Petro Poroshenko met for the first time in many months. Awkward!

Although Moscow had adamantly denied any involvement in the unrest in Ukraine, Kiev remained convinced that Russian soldiers were fighting alongside the local forces, disguising themselves and their military equipment when needed. Until this incident, Ukrainian officials made due with accusations. Now they had actually captured soldiers to put on display. And put them on display they did—by way of a post on one of the government's Facebook pages.

Moscow downplayed the incident, claiming that these particular soldiers entered Ukraine "accidently" at a part of the border that was not clearly marked. Could have happened to anyone, really! But Kiev was not buying the "wrong turn" explanation, insisting that the Russian soldiers were sent into the country intentionally and as part of a definitive military plan. Gaining further territory in Ukraine would be useful to Moscow in order to provide additional land access to the recently annexed Crimea.

In prior weeks, Kiev-backed forces, including a number of independent militias raised by private individuals, had gained the momentum in the disputed eastern region of the country, although separatists continued to resist efforts by the central government to exert control over their Russian-speaking enclaves. According to NATO's secretary general Anders Rasmussen, the Russian military had been actively supporting the separatists from within Ukraine. Although Ukraine is not a member state of NATO, several members sit on the border of Russia and Ukraine, causing concern for the military alliance. NATO members met in Britain the following week, and security in this region was a high priority, as well as how to best keep Russia in check.

What were the long-term consequences of Russian incursions into Ukraine? Would these escapades embolden Putin to cast a wandering eye on other former Soviet territories that could fit nicely within a newly assertive and expansionistic Russia?

Unfortunately, peace was still a long way away for many Ukrainians. Ambiguities over the Kiev coup and questions over the legitimacy of the current government provided ample space for separatists to rally support. Poroshenko made the risky, although anticipated, decision of dissolving the Ukrainian parliament in order to gain an edge in the snap elections that eventually followed. He claimed that supporters of deposed president Viktor Yanukovych held too much power in the current parliament and therefore they had to be replaced.

Given the run of successes that Putin had enjoyed previously on the diplomatic front, it was unsurprising that the Kremlin was emboldened to assert its interests in different quarters. Washington and Brussels were unable to gain an upper hand when dealing with Moscow, and the cumulative effects of these shortfalls could possibly lead to seismic changes in the balance of powers in coming years.

Both Putin and Poroshenko were in Minsk, the capital city of Belarus, on the day the Russian soldiers were captured. They were in the midst of negotiations involving the European Union and the recently established Eurasian Customs Union. Despite claims from both sides that peace is their mutual goal, the death toll in the region continued to mount. According to UN estimates at the time, more than 2,000 people had died since fighting first began four months earlier.

The annexation of Crimea had by now been accepted tacitly by the international community as a "done deal." Putin had suffered few serious consequences from his bold land grab. Questions of Russian involvement in the unrest in eastern Ukraine were much more contentious. Sanctions were imposed, but it was still highly uncertain whether these sanctions would be enough to put Russia on notice that further assertions of national interest would result in unacceptable consequences.

Interestingly, earlier this same week it was the pro-Russian separatists who appeared to have the upper hand when they forced Ukrainian prisoners of war to march through the rebel-controlled city of Donetsk on a day celebrated as the anniversary of Ukrainian independence twenty-three years before.

After four months of unrest in the east of their country, the new regime in Kiev still had much to prove, while Putin appeared to be dictating terms far more than negotiating them. The capture this same week of Russian soldiers may have been a social media coup for Kiev, but a lasting peace in the region was still a long way away.

* * *

Beleaguered Russians rang in the New Year in 2015 with a special gift from the Kremlin—a cap on the price of their much-beloved vodka. Facing an economy seemingly on the verge of collapse, President Vladimir Putin took decisive steps to ensure that a plummeting ruble would not prevent his country from drowning its sorrows in cheap alcohol.

Russians love a drink. Therefore, it is a brave Kremlin leader who stands in the way of his countrymen's desire for a reliably inexpensive tumbler of vodka. To this day, Mikhail Gorbachev remains a target for abuse and hatred in Russia for the limitations he tried to implement on alcohol consumption. So much for the grand image of reformer and peacemaker that Gorbachev enjoys among many intellectual elites in the West!

The fall of the ruble in December 2014 and the announcement this same week that its gross domestic product contracted over the past year by 0.5 percent further highlighted the inherent fragilities of Russia's oil-dominated economy. As Putin wrestled with declining oil prices and the sanctions his government faced over their escapades in Ukraine, experts were forecasting an additional 4 percent contraction in the economy in 2015. The fall in crude oil prices by nearly half, from the $115 a barrel last seen in June 2014, put enormous pressure on Russia, which until recently had been projecting an image of strength around the world.

Inflation was reaching 10 percent by this time, making daily life for working Russians harder and harder. With their purchasing power halved and prices still rising, Russians needed all the help they could get over the festive season in order to enter 2015 as happy and optimistic as possible.

While the Russian finance minister Anton Siluanov announced on Christmas that the ruble's rally had begun, Putin was taking the more pragmatic step of curbing grain exports so that no matter how the country was buffeted by external economic pressures in the following months, there would be bread and vodka for all!

Unsurprisingly, for the wealthiest Russians who had managed to move their fortunes out of the country and into other currencies, prospects looked considerably better. Britain continued to be a safe haven for Russian money looking for security and growth. The high-end real estate market in and around London remained buoyant in 2014 and 2015 as oligarchs decided that a nice town house or country pile was a lucrative way to hold $20 million until the global economy stabilized. Of course, the appeal of Britain to über-wealthy foreigners has traditionally been—and continues today to be—significantly higher than other European Union member states.

However, not everyone who remained in Russia during these difficult times was willing to be bought off by Putin's cheap vodka. In early January 2015, Alexei Navalny, a leading opposition leader, disregarded his recently imposed sentence of house arrest to join in protests at Manezh Square in central Moscow in support of his jailed younger brother Oleg. Both had been recently convicted of fraud, although they loudly denied the charges. Even the internationally famous punk band Pussy Riot issued a video showing their support for the Manezh Square protests.

Alexei Navalny was a persistent critic of Putin in recent years, although his fraud conviction prohibits him from running against Putin in the 2018 presidential elections. By giving Alexei a suspended sentence and house arrest, rather than a custodial sentence like his brother Oleg received, perhaps Putin loyalists felt this would be the most effective way to silence Alexei's fierce and relentless criticism without making him a martyr in the eyes of his supporters.

The Sochi Olympics, where Putin attempted to demonstrate the full reach of his power and popularity, by now seemed a very,

very long time ago. Instead of a lazy reliance on bombastic propaganda, Putin was maintaining his grip on domestic power more firmly, but perhaps less elegantly, than in the past. In the end, though, the firmness with which he is able to grasp the tiller does little to make his vessel—the vast remnant of the Soviet Union—any more seaworthy.

Russia faced severe problems—some of Putin's own making, although many were inherited from his predecessors over the last century. Blessed with vast natural wealth but cursed with a social, political, and economic order that does little to foster widespread prosperity, Russia must eventually implement comprehensive reform in order to put itself on the path of meaningful and lasting development.

Rather than making the difficult choices that his country so desperately required, Putin preferred to offer "bread and vodka" to his beleaguered subjects while making his top priority the retention of his own personal political power. Unlike earlier occupants of the Kremlin who were able to keep Russia largely isolated from the unpredictable forces of the global economy, Putin must today oversee a country dependent on oil exporting and unable to hide itself away.

Cheap vodka may have given Putin a little breathing room, but the mounting challenges that Russia faces would not be so easily swept aside.

* * *

Ukraine suffered a stunning defeat in February 2015 when separatists in the east of the country finally seized the strategic city of Debaltseve, much to the embarrassment of President Petro Poroshenko. The much-touted cease-fire agreed upon days before in Minsk, Belarus, did little to stop rebel fighters from pushing out government forces and taking control of the town before the agreement's provisions were fully in effect.

Germany and France had taken the lead in nudging Ukraine and Russia to the negotiating table. When announced, the cease-fire seemed to mark a meaningful step toward a lasting settlement between these two neighboring countries. According to UN reports, more than 5,000 lives had been lost in the first ten months of fighting, and a million people had been displaced.

Poroshenko vehemently denied separatist claims that Debalt-seve was encircled at the time the agreement was reached in Minsk. This was a crucial point for negotiations because if that were the case, then it would be behind the frontline of fighting and therefore not covered by the cease-fire. He claimed that the government had control over the town until Ukrainian forces were driven out by a relentless rebel attack after the cease-fire had been agreed on. The separatists argued that Debaltseve, an important transit hub that linked rebel territory in eastern Ukraine, was clearly within territory that they controlled and therefore not subject to the Minsk cease-fire.

Both the United States and Germany condemned the action, and because of the Russian support provided to the separatists, again threatened Moscow with further repercussions, including additional sanctions. Meanwhile, Russia continued its multifront publicity offensive by pursuing a motion in the United Nations that would promote peace in eastern Ukraine, much to the annoyance of Washington's UN ambassador, Samantha Power.

Putin took advantage of a visit to Hungary to urge Kiev to allow Ukrainian soldiers to retreat from Debaltseve and not dig in for a futile battle. As has been his custom over the prior year, Putin spoke favorably of the separatists in the self-proclaimed republics of Donetsk and Luhansk, whom he described as "former miners and tractor drivers." The Kremlin continued to deny that it was providing either weaponry or troops to support the rebels, although many critics argued that such support was significant and ongoing.

The inability to secure Ukraine's borders and strike a meaningful peace deal with Putin meant that Poroshenko faced increasing criticism at home just one year after antigovernment protests drove his predecessor Viktor Yanukovych from office.

Those who believed that Putin's assertiveness on the international stage would be put in check by a few sanctions imposed by Brussels and Washington were quickly disappointed. Although Russia's economy suffered from the decline in oil prices, Putin steadfastly refused to dance to the West's tune. Critics accused him of Bonapartist adventurism and a general disrespect for international norms, but what they could not accuse him of was being ineffective.

As the world's attention continued to focus on the fighting in Donetsk and Luhansk, it is interesting to reflect on what had almost entirely dropped out of the wider conversation—namely, Crimea!

At the time that Crimea seceded from Ukraine and negotiated its reunion with Russia, arguments were being made among diplomats and in the opinion pages of major newspapers that this secession violated international law and must be reversed in order to protect Ukraine's territorial integrity. By the time of these ceasefire negotiations, Crimea had fallen off the agenda. Instead, the concern was over how the Kiev government could regain effective control of the territory that remained to it. Regardless of the scale and scope of Russian assistance, the success of the separatists in resisting Ukrainian authority was a constant reminder of the weakness of Poroshenko and his government. For so long as open fighting was occurring in Donetsk and Luhansk, relatively little attention would be given to the legal niceties surrounding Crimea's reabsorption into a resurgent Russian Empire.

As bad as things were in Ukraine in 2014, when the Maidan protests led the Ukrainian parliament to unconstitutionally remove Yanukovych from office, few observers would have said that the situation in early 2015 was an improvement.

* * *

The United States used to be the type of country that sent brave men and women into space. No longer, of course. Americans must now be content to watch other countries, such as Russia, engage in the exploration of space, as was the case in 2015 when a Russian cosmonaut set a new world record for the most time spent in space.

Gennady Padalka, commander of the International Space Station (ISS), broke the previous record of just over 803 days, which was held by a fellow Russian, Sergei Krikalev. It took Padalka five separate trips to amass his total, and at fifty-seven years of age he seemed eager for yet another trip into space to ultimately break the 1,000-day barrier.

By contrast, the US space program continued to underachieve by almost all metrics. After ceding much of American efforts to an array of private companies, the United States was largely on the sidelines in recent years. In the same week as Padalka's impressive record, a rocket owned by US firm SpaceX exploded moments after liftoff. Its mission had been to resupply Padalka and his fellow travelers, but have no fear—the Russian Space Agency (now rebranded as Roscosmos) sent up its own resupply rocket just a few days later!

Despite the continued success of the ISS, Russian-American collaboration is actually quite rare today, especially since the United States–imposed sanctions covered Moscow's space program in response to President Vladimir Putin's Bonapartist adventurism in neighboring Ukraine. Given the Russian space program's continued success, while America's remaining efforts stall, it would seem that US sanctions achieved little except to highlight the differences in current capabilities between the two countries.

Although the "space race" was a key part of American rhetoric during the Cold War, and the successful attempt to land a man on the moon rallied most corners of the country during the

1960s, America's commitment to exploration has always lacked the breadth and depth of Russia's love affair with space.

The quest to conquer space at times takes on an almost mystic quality to Russians. From Yuri Gagarin's first orbit of Earth in 1962 and Alexei Leonov's first spacewalk in 1965, cosmonauts racked up a series of impressive accomplishments that motivated subsequent generations of Russian children to believe that one day they could also push beyond the inky-black boundaries that encompass the planet. This was despite the huge risks the original cosmonauts faced in their early adventures. For example, Leonov lost twelve pounds during his twelve-minute spacewalk due to anxious per-spiration when he realized that his spacesuit had swollen and he might not be able to fit back inside the small landing module!

Despite the diplomatic friction between Washington and Moscow, the Obama administration knew that if the United States wanted to put an American into space, there was only one place to send him or her—the Baikonur Cosmodrome in Kazakhstan. Despite the collapse of the Soviet Union and the turmoil that Rus-sia has faced over the past two decades, manned-space flight has remained a priority for both Moscow and the Russian people. By contrast, within months of the United States' historic landing of men on the moon, it seemed that American political leaders lacked serious commitment to further manned space exploration. While the US space program was intent on beating their Russian coun-terparts to victory, little else seemed to motivate the Americans.

In that light, the ultimate abandonment of ambitious plans for manned spaceflight by the Obama administration was per-haps only the most direct admission of what had been obvious for years—namely, that Americans generally lack a deep and abiding desire to explore space and face the associated risks and burdens, at least when compared to their Russian counterparts.

Padalka's record demonstrated both his impressive personal achievement as well as the long-standing commitment of his coun-try, Russia, to pursue the ambitious dream of space exploration, despite the challenges and costs that provided ample excuses to turn away from the vast promises of space in favor of more parochial, Earth-bound concerns. In its continued aspirations to push boundaries and drive global affairs, Russia demonstrates what a single country acting in its national interest can achieve if its leaders and citizens set their minds to it.

10

A Better Tomorrow?

A leader is a dealer in hope.

—Napoleon Bonaparte

By the end of 2012, France's Constitutional Council overturned President François Hollande's controversial 75 percent supertax on people earning more than 1,000,000 euro a year, dealing a humiliating blow to the increasingly marginalized leader. Although estimates were that the tax would apply to only approximately 1,500 individuals, the proposal had great symbolic importance for Hollande and many of his leftist supporters with the Socialist Party, who stressed the need for the rich to demonstrate adequate levels of "economic patriotism" during the lingering financial crisis.

Critics blamed the supertax for a spike in the number of wealthy French citizens moving abroad. Even cinematic icon

Gérard Depardieu announced plans to move to Belgium. In an article published by Depardieu in response to accusations by the French prime minister Jean-Marc Ayrault that he was behaving in a "shabby" manner, Depardieu defended his actions in the strongest terms: "I'm leaving because you consider success, creation, talent, in fact being different, must be punished." Even Vladimir Putin eventually weighed in on this colorful debate by kindly offering Depardieu a Russian passport, should he need one.

Hollande has never hidden his strong dislike for the rich. With official estimates that the tax would raise only 500 million euro the following year, which is less than 0.3 percent of all the money collected in the form of income tax, the proposal was seen as more of a statement of political confrontation than a meaningful contribution to the uphill battle to balance the French budget.

The French court struck down the law as unconstitutional on the grounds that two families with the same aggregate income could be charged significantly different tax rates, an outcome that offends the deep-seated French belief in equality. The overturning of the tax was an embarrassment to the governing Socialist Party. Hollande was swiftly branded by many critics across the partisan spectrum as a political amateur, prone to ineffectiveness and incompetence. By mistakenly drafting the tax law to target individuals instead of households, which are the basis for the rest of the French tax code, Hollande's government displayed an embarrassing lack of basic knowledge about the country's own laws.

Regardless of this procedural setback, Hollande took to the airwaves on New Year's Eve to defend his stewardship of the country and to reiterate his belief that "those who have the most will always be asked for more." Unfortunately, as Hollande continued to battle for his pet tax policy, unemployment in France rose for the nineteenth consecutive month. He stressed the need to win the great battle for employment, although it was not clear at the time or in the months and years that followed how Hollande would create the jobs that so many French men and women desperately needed.

Interestingly, many French were by this point already reminiscing fondly about Sarkozy's time in office, with the frenetic former president polling twice as high as the Élysée Palace's current occupant in approval ratings at the time. The French electorate eventually tired of Sarkozy and his manic approach to presidential duties and turned to Hollande in pursuit of a more normal and traditional head of state. Unfortunately, by the start of 2013, many now felt that the mediocre Hollande was unable to deliver the leadership and vision necessary to help France overcome its current economic challenges.

Even after the court ruling, the supertax remained broadly popular in France, with approximately 60 percent of French surveyed approving of the proposal, far higher than the favorable polling that Hollande himself received. However, France needed effective policies far, far more than it needed popular policies.

The lesson that is ultimately learned again and again from punitive tax rates that are adopted as a result of base political calculations in order to "soak the rich" is that, at the end of the day, they lower, rather than raise, the amount of money actually collected by governments in tax. Unfortunately, this lesson is soon forgotten by those on the left keen to rally the discontented and envious fringes of their party.

If taxation was a priority for Hollande, then the entire French tax code was in serious need of reform. Entrepreneurs needed encouragement and support. Job creators needed rewards, not punishment. Tough questions needed to be asked about the competitiveness of French companies and the productivity of French workers.

France faced considerable challenges, and its president needed to be willing to take those steps necessary to change the direction his country was headed. Simply clinging to populist campaign rhetoric was not enough. Real leadership on a Bonapartian scale was required.

* * *

Hollande's weak position with French voters was again on display in May 2013, as Sarkozy let it be known that he would be willing to reenter politics in order to save his country. Referring to Hollande as "really useless," Sarkozy believed that France was headed toward a "social explosion" unless serious changes were made. These revealing insights hit newsstands when a Parisian newspaper published an article about Sarkozy's life since leaving the Élysée Palace. Friends of the former president indicated that he would be willing to return to national office, if and when necessary.

Hollande was meant to be a refreshing change of pace from his frenetic predecessor. Unfortunately, rising unemployment and scandal within Hollande's cabinet saw his popularity rapidly drop. Where Sarkozy was seen as heavy-handed and vain, Hollande appeared to be unable to control his own government. To many French, boring and workmanlike Hollande now seemed to lack both the leadership skills and the vision necessary to govern a country with as many challenges and complexities as France possesses.

Hollande's unilateral attack on the rich, by raising taxes significantly on high earners, failed to earn him lasting friends or allies. Soon, even parts of the left-wing press were abandoning him. Embarrassingly, he was forced to fire his budget minister, Jérôme Cahuzac, when accusations were made that Cahuzac illegally held money in a Swiss bank account. This was particularly awkward for Hollande because Cahuzac had special responsibility for pursuing tax avoiders.

Many observers began making the claim louder and louder that this boring, poorly dressed bureaucrat was as unable to manage his home life as he was unable to manage his country. Tabloids continued to feast on stories of his current girlfriend, Valérie Trierweiler, and her fits of jealousy in the face of Ségolène Royal, with whom Hollande had a lengthy relationship and four children.

This situation made Hollande's political life even more awkward, as Royal was a senior figure in the Socialist Party who previously ran against Sarkozy for the presidency in 2007.

The path to a triumphant return to the Élysée Palace, however, would not be an easy one for Sarkozy. Unrest in the Socialist Party and mounting French disappointment in Hollande would not be enough to give Sarkozy another chance at power. His political party, the Union for a Popular Movement, has been ineffective in opposition. Two separate investigations were launched against him personally as well. One involved a tabloid-friendly accusation that he exploited the senile billionaire heiress to the L'Oréal fortune, Liliane Bettencourt, in order to obtain funding for his 2007 presidential run. The other involved a payment of approximately $500,000 made to him in 2008 by none other than Muammar Gaddafi, the former ruler of Libya. The "Bettencourt scandal" developed a life of its own when the ninety-year-old heiress was put under court protection in 2012. Seventeen people had been charged by this time with "abuse of weakness" by the team of magistrates leading the inquiry. If convicted, Sarkozy could face three years in prison.

The 2017 elections were still some time away, but these accusations weakened the man who was seen by his supporters as the candidate best placed to deny Hollande a second term. Of course, former French presidents were never strangers to postretirement criminal charges. Jacques Chirac, the center-right president who preceded Sarkozy, was ultimately convicted of corruption in 2011 and given a suspended sentence of two years.

Partisan political machinations aside, France was facing massive problems that at times seemed insurmountable. Its economy was sputtering and by the spring of 2013, government debt was more than 90 percent of the GDP. Unemployment sat at a dizzying 10.8 percent, the highest rate in more than fifteen years. Young people were fleeing France for opportunity elsewhere, like nearby London, with its promise of a pro-entrepreneur and pro-business regime.

Hollande was now forced to admit to himself that he won the last election solely on the basis that he was *not* Nicolas Sarkozy. Having brought with him no concrete policy initiatives or comprehensive governing philosophy, Hollande was adrift. As a result, French voters were increasingly drifting away from him as they recognized more and more that their leader was incapable of actually leading.

* * *

The posher neighborhoods of central Paris, such as the 16th arrondissement, have a unique charm and upscale appeal. Unfortunately, in October 2013 many residents feared this could be irreparably damaged if a government plan to establish Roma camps across the city was fully implemented. The proposal was backed by both the Paris city council and the national government led by President Hollande, a socialist.

The short-term goal was to better share the burden between the wealthier and poorer parts of Paris when it came to addressing the steady influx of Roma from Eastern Europe. This was to be accomplished by establishing so-called integration villages in areas such as Bois de Boulogne park in the 16th arrondissement to host homeless Gypsies. Roma camps have historically been found predominately in the most destitute suburbs of Paris. The thought of large numbers of Gypsies living adjacent to some of the best restaurants, boutiques, and high-end real estate caused great outrage among residents.

Unsurprising, of course. The concern over "not in my backyard" is fairly universal and can be found quite as naturally in contemporary France as anywhere else. Even those who may passionately support more government action to address the plight of Gypsies would quickly oppose such action when it puts at risk the value of their homes or the quality of their children's schools.

Many French otherwise sympathetic to the plight of Gypsies, who have been persecuted for many years, were still very concerned over the damage and lack of upkeep that allegedly occurs at the shantytowns and makeshift caravan parks that Roma frequently establish. Roma had been entering France for years from countries such as Bulgaria and Romania, and many remained largely unintegrated into wider French society.

As a result, the issue had become a particularly divisive one for French politicians. The 2013 proposal to set up "integration villages" may have begun as a bit of political rhetoric by far-left members of the Paris city council but soon had a life of its own.

The problem of what to do with the Roma divided both the left and the right. For example, the left in France had been suffering steady losses at the ballot box to the far-right National Front, which was gaining support from growing numbers of the unemployed working class frustrated by politicians in Paris and in Brussels who seemed indifferent to their fate. Focusing attention on the plight of the Roma was a way of better differentiating themselves from the National Front, which had traditionally handled a wide variety of immigration-related issues with tremendous amounts of suspicion and rhetoric.

A foundation stone for the European Union is the free movement of people around member states. As the continental superstate has grown in members in recent years, more and more ethnic groups have taken advantage of these freedoms to look for a better life elsewhere. Gypsies were simply part of the wider consequences of intra-European immigration, but like countless waves of migrants who have preceded them, their growing presence caused alarm among their new neighbors.

Reactions to the Roma led to a variety of responses, sometimes contradictory, from the French political class. In September 2013, the interior minister, Manuel Valls, created controversy when he said that since Gypsies had no intention to integrate into wider society, his goal would be to deport them. Valls, himself the son of immigrants from nearby Spain, had been leading an effort to close down illegal Roma camps. His remarks led to another member of Hollande's Socialist government, Arnaud Montebourg, the industry minister, to challenge Valls publicly. A variety of human rights groups also spoke out against Valls.

Earlier that summer, Gilles Bourdouleix, a center-right French MP, was recorded by a reporter as muttering that Hitler killed too few Gypsies, while he was trying to disperse a Roma camp illegally established on municipal land. Interestingly, at that time Valls announced his intention to initiate proceedings against Bourdouleix for condoning crimes against humanity.

As the economic situation in France continued to drift sideways with little chance of meaningful economic recovery, difficult questions were being asked by French men and women about their state's ability to support more and more claimants for public assistance. At the root of so many problems currently facing France was an economy that was not "fit for purpose" in the twenty-first century. The issue of how to cope with the influx of Roma merely displayed this underlying challenge in a slightly more sensationalist and headline-grabbing light. In the autumn of 2013, President Hollande seemed unable to push his reluctant country down the path of significant change necessary to jumpstart economic growth. Arguing about Gypsies was a poor substitute for meaningful and comprehensive reform.

* * *

As France continued to struggle with its mounting economic problems, Marine Le Pen, leader of the National Front party, warned in November 2013 that her country was on the verge of civil war. This precarious situation was, according to Le Pen, a direct result of an open-borders policy forced upon France by Brussels that had undermined the economic and social stability of her country.

These warnings came at a challenging time for France. The National Front was leading French polls as the most popular party, while President Hollande was the most unpopular president in recent history. Hollande, a Socialist, was seen by many as an ineffective technocrat who lacked a real vision for France and any real solutions to its growing list of structural problems.

By focusing the attentions of dissatisfied and anxious French voters on the negative consequences of immigration and the destructive aspects of EU regulation emanating from Brussels, Le Pen and her supporters gained traction in the polls. For many French, the status quo was simply not working. Despite the wave of optimism that brought Hollande to office eighteen months earlier, little had occurred since the election to meaningfully slow or stop France's perceived decline.

At the heart of Hollande's unpopularity was a French economy no longer "fit for purpose." High unemployment and anemic growth turned more and more attention toward immigrants who were believed to be taking jobs away from French citizens. This rhetoric was not coming from just the National Front. Even left-leaning members of Hollande's cabinet were pointing fingers at foreigners as a way of explaining away their government's inability to make progress in addressing these problems.

Importantly, distrust of Brussels and concern over the effects of unrestricted immigration were not unique to France at this time. Le Pen had also recently teamed up with the Dutch far right and its leader, Geert Wilders, to form a wider coalition of anti-EU groups across a number of EU member states. Since the global financial crisis demonstrated the weakness of European banks, as well as the flaws with the euro, EU institutions previously beyond criticism had found themselves in the firing line for the first time. The long-standing consensus that Brussels would inevitably bring economic growth and political stability through free trade, a single currency, and open borders was now being widely questioned.

By attacking globalization and its consequences, Le Pen was moving the National Front away from the types of unsubtle racist demagoguery that had been at its core for several decades. Instead, the focus would now be on protecting national sovereignty and limiting the encroachment of Brussels.

Britons, always more awkward Europeans than their continental cousins, had already been wrestling with these issues for many years. A split among those on the right into distinct pro- and anti-EU camps had become a recurring feature of British politics. Resentment toward Brussels eventually reached such a state in Britain that a new political party, the UK Independence Party (UKIP), was launched to funnel this sentiment away from the center-right Conservative Party. Interestingly, however, UKIP did not join the coalition with Le Pen, Wilders, and the other anti-EU parties, due to concerns over the racism that permeates many of these organizations. UKIP was more narrowly focused on exposing EU flaws and shifting sovereignty back to Britain, without being sullied by the far-right history and connotations these other parties bring with them.

With the level of "Brussels bashing" that was taking place across Europe in 2013, it would be easy to forget that only one year earlier the European Union had won the Nobel Peace Prize in recognition of the good work it had done to bring peace and stability to a continent that had seen years of bloody war during the last century. Unfortunately, the opinion of the selection committee in Norway—a country not even a member in its own right!—was not universally held among those men and women who have to live under Brussels' tsunami of rules and regulations.

By using inflammatory rhetoric to describe her country as on the verge of a civil war, Le Pen gave voice to the large number of French frustrated with their country's current predicament and worried about what is still to come. With the Hollande government unable to voice an alternative view of France's future, this vision of division and potential conflict would continue to build momentum.

★ ✳ ★

A new hand gesture was gaining popularity as 2013 drew to a close in France, which soon began working many politicians, bureaucrats, and commentators into a near frenzy over the possibility that it was in some way anti-Semitic. Or maybe it wasn't. This lack of clarity did not prevent intense debates and recriminations from breaking out in the media.

The *quenelle* is gesture made by holding the right arm in a straight position pointing to the ground some short distance ahead of you. The left hand then grasps the extended arm usually somewhere above the elbow. Created by a controversial French comedian named Dieudonné M'bala M'bala, it gained international notoriety when a French soccer player playing in England used the gesture as part of a goal celebration in December 2013. Nicolas Anelka was promptly branded an anti-Semite, unleashing a flood of accusations and counteraccusations that has left finger pointers competing very aggressive for the honor of being the most offended. To avoid any ambiguity on his inspiration for using the quenelle, Anelka tweeted afterward that the gesture was a "special dedication" to his friend Dieudonné.

In February 2014, Dieudonné was denied permission by the British government to enter the country to demonstrate his solidarity with Anelka, who was facing a disciplinary action by the Football Association, the sport's governing body in England. They ultimately retained a special expert to help determine whether the quenelle was actually racist or simply obscene. I suppose it is actually quite impressive that an individual has spent so much time studying and researching and publishing learned articles that he develops a reputation for expertise in the field of "offensive hand gestures," although it is hard to imagine that he sees much in the way of regular employment!

Anelka's team, West Bromwich Albion, issued a statement acknowledging that the gesture may have caused offense and

Anelka agreed not to use the quenelle again. Despite the team's principal sponsor, Zoopla, canceling its endorsement deal because of the furor, Anelka continued to play for his team.

For Dieudonné, whose name means "gift of God," the exclusion order handed down in London was only the latest in his legal troubles. He has been repeatedly prosecuted for inciting racial hatred in France because of the inclusion in his stand-up comedy act of anti-Semitic jokes, as well as offensive comments about the Holocaust. As the quenelle furor gained momentum, a number of his shows were canceled over fears of potential violence. When bailiffs went to his house in Dreux, in the north of France, to collect fines from him in relation to these earlier convictions, Dieudonné fired rubber bullets at them. He was promptly taken into custody, together with his partner, Noémie Montagne. Both quickly claimed that they were the subject of police harassment.

For opponents of the quenelle, it is clearly an inversed Nazi salute that was created by a convicted anti-Semite, leaving no ambiguity as to its meaning. Others argue that it is nothing more than simply an antiestablishment gesture that is not tied to any particular ethnic group. The word *quenelle* itself refers to a small dumpling in the shape of a sausage that is said to bear a striking resemblance to a suppository. Hence the argument that the gesture is simply an obscenity.

Dieudonné had been a popular comedian for many years, who only recently had begun to feature anti-Jewish humor more prominently in his act. Notably, when he began performing, he partnered with a Jewish comedian, Élie Semoun, and was identified with the left of the political spectrum. His drift toward the far right picked up momentum after 9/11, when he began to focus his comedic talents more and more on Jews.

Unsurprisingly, the more French authorities have cracked down on Dieudonné for his extremist remarks, the more momentum he developed among his young fans, both on social media and at his live performances. By the end of 2013, he was seen by many as a symbol of free speech who was being unjustly persecuted for his controversial views.

The sincerity and concern behind France's vigilance in combating anti-Semitism was certainly admirable, although perhaps this sentiment would have been much more effective if it had been demonstrated as forcefully in the early 1940s as it is being shown today!

Regardless, while committees and courts wrestled with the philosophical conundrum of what a recently made-up hand gesture actually meant, France continued to drift toward further disharmony and disruption. A stalled economy and an ineffective government left little cause for optimism in the minds of many French youth.

Instead, they were able to find common cause in Dieudonné's "shock-value" stand-up routines and his newly minted "up yours" gesture. For whatever good that will do them.

11

One Nation

Imagination governs the world.

—NAPOLEON BONAPARTE

When the global television viewing audience sat down to watch the 2012 Summer Olympics, they weren't tuning in to see an Austerity Britain racked by public debt and dubious economic growth prospects or plagued by runabout youth gangs or packs of pedophile grooming rings. No, they were looking for a vision of Britain that was positive and reaffirming. Fortunately, the festivities' opening ceremonies provided that vision.

The American diplomat Dean Acheson once famously remarked, "Great Britain has lost an empire and has not yet found a role in the world." Award-winning film director Danny Boyle's eccentric, yet deeply resonating, kick-off for the London Games succeeded artistically on many levels, but perhaps its most unanticipated success was to pose a compellingly idiosyncratic answer to this blunt accusation.

Boyle's fanciful pageant could not have been more different from the massive display of synchronized human endeavor that was offered up in Beijing four years earlier. The Chinese pursuit of spectacle and scale unfortunately teetered at times on the brink of tedium. Instead of superficial displays of wealth and power designed to leave viewers feeling shocked and overwhelmed, Boyle took a more British approach. He enthusiastically told a compelling story, with ample amounts of drama and humor.

The London opening ceremony was not nostalgia, in the trite and manufactured sense, although it dealt very directly with the role nostalgia plays in helping us understand and relate to our past. Instead, it was theatrical in the very best sense of the word. And no country on the planet does theater as well as Britain!

Literally featuring a cast of thousands, the role of the British people in the monumental transformation of their country was consistently at center stage. Kenneth Branagh's reading of *The Tempest*, before unleashing the rise of dark mills and smoke-spewing factories, demonstrated how the arts and artifacts of the past can survive and inspire us as the world changes around us almost beyond recognition.

American viewers may have been particularly shocked to see the affection toward Britain's National Health Service (NHS) that underlined the middle act of Boyle's elaborate performance. Like all human institutions, the NHS is imperfect and flawed. Although it has been constantly subjected to questions about the efficiency and reliability with which it attempts to meet the needs of a country growing in size, diversity, and complexity, the simple goals of the NHS have been quite effective at binding this country together.

As is their prerogative, Americans place other goals and aspirations above the welfare and well-being of the youngest and the weakest and the most vulnerable in their society. American society reflects these priorities, and Boyle made sure that these differences were clearly shown. The portrayal of Britons as groups of individuals, from various backgrounds, who have come together to pursue overlapping and interwoven agendas contrasts markedly with both the solipsistic consumerism of America and the dehumanizing top-down regimentation of China.

The postmodern world, with its complexities and contradictions, was not ignored. Boyle presented scenes from contemporary British life that were both familiar and prejudice-breaking. In an age of text messaging and social networking, downloading and updating, the digital youth of today's Britain were well represented in all their exuberance and originality.

As memorable as these 2012 Games were, London had been there before. The British capital now has the unique record of having hosted the Olympics three times. First in 1908 and then again in 1948, when London stepped up on short notice to ensure that modern Olympic movement would continue and thrive after the devastation of World War II, the Olympics came home again in 2012, and the British went to great lengths to ensure that the world felt welcome.

Of course, there was a hefty dose of British pessimism on offer during the first week of the Games. A debacle concerning missing security staff and a fiasco over empty seats in venue after venue were just two incidents where Olympic enthusiasm did not prevent direct questions being asked about why things weren't handled better. This was never going to be a Games "in the middle of nowhere." London is one of the world's most cosmopolitan capitals, and these Games were being played at its very heart.

While Europeans were continuing to wrestle with what it means to be a "multicultural Europe," Britain at least has some serious track record in this area. As a historically sea-faring country and former colonial power, Britons have a much longer history of dealing with cross-cultural issues. Think *HMT Empire Windrush* and the Ugandan Asians as only two post-War examples. Interestingly, the casual descriptions of London as a "melting pot"—using the American colloquialism—that appear in magazine articles and news reports often fail to note that the great breadth of non-European nationalities and languages is far more impressive than the sampling of Europeans that transit in and out of Britain every year.

The Olympics are, of course, about much more than simply sport. The millions of tourists who descended on London were there to spend money, take photos, and craft in their minds memories that will shape their view of Britain for the rest of their lives. As a result, 70,000 volunteers turned out to ensure that these visitors got an experience they will never forget. In this regard, Britain followed the example first set in 2000, when Australians made an unprecedented effort to ensure that the Sydney Games were welcoming and hospitable and enjoyable for all.

The confidence of modern Britain has never been more clearly displayed than during Boyle's film clip featuring the Queen and James Bond, portrayed by an urbane and mildly threatening Daniel Craig, on their short commute from Buckingham Palace to the Olympic Stadium. The British are known around the world for their sense of humor and their eccentricities. On closer inspection, these are often two sides of the same pound coin.

By staging the 2012 Games in their capital city, the largest city in Europe with a population of 8 million and covering more than 600 square miles, the British played host to the world. As athletes and spectators enjoyed the sports on offer, and as billions more watched these successes from their homes, images of modern Britain were being offered as well. Danny Boyle's personal (and slightly bonkers) vision of Britain was, of course, only one. But it is one that has proven itself to be utterly unforgettable.

* * *

Of all the many visions of Britain, one particularly powerful and divisive vision was the one promoted by Margaret Thatcher during her years as prime minister. Her passing in April 2013 caused many in Austerity Britain and around the world to focus on a woman who had her own very strong view of her country's past and its future. Any assessment of Thatcher's legacy will always be made more difficult by the intense divisiveness that she inspired, both among her more obvious opponents as well as within the political party she led. More so than any other British leader in recent memory, she was the ultimate "Marmite politician"—you either loved her or you hated her. Indifference was not an option.

As she did during her time in office, Thatcher still invoked broad praise and bitter resentment upon her death. She had a tendency to "handbag" those she felt stood in the way of the changes that were necessary to fix Britain. Although she was more prone to compromise and deft action than her critics often acknowledge, she would not step back from a fight if a fight was necessary to accomplish her goals.

When she first came to national prominence as education secretary, and the only woman, in Ted Heath's government, she soon became known as "Thatcher the Milk Snatcher" for taking away universal free milk for British schoolchildren. Few would have picked her out at this stage as eventually reaching the highest rung of British politics and joining the top table of international leaders.

Interestingly, her eventual political demise came from her own party and the men whose careers she had developed during her time in office. Her opponents in the Labour Party and other left-wing groups were not able to displace her at the ballot box. In the end, she was too powerful a campaigning force to be defeated in a head-on confrontation. Instead, she was dispatched ruthlessly by those whose loyalty she needed to rely upon. Perhaps that failure has embittered her critics even further as the years passed.

Although polls conducted on the day she died indicate that half of Britons thought she had made a positive contribution to the country, the voices of anger and disgust could still be heard very distinctly. Of those surveyed, 20 percent still rated her as very bad, while only a quarter of the Scots and a third of the Welsh felt she was good for the country. Those who stood against her—whether at the miners' strike of 1984–1985, at the Brixton riots, or along the campaign trail—repeatedly failed to get the upper hand. Those who disagreed with her didn't see principles or ideals but simple divisiveness.

Some of her positions, such as her views on South Africa, have not aged particularly well. The shadow of the Cold War polarized the world, and this polarization was readily seen in her approach to international affairs. However, she did champion Gorbachev when he came to power in the Soviet Union, and she was willing to negotiate with the Chinese over the handover of Hong Kong. She took several steps to strengthen the European Union before doubts arose that made her question the entire endeavor. There were subtleties and compromises to be found in Thatcher's approach to governing, just not as many and not as frequently as her critics would have preferred.

Obviously, as Britain's first female prime minister, Thatcher earned a place in the history books simply for earning a term in Number 10 Downing Street. This, however, was not enough. She chose not to sit on her laurels. With her country overwhelmed by a series of interwoven problems that had built up over generations, she decided to refashion the country and its institutions into a likeness of herself.

Much has been written about Thatcher having been born above a shop in Grantham, far from the corridors of power and the chattering classes that encircle them. Her goals while in office, although large in scope and controversial in execution, were simple to explain. She wanted to do away with institutions that failed to deliver what was needed and a worn-out consensus that no longer functioned in the grim realities that Britain found itself in during the late 1970s.

Perhaps her greatest triumph, however, was not the changes she wrought on her country or even on her own party. Perhaps it was the changes she forced upon the opposition Labour Party, as it was dragged kicking and screaming toward the middle ground. Thatcher's legacy was not ultimately secured by the tepid and wobbly government of her Conservative successor, John Major, who followed on after her unceremonious departure, but instead by the flash and dazzle of the New Labour parade that Tony Blair marched into Downing Street in 1997.

Blair's own success at the polls three times mirrored Thatcher's. Even though he was prevented from beating her record in office by the internal machinations of his own party, in a fashion similar to what she experienced in the end, Blair's government demonstrated in countless ways that, rather than undo Thatcherism wholesale across the country, accommodations would be offered here and there to please Britons who had become accustomed to the benefits of low taxes and the pursuit of individual opportunity.

And David Cameron's highly unexpected—but still quite definitive—victory in the May 2015 election again validated the appeal that Thatcher's policies of fiscal responsibility (in its current guise of "austerity") and British optimism still resonate among the electorate in the twenty-first century. Even the regionalism that took the form of insurgents within the Scottish National Party questioning the ongoing value of the Union would be recognizable to the former prime minister.

Many aspects of Thatcher's vision for Britain remain on display in the country today. The London that hosted the 2012 Summer Olympics reflected much of the courage, drive, and self-belief that she hoped to unleash through her reforms. The debate over austerity divided contemporary Britain in the years following the global financial crisis but still managed to retain ardent support among those Britons who recall the state of the country that Thatcher inherited thirty-five years earlier.

Britain, though of course still a work in progress confronting the social, economic, and political challenges it faces in the twenty-first century, was never the same after Thatcher, nor will it ever be.

★ ★ ★

When it comes to swearing in new citizens, no one in Europe does it quite so enthusiastically as Britain. In November 2014, it was reported that of all new passports handed out in Europe, one-fourth of them had the British seal on the cover. Clearly, when people are voting with their feet, they are casting a clear vote for Britain over other European countries.

Who are these newly minted Brits? Unsurprisingly, given the country's colonial history, India and Pakistan top the list. Then comes Nigeria, and in fourth place, somewhat surprisingly, the Philippines. However, when one bears in mind that the NHS is often referred to colloquially as the third largest economic organization in the world—after the People's Liberation Army in China and the Indian Railways system—it would, of course, be difficult to deliver medical care on such a vast scale without an ample supply of highly skilled Filipino nurses!

This trend may, in fact, have been accelerating. British authorities reported applications went up an additional 27 percent in 2013, fueled by new requirements on the horizon that would mandate minimum English language capabilities for new citizens.

However, migration—of both the legal and illegal varieties—was on the rise in 2014 across Europe. National governments were wrestling with how to react to the waves of new arrivals. Even Germany, which had so ardently supported the free flow of individuals across the continent, was beginning to reconsider whether its generous social safety net should be trimmed back. Italy, with is vast coastline, was a perennial target of boats full of eager new arrivals from North Africa seeking asylum.

Not all Europeans wanted to stop migration, though, at least for their own citizens. Since the first eastern expansion of the European Union in 2004, Poland has been outspoken in its insistence that the treaty guarantees that allow Poles to live and work wherever they want in the Europe be left sacrosanct. Britain has been a particularly attractive destination for many Poles—especially after then-Prime Minister Tony Blair decided to not take advantage of phasing-in powers that Brussels had granted existing

EU member states. As a result, it soon became a common refrain in London that it had become particularly hard in that cosmopolitan city to find a plumber who was not Polish! A good number of Romanians and Bulgarians were also finding their way to Britain during the next wave of eastern expansion in 2014, a full seven years after these countries joined the European Union upon the expiration of the transitional legal barrier that had prevented them from working and claiming benefits in other EU member states.

Political parties were being formed across the continent on the back of concerns over migration and how it should be managed. Whether through far-right parties like the National Front in France, led by Marine Le Pen, or the by-the-book euro-skeptics in the UK Independence Party, voters were voicing their fears and frustrations over both legal and illegal migration.

Even a statesman as middle of the road as former British prime minister John Major was by 2014 going on television to warn his fellow Britons that some sort of fix would be needed to address the large number of poor Europeans seeking their share of Britain's resurgent prosperity. While not seeking to end the freedom of movement enshrined in the Treaty of Rome, which is the constitutional cornerstone of the European Union, Major saw the challenge facing his country as a short-term problem that must be addressed with a short-term solution. A government report at this time put the number of EU migrants working in Britain at 1.8 million.

With UKIP gaining ground in local elections, current prime minister Cameron saw this as a direct attack on his party's continued grasp on power. Cameron had promised to cut migration to under 100,000 a year, but a perverse effect of the strengthening British economy under his government was that his country had again become a magnet for the unemployed elsewhere in Europe.

Of course, the difficulty with any discussion around migration was that the movement of individuals into a new country can be both very good and very bad for that country, often at the same time. If you are an employer, seeing a wave of eager new applicants willing to work for the wage you are willing to pay is an encouraging sight, especially if you are concerned about how strong and lasting the current British recovery really was. Unfortunately, though, if you are a Briton (especially a young Briton with limited experience) who is competing against these migrants for low-skilled jobs, you will see them as a threat to your own personal prosperity.

Perhaps there was a small nugget of good news for Britons of all stripes in the significant numbers of migrants who apply for British citizenship. At least by doing so, these individuals were consciously shifting out of a transient migrant mind-set and instead expressing their willingness to take on the full duties and obligations of a citizen.

They were declaring themselves not short-term carpetbaggers, but rather individuals committed to the long-term future of Britain.

★ ★ ★

Britain's millennium-long identity crisis as to whether it is fundamentally a European country or simply a country that is "Europe-adjacent" reared its ugly head again soon after Cameron's surprise win in the May 2015 parliamentary general election. On his way to leading a Conservatives-only government for the first time since 1997, Cameron had pledged to hold a popular referendum vote on his country's future in the European Union. Questions over which way the vote would go caused much hand-wringing in both London and Brussels as the groundwork for the referendum was being laid.

Cameron led a Conservative party that was torn between a wing that felt a Britain outside the continental super-state would be weakened and exposed and a wing that felt continued membership would erode Britain's democratic institutions and economic vitality. Even within Cameron's Conservative-only cabinet, senior political leaders were unable to form a unified front either in support of or opposition to the Brexit referendum.

As the public debate raged on, Cameron negotiated with Brussels for a radical change in British obligations under the various EU treaties in order to enable him to campaign effectively for staying in the multinational organization. Without serious concessions on a number of hot-button issues, it seemed increasingly unlikely that a highly emotional referendum battle would leave Britain within the European Union.

Cameron realized the serious collateral effects that Brexit would have on the EU's continuing effectiveness. This meant he had a unique opportunity to extract maximum accommodations from the other twenty-seven EU member state leaders, as well as the bureaucrats in Brussels who quietly run the EU machinery day to day. Their reflexive belief in the supremacy of their managerial Bonapartism would need to be set aside in order to accommodate Britain's reasonable demands. Unfortunately, Cameron failed to come home with concessions sufficient to quiet the Leave campaigners and break the momentum they were slowly gaining across the country.

The in/out vote was an attempt by Cameron to settle what had become an ongoing debate within the Conservative Party—as well as much of Britain—on whether EU membership was actually a net benefit to the country. It was a perfectly valid question to ask, but definitive positive answers were elusive. Unlike many other member states, there was a widespread belief that Britain could in fact survive and thrive on its own, in light of both its history and its current global profile. The same could not be said, for example, of Luxembourg or Belgium!

Cameron, however, was a pro-European at heart. He sincerely believed that in terms of both economic growth prospects and strategic security in the era of Islamic State and extremist terror, continued EU membership simply made more sense. Unfortunately, he knew all too well that members of his cabinet opposed him wholeheartedly on this issue, and the referendum campaign would lead to senior figures resigning from their posts and creating a schism within the party that might last a generation.

As a result, Cameron faced a two-front war—while negotiating with European leaders to accommodate British demands, such as suspending benefits for EU migrants until they have lived in Britain for four years, he had to be mindful of how British voters would view these concessions.

The case that Cameron made was, in essence, that the best for Britain would be a reformed European Union. The reforms that he pursued, therefore, were at the very heart of the case he was to make to the country when the referendum was held in June 2016. From a tactical perspective, these reforms could have dismissed out of hand many of the complaints concerning the current EU arrangements being raised by UKIP and the Leave campaign and replaced them with a debate of the future potential of a new configuration that reflected Cameron's demands.

Unfortunately, the negotiations were unsuccessful. Voices of discontent were regularly heard in Brussels claiming that Britain was asking for too much and shouldn't be accorded a special deal. To be fair, the issues that were being discussed were not simply exercises in political horse-trading. They represented concerns that went to the very core of the EU constitutional structure. There was also the elaborate structure of EU law that has grown up over the previous several decades that cannot simply be wished away or ignored. In fact, the accommodations that Cameron sought were required to be "legally binding and irreversible." The British people wanted certainty that their rights would be protected going forward if they voted Remain. A handshake deal or a few kind words would not be enough.

Having just recently survived a Scottish referendum in September 2014 that would have seen the United Kingdom united no longer, Cameron again faced the risk that a loss at the ballot box could radically transform the country he led.

Many observers believed that there was a deal to be had between Britain and Brussels that would provide significant concessions and address many—but not all—of the key issues raised by Cameron. Such a deal would have clearly strengthened the case for Remain and ensured that the British people would vote for continuity and stability within a reformed European Union. Too bad Brussels refused to oblige.

* * *

Migrants desperate to reach the promise of prosperity in Cameron-led Britain rioted yet again at the French port of Calais in July 2015. As a result of the ensuing chaos, British roads were gridlocked and local police were forced to intervene to bring some semblance of normalcy to British drivers. Dubbed "Operation Stack," authorities in the English county of Kent were forced to close a number of freeway off-ramps to allow freight-carrying trucks a means to approach the British end of the Channel Tunnel and await an opportunity to cross.

In total, an estimated 2,000 migrants attempted just before midnight to "bum-rush" the Calais terminal that permitted cars to be transported under the English Channel, the narrow body of water that separates Britain from France. As a result, trains were severely delayed, causing chaos on both British and French roads. This was not a unique event. Over several preceding weeks, an increasing number of migrants had been trying to illegally cross through the Channel Tunnel into Britain.

One viral video the prior month showed a migrant brazenly entering the front of a cargo truck and subsequently attempting to open up the trailer to allow more migrants to hide in there. Individuals typically waited until nightfall and then cut their way through fencing and boarded trucks headed across the Channel, in the hope that they would make it undetected out of France and into the "promised land" of Britain. Cargo trailers were a favorite target of migrants, as they offered numerous options for stowing away.

Estimates of the number of migrants in the small town of Calais increased significantly during the beginning of 2015, rising from 600 in January to approximately 5,000 by July. As the number of migrants became larger, the scale and level of coordination of the nightly attacks became more evident.

Neither the French employees at the Eurotunnel station in Calais nor the local French police had the manpower to withstand sustained attacks by increasing numbers of migrants. In order to assist their European colleagues, the British government eventually agreed to provide an additional $10 million to fund French port security. The money was earmarked for video surveillance, better fencing, and well-trained police dogs.

The chaos at Calais came at a time when larger waves of migration were crashing on European shores of the Mediterranean as more and more men, women, and children attempted to make the perilous crossing from North Africa. Uncertainty across Africa and the Middle East was leading to record numbers of migrants attempting to find a foothold in Europe and, eventually, make their way to the prosperity of Britain.

The chaos on both sides of the English Channel raised awkward questions about how European rules and regulations would best address the problem of increased economic migration into the continental trading bloc. At its best, Operation Stack was a short-term solution to keep roads opens and traffic moving under increasingly difficult circumstances. Reportedly, businesses in the county of Kent in England lost $2 million each day that the Channel Tunnel was closed. Given the importance of European commerce in and out of Britain, the country's entire supply chain was effectively compromised by the Calais chaos.

Although urgent solutions were required in Calais, it was unclear whether either the French government in Paris or the European bureaucrats in Brussels had the resolve to address the problem head-on. And as the powers-that-be wrung their hands in consternation, the fate of the men and women encamped in the French port city was steadily becoming more and more dire.

Observers were calling the situation in Calais a humanitarian crisis, made worse by a stereotypically French strike by ferry workers a few weeks earlier and an increasing reliance on razor-wire fencing to contain the growing populations of the shantytown that had sprouted up.

Some commentators pointed out that the current migrant camp was better organized and seemingly more permanent than the numerous camps that had preceded it. The Calais encampment boasted a church, two mosques, a school . . . and a nightclub!

In response to French containment efforts, migrants were becoming increasingly aggressive in their attempts to escape the barricades and get to their final destination—Britain. No matter how many times French authorities bulldozed the migrant camps, the flow of more migrants into Europe looked set to continue for many more years to come.

The difficult issue for Paris and Brussels was to establish both an effective protocol to prevent migrants from undermining their border-control initiatives and a humane policy that effectively refocused the desire of these men, women, and children to abandon their homes and seek opportunity elsewhere. Until they accomplished this, chaos at Calais—and potentially the other side of the Channel—would continue to be a recurring feature of European life.

British voters would bear this in mind when they went to the polls less than a year later to decide on their future membership in the grand experiment in shared sovereignty that is the European Union.

12

Chaos Theory

*A throne is only a bench
covered in velvet.*

—Napoleon Bonaparte

Many German television viewers were scandalized in October 2015 when a news program chose a controversial screen graphic when covering the migration debate—a picture of Chancellor Angela Merkel dressed in conservative full-length Islamic dress. For good measure, a skyline of Berlin was Photoshopped to include numerous minarets as well.

The graphic ran during a commentary piece by Rainald Becker on the *Bericht aus Berlin* program. Becker expressed concern over how liberal German values would be impacted by the large numbers of migrants from the Middle East and North Africa. Angry viewers complained that the imagery was blatantly anti-Islamic propaganda. The station, however, defended the graphic as an attempt to visualize Western freedoms.

Germans in autumn 2015 were growing increasingly anxious over the new arrivals from Syria, Iraq, and elsewhere. Estimates circulating at this time forecasted that before the end of 2015, approximately 1.5 million asylum seekers would arrive in Germany, almost double the 800,000 initially put forward by the government. The asylum seekers who had already arrived were putting a significant strain on their host's resources. Government officials scrambled to ensure that adequate food, shelter, and sanitation were being provided.

Although initially popular, Merkel had in recent months seen her approval rating decrease as hostility toward her open-door migration policy grew steadily. Her insistence on opening the borders proved divisive among her EU partners but was seen by the international community as a grand gesture of charity and humanitarianism.

It is worth noting, however, the pragmatic reasons Merkel had in mind when setting her migrant policy. Germany might have been Europe's largest economy, but it faced significant challenges to continued growth and prosperity. The culprit was a low rate of population growth, which had several pernicious trickle-up effects. For example, the lack of skilled and unskilled workers meant that companies operating in Germany could find it very difficult to get the levels of staffing they needed. In addition, someone would need to contribute to the country's generous social welfare benefits programs if their workforce dramatically declined in the near future!

Regardless of her motivations, Merkel's decision led to increased tensions with other European leaders. Britain was already facing an increasingly bitter and noxious Brexit referendum on continued EU membership even before the migration crisis hit during the summer of 2015. In the months following Merkel's unilateral decision, the debate between the Leave and Remain camps became even more heated. British prime minister David Cameron was being forced to navigate a growing euroskepticism at home while trying at the same time to renegotiate the terms on which it participated in the EU. At the same time, his reluctant continental counterparts were focused primarily on the migrant crisis and the Greek economic debacle.

Having barely survived the 2014 Scottish independence referendum with his country intact, Cameron was now being forced to navigate the sharp corners of Brussels' bureaucracy in order to extract enough concessions to satisfy those back home who felt that Britain had been given short shrift during its four decades of EU membership. Of course, Britain at the time sat outside of both the euro-zone and the EU's Schengen borderless area, preferring to select, "cafeteria-style," which parts of the European experiment that it participated in, rather than simply accepting each wave for further integration as a foregone conclusion.

The European Union and its predecessor organizations were conscious creations in the aftermath of World War II. The founders and early proponents of the multinational bloc saw integration and harmonization as an attempt to prevent the horrors of war from ever returning to the continent again. The EU institutions that have developed since were greatly tested in recent years, first with the euro crisis resulting from Greece's near collapses and then by the increasing number of migrants seeking a better life in Europe.

Merkel, as German chancellor, had a key role—both symbolic and pecuniary—in setting the course for Europe's future. Her preferences and prejudices were clearly seen in her response to each of the euro and the migration crises. As a result, it was perhaps unsurprising that the television images of her in a burka created such an uproar among German viewers.

German moviegoers also got a special treat when the movie *Look Who's Back* hit theaters in this same time to much fanfare and hand-wringing. The movie, based on a bestselling novel, imagines what it would be like if Adolf Hitler awoke from a coma and reentered modern German society. A comedy, *Look Who's Back* includes Borat-like scenes in which the actor playing Hitler is filmed unscripted interacting with unsuspecting Germans.

The contrast between Germany today and in the time of the Third Reich is stark. Rather than seeking strength through racial purity, Berlin's current leaders are embracing a wider world full of ethnic differences. However, the next seventy years could see the country thoroughly transformed yet again, as the recent arrivals from the Middle East and North Africa—and their children and grandchildren—adapt themselves to Germany, and vice versa. Perhaps by then, a German chancellor in a burka will be, if not a reality, then at least a concept that sits in the realms of pragmatic possibility.

* * *

For more than one hundred women in Cologne, 2016 did not begin well, as they found themselves victims of sexual assault and other crimes. Germany achieved international fame during 2015 for its willingness to accept unprecedented numbers of refugees from Syria and other Muslim-majority countries. However, despite the initial hospitality she showed, Merkel stated in response to these attacks that their policy on deportations was under continuous review and any asylum seekers who refused to follow German law could expect to be expelled from the country.

On New Year's Eve, Cologne's main train station became the site of two reported rapes and a variety of sexual assaults and muggings, initially overwhelming local police. Victims described their attackers as Arab or North African men. A crowd had assembled in the square outside the station, next to Cologne's famous Gothic cathedral, and soon became rowdy. In the official police report, they were described as several thousand "mostly male people of a migrant background." When police initially arrived after the first reports of assaults were received, the crowd appeared to take little notice.

In the days that followed, allegations quickly circulated within Germany that a cover-up by both the government and the media was under way in order to avoid stoking antiforeigner sentiment.

In 2015, Merkel had unilaterally adopted an "open-door" policy regarding Middle Eastern asylum seekers. In the course of a year, German accepted more than 1 million refugees.

Cologne was not the only place where violence occurred. Several other German cities were affected, including Hamburg, where fifty-three police reports were made. Initial statements from police spokesmen indicated that it looked unlikely there would be any convictions, given the lack of evidence.

It took four days for the state broadcaster ZDF to report on the attacks, a delay that they later were forced to apologize for. Decisions by mainstream media to silence negative stories about refugees played into the mounting concerns of many Germans that the government was imposing a "blackout" on any bad press.

Simply put, if evidence were to emerge that the perpetrators were asylum seekers, the antiforeigner sentiment that had been building up in Germany during 2015 could have reached new heights. Under German law, a criminal conviction that results in a sentence of one year or more is grounds to have a refugee claiming asylum deported.

The problem facing Merkel's government was how to govern in a responsible manner without being seen to cave in to the daily spikes in public anger toward the influx of refugees. Of course, law and order is central to any government's legitimacy. Failure to ensure that Germans were safe on their own streets would put Merkel's mandate at risk.

To discuss important issues effectively—such as Germany's migration policies—it is important for the government and the media to ensure that accurate and complete facts are available to base any judgments on. After an initial quiet period, Merkel and her cabinet eventually began to prioritize the incidents in Cologne and other cities, acknowledging the tensions that had been escalating in the country.

Even with a million refugees already in Germany at the start of 2016, thousands continued to arrive each day. Groups like PEGIDA gained momentum across the country by focusing attention on the possible threats posed by the acceptance of large numbers of unscreened migrants on an unprecedented scale.

In the absence of hard evidence obtained by the police indicating the attackers' immigration status, both sides of the refugee debate had staked out their predictable cases—namely, those supporting the "open door" policy stating that there is no evidence that any of the men were recent asylum seekers and those who opposed noting that there is no evidence that they weren't.

Unfortunately, whether out of an obsessive desire for political correctness or an excessive deference to the policy preferences of the current government, there was a distinct unwillingness in the German media to report the attacks in those initial days.

The media makes its most important contribution to public policy debates when it verifies and draws attention to awkward facts that disrupt or unwind the leading narratives on both sides of the political spectrum. Neither silence nor rote repetition of established talking points will do much to improve the quality of such debates or push them closer to any much-needed answers.

Merkel's unilateral decision to throw open Germany's borders to an unprecedented number of unvetted refugees was both unexpectedly bold and highly risky. The full consequences of this decision on the future of her country and her people will not be known for many, many years. Until then, ignoring embarrassing stories and covering up uncomfortable statistics will likely do much more harm than good.

★ ★ ★

Scandals involving sexual assaults by migrants in Europe expanded to include Sweden in early January 2016. Police covered up reports of assaults on teenage girls at a large music festival in the capital city of Stockholm, out of fear that the perpetrators' identity as migrants would derail government race-relation goals.

The We Are Stockholm festival lasts for five days and boasts 170,000 attendees. In numerous incidents at the festival, large gangs of men surrounded young girls and attacked them with no regard for the criminal consequences of their actions.

Unfortunately, the police's failure to report these attacks amplified the concerns of many Swedes that government officials cannot be trusted to speak honestly about the facts surrounding the increasing number of migrants in their country because of excessive concerns over political correctness.

It is a well-established statistical fact that crime has grown significantly in Sweden in recent decades. However, Swedish law prohibits the collection and disclosure of information concerning the ethnicity of perpetrators. Regardless, a significant number of Swedes believe that male migrants from the Middle East are responsible for many of the rapes that are occurring in the country.

Internal memos released in January 2016 revealed that Stockholm police explicitly considered the ramifications of reporting the assaults at the festival on fraying public opinion regarding migrants. With the recent rise of an antimigrant party in Swedish politics, known as the Swedish Democrats, senior officials were concerned about the electoral ramification of publicly disclosing the fact that the attackers were migrants from Afghanistan.

Critics argued that rather than simply do their job and keep the Swedish public safe, the police seemed more concerned about the political ramifications of an awkward fact. By favoring short-term convenience over long-term fulfillment of their duties, the Swedish police blatantly disregarded the safety and well-being of young women in order to avoid disrupting their employers' top-down narrative about the ease with which migrants were integrating into Swedish society.

Gangs of foreign men groping and raping young women are unacceptable in all societies, but particularly repulsive in a country such as Sweden that has taken so many strides over the course of the last century to promote the status and dignity of women in their country. Swedish prime minister Stefan Löfven eventually lambasted police for their glaring omission, claiming that the failure to fulfill their duties honestly and transparently represented a betrayal on numerous levels.

A police paralyzed and distracted by narrow political priorities risks undermining the broader faith that the Swedes have developed in them over many years. Routine policing should not be altered or manipulated in order to accommodate partisan political goals. In the long-term, the case being made by champions of an "open door" policy with regards to migrants is not strengthened by a categorical unwillingness to discuss the ramifications of this policy in a robust and candid manner.

Unsurprisingly, champions of the refugee cause in Sweden rallied to the defense of new arrivals, claiming that sexual harassment can be found among men from a variety of backgrounds, not just Muslims from the Middle East, in order to reassure nervous Swedes that most of the refugees arriving in Sweden actually have great respect for women.

As alluring as it may be to believe that these events can be dismissed out of hand as statistically insignificant and not representative of the behavior of the larger migrant community, the most disturbing element of these stories is the unwillingness of police officers and government officials to speak openly and frankly about crimes committed against Swedish, German, and other European citizens.

The debate over the most appropriate asylum policy to adopt in the context of both domestic and international factors is a very important one to have. For the debate to result in an effective consensus that can serve as the basis for sound public policy, all relevant facts must be made available and analyzed in an open and transparent manner.

Meanwhile, the situation in Germany continued to deteriorate during January 2016 as more reports of sexual assaults surfaced and the Merkel government was forced to take immediate actions that undermined its unqualified support of ever-increasing numbers of new refugees.

Steps must be taken to ensure that women are not put at risk simply because they decide to exercise their independence and walk unaccompanied by male relatives down the streets of their own towns and cities. The fact that a recently arrived refugee grew up in a patriarchal culture that banishes women from public life is simply no excuse. The standards that we uphold in our societies must be set higher.

If the leaders of Sweden, Germany, and other European countries continue to operate an "open door" policy for migrants, then they must demonstrate that they are taking adequate steps to address the risks that accompany such a policy, rather than indulging in cover-ups and media manipulation driven by concerns over political correctness.

★ ★ ★

As January 2016 was approaching its end, a new law adopted in Denmark permitted police to seize assets carried by refugees seeking asylum in the country. The move followed similar steps taken in Germany and Switzerland to address the record number of migrants arriving in Europe from North Africa and the Middle East during 2015.

The goal of the law was to attempt—at least in part—to cover the costs of processing and housing the refugees while their claims were being processed. Items worth more than $1,500 were subject to seizure if they were nonessential and lacked sentimental value. In simple terms, the new law was perhaps just an attempt to dissuade migrants from coming to Denmark. The risk of forfeiting their belongings incentivized them to either stay at home or select another destination in which to seek asylum.

While the United Nations promptly condemned the decision and champions of migrant rights drew expected comparisons to the Nazi's treatment of the Jews, defenders of the law claimed that it tracked similar requirements imposed on Danes who claim welfare assistance from the government.

To many, Denmark and the other Scandinavian countries have served for decades as a role model for the rest of the world when it comes to humanitarian efforts. This forfeiture law was being criticized as an abdication of responsibility and a big step back from the open arms that they have historically presented to the needy.

No less an international cultural celebrity than Chinese artist Ai Weiwei made his view of the new seizure law known when he ordered the immediate closure of his exhibition, Ruptures, at the Faurschou Foundation in Copenhagen!

Frustrations were mounting within Europe as the number of refugees arriving each week showed little sign of abating. EU ministers began speaking openly of repealing the Schengen Agreement, which permits document-free travel within much of the continent. Such a move would have effectively sealed up the border with Greece, which was simultaneously suffering the continued effects of an economic meltdown and the presence of hundreds of thousands of refugees intent on making their way to the promised land of Germany and Northern Europe.

Athens quickly voiced its displeasure at the thought of being cut off from the EU brethren and left to deal with the mounting refugee crisis alone. With asylum seekers arriving every day, Greek authorities had few options open to them to stem the flow—short of opening fire on them! Unemployment in Greece stood at 25 percent, and the effects of the current economic depression were still clearly visible in the towns and across the countryside. For Athens to adequately cope with the asylum seekers, significant financial assistance—as well as logistical assistance—was required from Brussels and the other EU member states.

For decades, the European Union prided itself on its ability to find common solutions to common problems, even winning a Nobel Peace Prize for serving as a glowing example of what multinational collaboration could look like in the twenty-first century. Unfortunately, the refugee crisis instead put Europe up as an unenviable example of a blame-shifting, name-calling, go-it-alone policy vacuum.

While EU officials dithered, men, women, and children continued to risk their lives to make their way to Europe in the hope of starting a new life free of the dangers and threats that they faced in their home countries. Even if Greece was effectively walled off from the rest of Europe, some experts warned that desperate refugees would simply find other routes in, whether by land or by sea. New routes could mean new dangers and higher risks, leading to further casualties.

No matter what Trump-style walls they could try to build across land borders, Europeans have few options when it comes to their maritime border—the Mediterranean Sea. A source of numerous fatalities over previous years, the closing of overland routes would inevitably drive more asylum seekers either into the hands of dodgy human traffickers or into high-risk crossings by boat.

A particularly awkward source of disagreement with Europe at the time was trying to decide which particular asylum seekers should be welcomed and which turned away. Many countries were beginning to limit their hospitality to Syrian, Iraqi, and Afghani refugees, sending back those most recent arrivals who sought to jump on the bandwagon and take advantage of Chancellor Merkel's generous offer of hospitality.

Many would-be migrants sitting at home in impoverished countries saw these recent waves of asylum seekers as encouragement to make their own journeys to seek relative prosperity in Europe. Merkel's one-woman open-door policy had started a stampede that would confound and perplex European officials (and many Brexit referendum voters) for some time to come.

* * *

European voters loudly voiced their frustration and anger with a series of elections across the continent during 2015 and 2016, resulting in weak coalitions and unstable governments. At a time when Europe needed strong leaders capable of make making bold decisions, it was instead grappling with insurgent populist groups carving support away from traditional center-left and center-right parties.

The challenges facing Europe were clear—militant jihadi terror, mass migration from North Africa and the Middle East, and the continued fragility of the euro-zone economy. Any one of these would put a serious strain on governing for most mainstream politicians. The three together posed a particularly serious risk for the continued security and prosperity of the continent. British voters were just months away for deciding whether to cast their votes for Leave or Remain, and their European compatriots were doing little to reassure them that the Brussels political infrastructure was up to these challenges.

Given the predilection of parliamentary systems to produce large numbers of parties with none having a sufficient majority to govern by itself—especially where proportional representation ensures that even small niche parties receive a certain minimum number of representatives—coalitions are a recurring feature in Europe. Often these coalitions can be large and unwieldy. Other times they can produce strange bedfellows, where parties with vastly different visions are forced to cooperate in order to avoid institutional paralysis.

The 2015 regional elections in Germany were just one example of the inability of mainstream parties to prevent the allure of anti-migrant and anti-EU parties from draining away their support. At the national level, voters in Ireland, Portugal, Slovakia, and Spain returned an array of parties to their parliaments, many openly hostile to one another, and none had a convincing mandate to lead their country. Meanwhile, Belgium, Denmark, and Sweden were governed by precarious governments dependent on the whims and follies of small "king-maker" parties.

In the case of Spain, for example, in the first three months after the election, a government still had not been formed. Instead of providing a clear mandate to either of the two traditional mainstream parties, a pair of newly formed insurgent parties captured over a third of the vote, just enough to produce a highly effective stalemate.

Consensus was proving elusive in many European countries and across the European Union as a whole. As a result, fragmentation was the new normal. Parties farther out across the political spectrum were proving adept at giving voice to popular frustration and gaining votes on Election Day as their reward.

In addition to antiausterity parties on the far left, far-right parties were effectively tapping into widespread antimigrant sentiment. Normally dominant center-left and center-right parties were in retreat, as many voters deemed these parties no longer fit for purpose and lacked compelling solutions to the pressing problems facing their countries. Perversely, rather than enabling their governments to take tough, controversial decisions, the decision by voters to back niche protest parties usually made the task much more difficult as their parliaments fragmented and ground to a halt.

If the pendulum of voter sentiment did not swing back in favor of consensus in the near term, mainstream parties would have little chance to get much better at assembling effective governing coalitions from larger numbers of highly opinionated, ideologically pure splinter groups. Failure to do so would mean inertia and indecision at just the time when the security and prosperity of Europe faced its greatest threats since 1945.

Much hand-wringing was occurring at this time over the rise of far-right parties in many European countries. Comparisons to the 1930s were frequently being made by grim-faced commentators and political leaders. They looked down on the economic wreckage from the global financial crisis that still remained strewn across the continent and worried about youth unemployment rates on the continent that varied from 25 to 50 percent.

Nervous eyes then gazed over at the far-right parties who have been doing increasing well lately in winning seats at elections by pointing the finger at the "real causes" of misery in their countries. Whether it's France's National Front, Sweden's Sweden Democrats, Italy's Northern League, Austria's Freedom Party, Greece's Golden Dawn, or Germany's Alternative für Deutschland, support for extreme solutions—or at least the willingness to verbalize such solutions as alternatives—was gaining traction.

Of course, there was also increased antiausterity agitation at the time, most notable in Spain where the Podemos group had won power by pushing for an alternative to the harsh budget cuts that many blamed for the continued fragility of the European economy. But it was the populist spread of antimigrant and anti-Brussels sentiment by the far right that had produced the most alarmist warnings from pro-EU observers.

The most crucial question facing European voters during these months was not whether they would approve of the mainstream parties in their counties. Instead, it was simply whether they wanted an effective government addressing the challenges facing their country or an ineffective morass of niche voices more comfortable in the echo chamber of never-ending debate than in constructing and implementing public policy.

British voters were watching these unfortunate developments with mounting concerns.

13

A Kinder,
Gentler Tsar

*The best way to keep one's word
is not to give it.*

—Napoleon Bonaparte

If you're Santa Claus, one thing is now certain—you better watch out whenever Russian president Vladimir Putin is coming to town. In August 2015, Russia submitted to the United Nations their claim for more than 400,000 square miles of Arctic seabed reaching all the way up to the North Pole. Experts believed that billions of tons of oil, natural gas, and other valuable resources could be found in this resource-rich area.

The Russian claim was made under the provisions of the UN's Convention on the Law of the Seas, which allowed a country to claim an exclusive economic zone as far as their territory extends beneath the water's surface. Moscow was arguing that key underwater features in the Arctic were actually extensions of sovereign Russian territory, giving them valuable rights in these areas.

Denmark made a similar claim a few months earlier, based on its possession of Greenland. Canadian and Norwegian officials had previously clashed with their Russian counterparts over Moscow's "colonial" attitude toward the Arctic.

It was unclear in the days that followed how the United States would respond to Russia's northern offensive. Alaska fortunately granted Washington a seat at the Arctic table and a basis to make further claims of its own, but there was little indication during the remaining months of the Obama administration that the White House intended to make these issues a priority. In light of Washington's limited success in prior years in containing Russian territorial ambitions, expectations were not high.

Putin believed that the Arctic was squarely within Russia's sphere of influence. He repeatedly demonstrated his willingness to back up his words with cold hard cash by allocating almost $5 billion over the following years to develop its claims to the region, including an increasingly visible military presence.

Notably, these expenditures came at a time when the Russian economy was still reeling from the one-two punch of low oil prices and Western sanctions over Moscow's Bonapartist adventurism in Ukraine. The International Monetary Fund (IMF) announced this same month that by their calculations the sanctions then in place would eventually cost Russia up to 9 percent of its GDP. Annual GDP growth rate had decreased significantly in recent years, from 7 percent per year in 2008 to a forecast of only 1.5 percent going forward. In 2015, it was estimated that the Russian economy would contract by more than 3 percent.

Contrary to the advice of the IMF and other august international bodies, the extensive role of the state in the Russian economy continued unashamedly. Putin's levers of control and influence extended deep into his country's economic infrastructure.

Of course, not all Russians were suffering equally from the economic downturn. Proximity to Putin unsurprisingly tended to be a good indicator of access to financial opportunity. For example, a scandal broke out in the Russian blogoshere this same month concerning Putin's spokesman, Dmitry Peskov, and the watch he wore to his recent wedding.

When Peskov married Olympic figure skater Tatiana Navka at an extravagant ceremony held in Sochi's top hotel, media attention on this "wedding of the year" was high. Interestingly, though, it was his choice of timepiece that ended up being the source of mounting criticism. A wedding photo of Peskov and Navka kissing clearly shows Peskov wearing a limited-edition Richard Mille RM 52-01, with a distinctive skull-shaped mechanism on the watch face. With only thirty ever made, the watch was estimated to sell at $600,000.

Anticorruption campaigners such as Alexei Navalny began to ask publicly on their blogs how the president's spokesman could afford a watch worth four times his officially declared annual salary? In response to ensuing media queries, Peskov responded that the watch was a gift from his wife.

Expensive watches on the wrists of Russian leaders had become a recurring target for opponents of the Putin regime. Even the Russian president himself had been accused of having an extensive collection of expensive timepieces!

Despite the economic challenges facing Russians at home, Putin was clearly not allowing his assertiveness on the international stage, nor his grip on power domestically, to diminish in any meaningful way. Moscow was demonstrating on several fronts that it would continue to push hard in pursuit of its national interests. Russian claims in the Arctic were just one more area in which Putin was ensuring his country's influence in the decades to come.

As Russia continued to wrestle with an economic downturn and Western condemnation, any hopes that Putin would emerge chastened and conciliatory were quickly dashed. The Russian president seemed intent on continuing forward with his key policy priorities despite whatever criticisms were launched at him.

So Santa Claus had better watch out in the years to come—or his lovely Christmas village might eventually begin to look a lot like Luhansk and Donetsk in eastern Ukraine!

★ ★ ★

Putin's support of Internet trolling—which would gain international notoriety following Trump's surprise victory—was first revealed in all of its glory in August 2015 when a Russian court awarded a former employee of a "propaganda factory" one ruble in symbolic damages. These revelations demonstrated the length that the Russian president was going to ensure that his opinions were adequately aired, although official spokesmen for the Kremlin denied any official link between the government and the trolling operation.

In exchange for a salary of a few hundred dollars each month, employees of the Agency for Internet Studies (AIS) in St. Petersburg filled social media and online comment pages with praise for Putin and championed the Kremlin's various talking points. Advertisements for jobs with AIS appeared innocuous at first, as the organization recruited tech-savvy young men and women to develop online "content." Lyudmila Savchuk, a freelance journalist, took a job with AIS to uncover the scope of its operation but was fired after only two months when she published news stories revealing the group's activity. She subsequently sued AIS for unfair dismissal and in the course of the proceedings was able to put the activities of the shadowy organization under public scrutiny.

Propaganda as an art form was perfected under the previous Soviet regime. It appeared that Putin was now unafraid to use such dark arts whenever needed. Of course, as the nature of news reporting and media had changed so dramatically over the last few decades, so propaganda must also evolve and adapt. In 2015, it was the comments sections of major websites and blogs where the battles for "hearts and minds" was taking place. And the viral video had taken the place of the polemic poster as a means to rally opinion.

AIS's efforts were well thought out. Web proxies hid the location of AIS and its legion of trolls. By burying occasional pro-Kremlin remarks in longer posts on a variety of other topics, the trolls hoped to appear as genuine and authentic as possible. Even YouTube videos ostensibly about video game minutiae were fair game for a bit of off-hand propaganda. An elaborate pecking order was established that allowed the most successful trolls to move up the ladder as their posts gained more viewers and they developed an audience, making a competitive game out of the process with cash bonuses paid to the most successful trolls.

A fair question to ask, of course, was how effective was this online activity at actually changing people's minds about Kremlin policy? One near-immediate response to disclosures about AIS was to wonder why Putin was so sensitive about public opinion that he would actually see money being spent on these activities. Didn't this in fact reflect an underlying insecurity with his grip on power?

Even a perfunctory reading of the tech and finance press reveals how important "social marketing" is in the modern economy. Perhaps the Russian president was actually ahead of the curve on this issue. The story of the 2008 US presidential election included the importance of grass roots, bottom-up efforts by Obama campaigners to tarnish the sense of inevitability that circled Hillary Clinton at the time. Facebook posts and Twitter messages played an important role in those early efforts and were being been studied and replicated by others with various degrees of success ever since.

With the conflict in Ukraine at this time showing little sign of resolution, tensions with the United States and Europe were high. Even in the face of Western sanctions and tumbling oil prices, Putin's support at home remained noticeably strong. The Kremlin even went so far as to impose sanctions of its own against international products as a tit-for-tat countermeasure, even as the economic situation in Russia continued to suffer. High-profile reports of "illegal cheese gangs" having their illicit European dairy products confiscated and destroyed and imported Dutch flowers being incinerated were now a regular occurrence in Russia. Putin was making clear that he had no intention to sit back and allow US and European leaders to dictate the terms under which he governed his country.

Winning "hearts and minds" has always been a crucial element of leadership, although the means by which this battle is won has changed significantly over the centuries. Given the importance of social media as a source of news and a forum for debate, it was entirely unsurprising that it eventually became a focus for politicians.

Putin's "troll factory" demonstrated the Russian leader's willingness to use all the tools available to his best advantage. Valid questions can be raised about the short-term and long-term effectiveness of such measures, but the intent of such actions remained clear—to allow Putin to secure the reins of power in Russia for as long as he chose to stay in office.

★ ★ ★

A curious spat bubbled up in the international media in September 2015 when a Kremlin spokesperson publically denied that Putin had spoken with singer and LGBT advocate Elton John. While many national leaders go out of their way to court and publicize celebrity contacts, Putin wanted to keep any relationship with John strictly on the "down low."

The British singer posted on his Instagram account that the Russian autocrat had reached out to him to discuss his country's controversial antigay laws and implied that further conversations on LGBT rights would be forthcoming. By contrast, Putin's people insisted that no such conversation ever took place.

Russian law had previously made it illegal to distribute any propaganda concerning "nontraditional sexual relations" involving minors. Critics claimed the real goal was to make it difficult for campaigners to circulate practical information to LGBT men and women.

Rather than back away from the controversial law, Putin embraced the hardline stance by handing out a prestigious award the previous week to Vitaly Milonov, an unapologetically antigay politician who was one of the inspirations for the nationwide ban. Among his many attempts to combat the "epidemic" of homosexuality, he has argued that Western pop stars such as Madonna and Lady Gaga violated the terms of their visas when they spoke out in favor of LGBT rights at their Russian concerts.

Despite the brusque Kremlin denial, LGBT advocates in Russia still praised John's efforts. John enjoyed significant popularity in Russia at this time, even in light of his public pronouncements against the antigay law at his concerts in Moscow and St. Petersburg.

The political traction of the Kremlin's antigay stance was perhaps more understandable in light of the fact that homosexual acts were only decriminalized in 1991. LGBT men and women, therefore, did not have a long public history in Russia. Many Russians were finding it difficult to adapt to a modern world where open validations of homosexual lives were a common occurrence.

It is worth remembering, however, that, until recently, antigay laws and policies were common in much of the West. Britain only repealed its ban on promoting homosexuality in schools in 2003 and the US Boy Scouts only began accepting gay scout leaders in 2015.

Of course, much has been written in recent years about the fact that Putin has himself become a gay icon of sorts. Shirtless astride a horse, it was hard for him not to! But still the Russian antigay law remained. Perhaps his metrosexuality had the perverse side effect of forcing him to strike an even harder line when it comes to sexuality-related issues.

Some observers of contemporary Russia might point out that the country actually has much more pressing issues to confront than attempting to contain alternative sexualities. For example, alcoholism remains a scourge of the Russian workplace and a blight on many lives. One report issued at the time by the Organization for Economic Cooperation and Development (OECD) estimated that approximately 30 percent of all Russian deaths were linked to alcohol abuse.

The problem was so vast in scale that Deputy Prime Minister Olga Golodets urged state-owned businesses to do more to combat drunkenness at work. Apparently of particular concern were factories operating in both the defense sector and the nuclear sector. Perhaps someone should consider installing a Breathalyzer that employees will need to blow into before they can sign out the enriched uranium!

Add to this plunging oil prices and a rapidly deteriorating ruble, and the scene was set for painful economic contractions and the possibility of prolonged recession. In 2015, though, Putin did not appear to be allowing any amount of economic uncertainty to weaken his grip on power. His popularity at home showed little sign of wavering in the near term, and the hardline antigay stance resonated with many Russians who resented aspects of the social transformation that Russia had observed since the fall of the Soviet Union and the loss of the old certainties.

From such a position of strength, one would hope that Putin wouldn't shy away from a free-and-frank conversation with someone who has the global following of Elton John.

Tip for Elton in the future: We know that Putin is a fan of karaoke, as the online videos of him crooning to "Blueberry Hill" clearly attest. The price of admission for a one-on-one chat, therefore, might be as simple as a quick a cappella duet of "Benny and the Jets." A small price to pay to air your grievances and make the case for LGBT rights in Russia.

* * *

When the Turkish military shot down a Russian fighter jet in November 2015, Putin promised "serious consequences." This was no idle boast. In the weeks following the attack, tensions escalated considerably between the two former allies. A diplomatic war broke out between Moscow and Ankara, with little certainty as to what the medium- and long-term consequences would be.

Emotions ran very high in Russia. As a result of the attack, the Russian pilot was shot and killed by militants when he tried to land in his parachute, while another Russian soldier died in the successful attempt to rescue a downed navigator who survived his landing.

One particular group felt the increasing animosity most directly—the 800,000 Turkish nationals living and working in Russia at the time. Reports circulated in the weeks that followed of individuals with Turkish citizenship being denied entry into the country or being deported, as well as Turkish students at Russian universities being targeted for harassment by police. In addition, the Turkish embassy, located in Moscow, was vandalized by people throwing paint and rocks—and even eggs!

Boycotts and bans were adopted by the Kremlin in order to put an economic price on what Russian leaders viewed as an unjustified and unprovoked attack. Initially, the import of fruits and vegetables from Turkey was banned, as well as charter flights between the two countries. With Turkey a common holiday destination for more than 4 million sun-seeking Russians, the impact of the flight ban on the Turkish hospitality and tourism industries was significant.

Russian state media also jumped wholeheartedly on the anti-Turkey bandwagon, broadcasting a series of negative pieces demonizing Turkey and claiming that Ankara had wider territorial goals in the Middle East. Even Putin himself made claims that Turkey profited from the export of Islamic State–controlled oil through its territories.

Unfortunately, Russia was not the only country with a confrontational, and occasionally abrasive, leader. Turkish president

Recep Erdoğan was also well known for his grandstanding and recalcitrance, laying the groundwork for a "perfect storm" of diplomatic breakdown between these two Bonaparte-esque figures.

Erdoğan publicly stated that Russia was "playing with fire" if Turkish nationals visiting the country were subject to abuse and mistreatment. These threats did little to rein in angry Russian officials. Meanwhile, Putin has made it clear that he would not meet with or speak to Erdoğan until the Turkish leader apologized for the attack.

Russia's increased military activity in Syria, as it simultaneously battled Islamic State and supported Syrian president Bashar al-Assad, had already placed it in a precarious position with regard to Erdoğan's Turkey. Since US and EU sanctions were imposed on Russia after its Bonapartist adventurism in Ukraine, Moscow had been moving closer to Ankara as an alternative trading partner, to the mutual benefit of each country. Unfortunately, that door was now closed.

The consequences of this public spat, however, meant more than simply a lack of fresh Turkish fruit on the shelves of Russian grocery stories. Given Turkey's status as a NATO member, the potential ramifications of a prolonged kerfuffle could have been severe, not only for the two countries involved but also for other NATO members, such as the United States. These treaty-bound allies could one day be in a position of having to defend Turkey from a Russian attack.

Adding to the complex nature of the anti–Islamic State coalition that had stumbled into existence after the Paris atrocities the prior month were the persistent rumors that senior Turkish officials had, in fact, provided support to Islamic State and undermined attempts to contain them. Erdoğan denied the claim, but the awkward rumors persisted.

Obama had urged Putin and Erdoğan to focus on the "common enemy" Islamic State and not to get sidetracked by their dispute over the downed jet. However, Obama was also clear that the United States supported Turkey's right to defend its own airspace and that he fully understood US obligations to Turkey as a NATO member.

Of course, the anti–Islamic State coalition of the United States, Russia, and France differed on one fairly fundamental point— namely, Assad's future role in a post–Islamic State Syria. The Russians had been clear that they backed Assad, in the face of French and American calls that he should have no role after the defeat of Islamic State.

As tensions between Turkey and Russia worsened, the complexities of combating Islamic State abroad and extremist terror at home were becoming increasingly evident.

⋆ ⋆ ⋆

In 2006, former KGB agent Alexander Litvinenko died of radioactivity poisoning in London. His murder became front-page news and an ongoing mystery that British officials have sought answers to ever since. A decade later in January 2016, a public inquiry conducted in the Royal Courts of Justice announced its findings, naming the two Russian agents who killed Litvinenko and stating that there was a strong probability that they were acting on orders from Vladimir Putin.

British home secretary (and soon-to-be prime minister) Theresa May subsequently called the murder an unacceptable breach of international law. Litvinenko's widow, Marina, immediately demanded that Britain hold Russia accountable for her husband's murder.

A spokesperson for then-prime minister David Cameron quickly said that the inquiry confirmed what many in the government had believed for some time but stressed that any potential response would have to be measured in light of Britain's and Russia's ongoing cooperation in fighting Islamic State. Adding a further layer of complexity to the situation was that shortly before he was murdered, Litvinenko had obtained British citizenship, placing Cameron in an awkward position if he tacitly condoned an assassination of one of its citizens by a foreign government.

As Litvinenko lay dying in a London hospital bed from exposure to the highly toxic polonium-210, he had no doubt who was responsible for killing him—Putin. Moscow responded to the inquiry's findings with claims that the investigation was politically motivated and its results a foregone conclusion, given the animosity toward Russia that emanated from London and other Western capitals in recent years. In addition, a Putin spokesperson took particular aim at the inquiry's verdict that the Russian leader was "probably" involved in the crime, noting that a verdict of "probably" wasn't a feature of the Russian judicial system.

Not all of the inquiry's proceedings were made public, due to the use of secret intelligence sources, leading to further claims by Russian authorities that the verdict was nothing more than an attempt to "whitewash" failures by Britain's own special services. British officials countered that the finding would be the equivalent of complicity in murder and would result in a criminal conviction, should Putin ever be tried in Britain.

Even the man accused of actually committing the crime, Andrei Lugovoi, laughed off the inquiry's findings against him. Now an elected member of Russia's parliament, Lugovoi linked the renewed interest in the Litvinenko case at the time to anger over the situation in Ukraine and dismissed the process as "pathetic." Attempts to extradite Lugovoi and his accomplice Dmitry Kovtun so they could face trial in Britain were rebuffed by Moscow.

Despite tensions with the Kremlin over its Bonapartist adventurism in the Crimea and continued efforts to destabilize Kiev, Putin had ensured that he was viewed as an essential partner when it came to addressing the threats posed in Iran and Syria.

Opposition politicians in Britain argued for a more assertive response, with some suggesting—yet again!—that the 2018 World Cup be stripped from Russia. Other critics insisted that London was awash in "dirty" Russian money and steps should be taken to clean up the capital.

State-sponsored assassinations on the streets of London are clearly a cause for concern, regardless of whether the mastermind is the Russian president or the head of an extremist terrorist organization. Given the rhetoric used against followers of Al-Qaeda and Islamic State who have committed horrific acts against innocent people in recent years, it would seem strange to many if the British government failed to take the necessary steps to hold the Kremlin accountable for the killing of one of its own citizens.

In addition, it was quite unclear whether allowing Putin to emerge from this incident unpunished would actually help the British–Russian relationship long-term. There were some who argued that Putin had no respect for weakness, at home or abroad. If Cameron decided to give Putin a pass on the Litvinenko murder, there was a real possibility that Putin would respond not with private thanks but instead with public disdain.

In many respects, the inquiry's 300-page report did not break new ground. Instead, the report simply confirmed what many observers had believed for the past decade. What was interesting about the findings, though, was the direct and prominent way in which it laid responsibility for the assassination squarely at the feet of Putin.

Even if diplomatic priorities required the British government to put its need for Kremlin support in Syria, Iran, and elsewhere above the desire for justice, the verdict against Putin was one that could linger against the Russian president for years to come. With the rapid approach of the Brexit referendum in June 2016, it would also raise awkward questions for some Britons about the actual value of sovereignty if it not used in situations so vivid and clear-cut as the execution of a British citizen on the streets of their nation's capital.

14

To the Barricades!

*I saw the crown of France
laying on the ground,
so I picked it up with my sword.*

—Napoleon Bonaparte

President Hollande saw his Socialist Party battered and bruised in local elections in March 2014. The embarrassing results sent a clear message—voters were frustrated with the lack of progress being made in the two years following Hollande capture of the Élysée Palace from the center-right incumbent, Nicolas Sarkozy.

The ferocious losses for the Socialist Party were widespread. Sarkozy's Union for a Popular Movement (UMP) party (later to be rebranded as the American sounding *les Republicains*) showed strong gains across the country. Unfortunately, the far-right

National Front, led by Marine Le Pen, also did very well, throwing a wrench into some of the electoral calculations for the runoff.

Under the French system, a candidate who receives more than 50 percent of the votes in the first round wins outright. If no one crosses the threshold, the top two vote-getters run again one week later. However, strategic voting is often used to see National Front candidates blocked from winning in runoffs. Under the "Republican pact" that has been in place for the past thirty years, mainstream French parties have consistently agreed to vote in such a way in the runoff election so as to block the extremist National Front candidates from getting into office. Interestingly, the "Republican pact" only applies to the far-right National Front. The Socialist Party does not similarly distance itself from far-left parties, an inconsistency that UMP leader Jean-François Copé repeatedly pointed out.

Only a few years earlier, in 2008, the National Front appeared to be well past its prime. Its subsequent resurgence was due in large part to the transfer of leadership from the party's founder, Jean-Marie Le Pen, to his daughter Marine, as well as the widespread resentment building toward unchecked immigration and the vast, out-of-touch European bureaucracy in Brussels. Where should French voters turn now? Who would be their new Bonaparte to put their country back on a path to greatness?

On the left, the Socialists under Hollande repeatedly failed to deliver the growth-without-austerity that they promised. On the right, Sarkozy was dumped after a single term when many in France grew tired of his bling-bling style and micromanaging approach to governance. Some on the right were now hinting, though, that Sarkozy was well positioned to swoop back into national politics and recapture the Élysée Palace once again. However, scandals continued to dog the former president, with prosecutions for corruption slowly working their way through the French judicial system.

There are important lessons to be learned regarding the recent rise of populist parties in Europe. France is not alone. Faceless EU bureaucrats in Brussels, out of touch with the needs and priorities of everyday Europeans, were driving more and more disgruntled voters into the arms of parties like the National Front in France and the Freedom Party in the Netherlands—and UKIP in Britain as well!

As the financial crisis rocked the economic foundations of Europe in recent years, cracks had become evident in the political foundation as well. The easy consensus that the European Union was unquestionably a force for good was now being questioned more often across the continent, and not just in perfidious Britain. Men and women were increasingly asking awkward questions about the priorities of the Brussels bureaucrats. Were they focusing at all on the impact of their directives, regulations, and white papers on the working-class families across the continent? Or were they simply prioritizing a set of goals that benefited a small cluster of social, political, and economic elites—the so-called party of Davos?

It was unclear in the spring of 2016 whether Brussels would be able to provide fresh solutions that resonated with European voters within the framework of a European Union whose doctrine of managerial Bonapartism was looking increasingly aloof and outdated. Perhaps even a European answer to the Tea Party was now in the works—but could the insular Brussels elite respond to such a broad-based challenge?

★ ★ ★

In late February 2015, Hollande found himself under scrutiny for his careless use of a racially charged term. By describing white French men and women as "Français de souche," a nativist term used by some on the far right in France, the unpopular French leader made yet another misstep in a country still tense and uncertain after the tragic killings at *Charlie Hebdo* several weeks earlier.

By using the controversial phrase "native French people" in a speech to a leading Jewish organization, Hollande was accused by critics of attempting to divide his country between first-class white citizens and the remainder who were relegated to an inferior and somehow illegitimate second-class position. Even the leader of the far-right National Front party, Marine Le Pen, denounced the president by stating that she didn't favor the controversial term!

The topic of Hollande's speech at a meeting with the Representative Council of Jewish Institutions in France was the mounting anti-Semitism that was gripping his country at the time. The group's chairman, Roger Cukierman, attributed the upswing in attacks on Jews to Muslims, while Hollande rebutted that there had also been recent incidents of vandalism involving "native French people." Hollande's inability to address these concerns and fears would be a key factor in determining his inability to retain the presidency when his first term ended two years later.

The increasingly frayed state of affairs in France was creating some awkward and unforeseen political bedfellows. For example, Cukierman went so far as to publicly endorse Le Pen this same week, a feat unthinkable only a few years ago. With the next presidential elections scheduled for the end of April 2017, it was believed that approximately 15 percent of Jewish voters could back the far-right National Front. Their motivation was a fear of radical Islamist terror and what that meant for the continued viability of the 500,000-member Jewish community within France.

The National Front, under the leadership for many years of Le Pen's father, Jean-Marie, was once very vocal in its anti-Semitism. He even went so far as to defend the wartime Vichy regime and was convicted on a number of occasions as a result. Under his leadership, the party attracted just over 4 percent of the Jewish vote when he ran for president in 2007. With the more media-savvy Marine Le Pen as the party's candidate, the National Front tripled that result in 2012.

By 2016, the focus of the National Front was on radical Islamist terror and the negative impact on France of Muslim immigration. Anti-Semitism, a staple of the far right for many years, had been set aside. With the 2017 presidential election steadily approaching, Le Pen was leading national opinion polls. Unfortunately, there was still considerable anti-Semitism among rank-and-file members of the National Front, and Le Pen had not yet formally renounced her father's past statements regarding Jews and the Holocaust. As a result, many French voters still doubted how sincere Le Pen's commitment was to her newfound Jewish brothers and sisters.

Unfortunately, the situation had become so strained that record levels of French Jews were leaving the country. Hollande was doing his best to try to persuade his Jewish citizens that they were safe under his watch, but considerable doubts remained. For example, more than 850 attacks on Jewish men and women were reported in France in 2014 alone. But the reach of anti-Semitism was broader than just physical violence and included far-flung conspiracy theories about the influence this community was exerting on the country's leaders.

Even the composition and integrity of Hollande's own cabinet was being called into question. Manuel Valls, the prime minister, was accused by Roland Dumas, a senior member of the ruling Socialist Party, of being "under Jewish influence." The reason? Valls' wife, Anne Gravoin, was Jewish.

Valls had been assertive in his stance on the threat of Islamist extremism and had campaigned aggressively against anti-Semitism. According to this argument, which featured prominently in a number of conspiracy theories, Gravoin, a successful violinist, was in reality a key member of a highly effective Jewish conspiracy to control the French government.

Others within the Socialist Party quickly distanced themselves from Dumas and his remarks, but many feared that such a statement would fuel further departures by French Jews for a safer home in Israel, Britain, or elsewhere. Despite Valls' pleas that "the place for French Jews is France," thousands of Jewish men and women were voting with their feet.

★ ★ ★

Having failed to deliver success in the March 2014 French municipal elections, the National Front quickly experienced divisions at
the very top of the party hierarchy. Founder Jean-Marie Le Pen
was publicly disowned that same week by his daughter, current
leader Marine Le Pen. Marine was seen by her father as a moder-
ating force who had betrayed the founding principles of his party,
while Jean-Marie appeared to his daughter as an anachronistic
throwback to an era where the party made trade in Holocaust
denial and anti-Semitic remarks.

Until the disappointment in these midterm elections, Marine
had been seen a modernizer within the far-right party, setting
aside much of its controversial rhetoric and making it electable
in a way that it had never previously been. Considered by many
as "toxic," the National Front had been transformed from a hate
group to a populist anti-immigration party that sought out alliances and collaborations with other French groups.

An interview with Jean-Marie published in April 2015 contained quotes from the former leader at his most controversial.
He defended the collaborationist pro-Nazi regime that governed
during World War II and oversaw the deportation of 78,000 Jews.
He attacked the recent increase in the number of National Front
members who were homosexuals. He lambasted the current prime
minister, Manuel Valls, who had the misfortune of being born in
Spain and having a Jewish wife.

In response, Marine stripped her father of his right to stand
in regional elections in December 2015. She was also reportedly
considering forcing Jean-Marie out of his post as honorary president of the party, a position he had enjoyed since stepping out of
the limelight four years earlier.

Jean-Marie Le Pen founded the National Front to give voice
to frustrations and anxieties that had been ignored by the mainstream parties. However, he had increasingly appeared out of step
with Marine's push toward mainstream acceptability. His vitriolic
outbursts raised in many French voters' minds the concern that
the party was still driven primarily by hatred, rather than genu-

ine attempts to legitimately address the challenges facing France today.

Some observers discounted the recent domestic meltdown as simple theatricalities gaining media coverage because of the party's failure to capitalize on its surge in national polls in recent months. Despite early indications that the National Front was poised to make important gains, the party was unable to win control of any councils. This failure caused critics to question whether Marine Le Pen's modernizations would ever lead to tangible electoral success. Her father had decided to take advantage of this period of self-doubt to relaunch a "greatest hits" selection of his more colorful theories.

Underlying the melodrama surrounding a very public father-daughter split was the less-reported controversy over the party's lurch to the left on a number of key economic points. In an attempt to sweep up support from disillusioned members of France's working classes, the National Front now championed several left-wing policies. Despite the tactical merits of such an approach, Jean-Marie Le Pen condemned the leftward lurch and the lack of concrete successes to validate the new approach meant it was clearly open to debate.

What many observers outside of France, however, were failing to realize was the deep sense of pessimism that remained among many of the country's most high-profile intellectuals. To many of these word-loving elites, their beloved France was being crushed from both an Anglo-American market capitalism and an extremist Islamist ideology, each of which sought to undermine uniquely French values and customs. In this narrative, France, and perhaps the entirety of Western civilization, was about to fall off the cliff in as spectacular a fashion as the Roman Empire did a millennium and a half before. Globalization, in all of its worst guises, had arguably left France unable to maintain the traditions that once made it the envy of much of the world.

Marine Le Pen's revamped National Front was attempting to simultaneously capitalize on and rebut this sense of melancholy and doom. Regardless of her changes, her father remained for better or worse the most potent icon the party had. How his daughter and the current leadership dealt with him and his legacy would go a long way toward determining whether the National Front could really transform this party into an election-winning political machine, as well as providing some insight into the future bounds of acceptable political discourse in France, and in Europe as a whole.

★ ★ ★

A small diplomatic kerfuffle broke out between France and Italy in June 2015 over one the biggest challenges facing Europeans today—Nutella!

The rich chocolate-and-hazelnut spread was targeted by French environmental minister Ségolène Royal as a cause of global warming. Perhaps the more obvious line of attack for the former Socialist presidential candidate (and coincidently ex-domestic partner of then-president François Hollande) would have been the threat that this creamy confectionary posed to European waistlines! Instead, Royal expressed serious concerns over Nutella's use of palm oil and how deforestation in Indonesia and Malaysia to increase palm fruit production was harming the environment.

With national pride at risk, Royal's governmental counterpart in Italy, Gian Luca Galletti, responded with a fervent defense of the beloved product, produced by the Italian company Ferrero, including a promise that he would be eating Nutella for dinner that same night!

Royal had suggested that given the potential impact that deforestation had on global warming, Nutella should have been avoided until it was produced with other more ecofriendly ingredients. In response, a Ferrero spokesman insisted the company exerted great efforts to make sure that any palm oil that finds its way into Nutella jars would be sourced responsibly from sustainable supplies.

An embarrassed Royal quickly apologized, although hers was not the first French attack on Nutella. Only three years earlier, the French National Assembly attempted to impose a 300 percent tax on the same ingredient—palm oil—to both protect the environment and combat childhood obesity, a growing threat across the developed world. Fortunately for Nutella's legion of French fans, the bill failed to pass.

Given the other health challenges facing France today, it was somewhat surprising to find Nutella a target of senior governmental policy. For example, French men and women were still facing at this time unacceptably high levels of alcohol consumption and smoking.

Approximately 50,000 people were dying in France each year due to alcohol abuse. On average, each French person consumes about 120 bottles of wine a year, while the European equivalent would be approximately 90 bottles. Although the French drank less in 2015 than they once did, they were still one of the leaders in Europe and the costs to their national health system were significant.

In an effort to cut smoking after a recent spike in usage, the French government mandated plain packaging on tobacco products. Of particular concern was the number of French women who smoke in the final months of their pregnancy.

As President Hollande continued to battle with wavering support among voters, a wobbly economy, and a resurgence of far-right opposition, it was particularly awkward that this same month also saw the 200th anniversary of Bonaparte's defeat to the British at Waterloo. Hollande boycotted the official commemorations of this battle, which remains to this day a sore spot in the collective French memory. For example, one of his predecessors in the Élysée Palace, Charles de Gaulle, once wrote a history of France that omitted Waterloo in its recounting of his beloved country's long history.

Bonaparte's own legacy in France remains multilayered and unresolved. He made the argument through words and deeds that France should be a great power and the leading country in a unified Europe. Since 1815, though, France had ceased to be one of the prime movers of world events and instead has been largely relegated to a position of keen observer and frequent spoiler of the plans and aspirations of others. Although military superiority is no longer a trait impartial observers attribute to France, the country still has an impact that far exceeds its actual size.

France's challenges today, like the challenges of so much of the developed world, include many that are actually quite mundane. The impact of palm oil and alcohol on French diets, as well as the potential environmental and financial impact of such personal decisions when aggregated on a large scale, are not the types of public policy decisions that would have sustained Bonaparte's attention for very long!

Of course, the world still faces challenges to the security of our countries that often only military force can fully address. But the expectations that citizens have for their governments and that governments have for their citizens have expanded greatly since Bonaparte took the field at Waterloo.

Debates over whether there should be a government policy on Nutella consumption might seem an absurd distraction from more important questions that our leaders should address. However, as the remits of governments expand to include the provision of a wide variety of social and economic benefits for its citizens, with taxpayers ultimately picking up the bill for bad decision-making by individuals, it's hard to say that these same governments can be wholly indifferent to the aggregated effects of such bad decisions. Especially if the state ends up stuck with the Nutella bill!

★ ★ ★

The French take their national cuisine very, very seriously. Their loyalties to Nutella are just the tip of the gastronomic iceberg. While American children braving a hot lunch in their school cafeteria might have to make due with turkey tacos, Salisbury steak, or the ever-reliable corn dog, their French counterparts enjoy a variety of high-end selections, such as veal stew, chicken pâté, and potted salmon.

A frequent ingredient, however, in many of these dishes is pork, a staple on French tables for hundreds of years. If you are a practicing Muslim, pork is anathema and must be avoided at all costs. Until recently, French public schools had been accommodating. Typically, any day when pork, ham, or bacon was on the menu, an alternative was provided for those who chose it.

In October 2015, a campaign to remove this option began building considerably in France, leaving Muslim students a stark choice—eat pork or go without. In practice, the latter means that observant children would need to bring their own lunch on days when pork was on the menu. The pro-pork campaign came after a prolonged attack on the wearing of headscarves in public. Both acts are seen by an increasing number of French men and women as an attempt by Muslims to flaunt the country's much heralded secularism—known as *laïcité*—and refuse assimilation into wider French society.

Apparently, consuming pig meat was central to the national identity of many French people—who knew!—and a wide range of politicians were jumping on the pork bandwagon. To its champions, pork was a cornerstone of French gastronomy. To deny the place of the pig in one's diet was to deny any possibility of being authentically French. From this perspective, any accommodation to account for the individual religious practices was a clear attack on the country's commitment to being secular.

Even the frenetic former French president Nicolas Sarkozy came out publically in support of pork on school menus. To Muslim parents, the issue was not the need to maintain state neutrality on religious matters, but instead a thinly veiled attempt to foster Islamophobia and further isolate their community. Despite the oft-repeated claims of Republican values of equality, liberty, and fraternity, many immigrants from the Middle East and North Africa found French life unwelcoming and exclusionary.

For example, a controversial law banning public employees from wearing symbols of their religious beliefs was widely seen as a direct attack on Muslims, even though the wearing of a cross or star of David is just as forbidden as wearing a headscarf, or *hijab*.

The terrorist attacks on the offices of *Charlie Hebdo* in January 2015 reignited the debate over how best to integrate Muslims into French society and prevent the radicalization of at-risk youth. This debate accelerated after the bloody attacks across Paris in November 2015. Secularism was now a prominent rallying cry of right-wing commentators and politicians seeking to thwart the next Islamic extremist atrocity. Their opponents responded that this corruption of *laïcité* was being used simply to enforce a stereotypical homogeny on individuals.

The National Front, led by Marine Le Pen, had for some time been at the vanguard of anti-immigrant politics, setting themselves up as the champion of traditional French life. Given her sustained success at attracting alienated French voters, other politicians were appropriating her themes and priorities in an attempt to win votes for themselves.

The question of religious practice sat awkwardly at the frontier of public and private life. No matter how confident a democracy may be, there was always at least a bit of nervousness and anxiety when the religion crosses into the public sphere. When British prime minister Tony Blair once spoke exuberantly about his faith, his political advisor Alastair Campbell famously retorted, "We don't do God." By contrast, the general omnipresence of religious imagery and references in the American political narrative is well known. Republican presidential hopeful (and eventual Housing and Urban Development Secretary) Ben Carson's remark that he could not envision a Muslim being elected to the highest office in the land would strike many Americans as crudely racist, but many others would see it as a clear statement of the obvious.

France is built around the state's preeminent role in two areas: the economy and enforcing the concept of *laïcité*—or secularism. Both policies may actually be exacerbating tensions with French

Muslims. There are currently 4.7 million Muslims in France. Importantly, it is a crime in France not to carry identification, providing French police with a convenient excuse for stopping individuals. In the *banlieues* to the north of Paris and across the country, there was a pervasive sense of exclusion and isolation.

As Sarkozy continued to ponder another run for Élysée Palace in 2017, and politicians continued to mine popular anxiety for the chance to gain a material electoral advantage, the issue of the place of Muslims in French society remained a highly contentious one. Having secured pork's primacy in school cafeterias, perhaps the next round of public debate would see French candidates eagerly demonstrating their authentic Frenchness by passing public bacon-eating loyalty tests to adoring crowds of supporters. *Vive le porc!*

* * *

With the memories of the deadly 2015 Paris attacks still at the forefront of their thoughts, French legislators voted in February 2016 in favor of several controversial constitutional amendments. They permanently enshrined security measures previously implemented by President Hollande on a temporary basis. Included in the amendments were provisions that allow French citizenship to be stripped from convicted terrorists.

The power to strip citizenship proved highly controversial, with one minister in Hollande's cabinet resigning in protest. Initially targeting only those French nationals with dual citizenship, of which there were more than 3 million in the country, the proposals were revised to read as applicable to all French men and women.

Since the November 2015 attacks, Hollande had attempted to reinvent himself as the next Bonaparte—a commander in chief leading his country at a time of war, rather than an ineffective middle manager, adrift and irrelevant. He used the current state of emergency powers, which had to be renewed every three months, to allow police and security forces to operate without judicial oversight. Critics claimed that the broad powers were being abused, while champions of the measures argued that they were essential in order to prevent another bloody attack by extremist militants.

By claiming that his country was at war, Hollande favored heated rhetoric that included a promise to eradicate Islamic State around the world. Comparisons between the French leader and US president George W. Bush in the weeks and months that followed the 9/11 attacks were easily drawn. However, while the threat posed to the United States fifteen years earlier was widely viewed at the time as a primarily external one, France faced a deemed enemy that was as much a domestic concern as a foreign adversary.

In many ways, Hollande was fighting for his personal political survival as well as against the jihadi terrorists who left 129 people dead on the streets of his capital city. Prior to the November attacks, Hollande was the least popular French president in modern history, widely seen as in over his head and unable to respond effectively to either the mounting terrorist threat or the wide-ranging problems dragging down France's economy.

With Sarkozy eyeing the country's top job once again, and far-right leader Marine Le Pen posed to make a serious run for the presidency as well, Hollande needed to be seen by French voters as effective in conducting his own personal War on Terror if he wanted to have any chance at retaining his job in 2017.

As a result, Hollande went further than many leftist politicians would to strengthen the ability of the government to identify and prevent future attacks and to punish those responsible. Unfortunately, there was only so much increased surveillance, warrantless searches, and house arrests one could do to address the day-to-day realities of the social apartheid that had divided France for many years.

It was soon clear to Hollande that his time in office would be largely judged by his ability to prevent anything like the November 2015 attacks from occurring on French soil again. Of course, declaring a war is much, much easier than actually winning one. There were still many who looked at the American response to 9/11 and saw more mistakes than successes, especially as Islamic State grew and metastasized around the Middle East and North Africa.

France notably did not take part in the invasion of Iraq in 2003 when Bush declared his War on Terror, but now Hollande insisted that he would take all steps necessary to declare total victory. In doing so, he faced accusations by members of his own party that he was betraying fundamental French values, although he could take some comfort that, by one recent survey, his citizenship proposal had the support of 94 percent of voters.

Perhaps the most successful argument against stripping citizenship from convicted terrorists was that it would have no practical impact on the challenges the country actually faced from jihadi terrorists. Many extremist attacks were, of course, suicide bombings. Their perpetrators have little desire to walk away from their crimes and suffer the criminal consequences of their actions. And those who did would probably not shed too many tears for the loss of citizenship in a country they actively sought to destroy.

As far as vote-winning rhetoric, Hollande's proposal no doubt had merit. However, the threat facing France at this time—together with much of Europe, including Britain—was much more nuanced and pernicious than a simple question over what passports an Islamist extremist may carry.

*　*　*

One sign that a country is in chaos must surely be when senior government officials make a point of stressing that their country is absolutely, positively not in chaos. Such was the case in June 2016 when French prime minister Manuel Valls told journalists who were questioning him about the widespread striking taking place to protest a comprehensive change in France's labor laws. Valls stated categorically that "it is not chaos in France."

Many of his fellow countrymen did not take much comfort in his words. Images of these strikes across France would prove to be a serious disruption to summer tourism, which was important every year but was particularly important in June as the Euro 2016 international soccer tournament kicked off. More than 2 million spectators attended matches across the country in the following weeks.

For many years France has wrestled with its reputation as a country where serious economic reform was simply not possible. Valls' goal was to streamline the process by which French workers were hired and fired. Unfortunately, powerful unions staged blockades at fuel depots, which caused significant travel delay. In addition, almost half of the train services were canceled, as were over a hundred flights across Europe, due to a parallel strike by French air traffic controllers.

Despite the strikes, Valls vowed to stand by his labor reforms. Regardless of the anger he incited in the strikers who opposed him, Valls was passionate in his belief that reform was essential to France and that compromise around a broad-based consensus was preferable to allowing a small group of militants to effectively hold a veto over national policy.

What made Valls' position particularly noteworthy was that he was a long-standing member of the Socialist Party and served in the highest ranks of a distinctly left-leaning administration, led by President Hollande. For his championing of pro-business, pro-market causes, Valls earned both the hatred of many of his far-left colleagues and generous comparisons to former British prime minister Tony Blair. Blair was one of the first center-left politicians in Europe to seriously attempt a "third-way" approach to governing that did not set them in direct opposition to market-oriented reforms.

The risk to Valls and to other reform-minded French politicians was clear—to cave on these important labor market overhauls would significantly undermine the prospects for any future efforts to liberalize the economy. In this regard, these reforms became highly symbolic, inflaming the passions of union leaders and necessitating high levels of resolve by Valls and other senior members of the French government, if they intended to see them fully implemented.

Revolution is near and dear to the hearts of many French men and women. Their tendency to support the plight of the abused worker in the face of overreaching capitalists is often marked. After many years of center-right presidents occupying the Élysée Palace, the Socialist Party regained it in 2012 with Hollande's victory. However, much of the goodwill that initially existed was squandered by Hollande, leaving him in the summer of 2016 at record low levels in the approval polls. Valls' labor reforms were a bold gambit to reposition his party for upcoming elections, but at the same time they were essential to put France's economy back on track toward growth and prosperity.

The chaos unfolding across the country was vivid and real, but the effect of this chaos could have been broader support among French voters for implementing the much-needed reforms, rather than capitulating to a small number of militant union leaders and their most extreme supporters.

The French must eventually decide whether they are willing to see necessary changes made to the way their economy works or instead see their reputation as being immune to reform be reinforced yet again. Having the political nerve to stand up to a little "chaos" may one day appear to have been a small price to pay if the result is an economy fit-for-purpose in the twenty-first century—but such political nerve tends usually to be in short supply, unless politicians genuinely fear that there might be actual consequences from their electorate.

And electorates have become more demanding—and much more unpredictable—in recent years.

15

The Morning After . . .

*Friends must always be treated as if
one day they might be enemies.*

—NAPOLEON BONAPARTE

Once the Brexit referendum votes were counted, the recriminations began. European Commission president Jean-Claude Juncker called Brexit "a tragedy." French president François Hollande demanded that Britain "pay a price" for its decision to leave.

Frankly, there is something distinctly sinister in the oft-repeated contention that Britain—and the British people themselves—must be made to suffer for having the temerity and the gall to upend the benevolent rule of Brussels' Eurocratic elite. It is hard to find another act of democratic self-determination that has been greeted by such widespread and casual vindictiveness. You would think that an entity held up as an example of enlightenment and virtue would not be based on a fear (or at least a strong dislike) of the individual men and women who it governs. Defending democracy shouldn't be quite so hard!

In addition to blame, there were also small pockets of wishful thinking. Many commentators argued that this democratic exercise would ultimately have no meaningful impact on British policy or the European Union's constitutional makeup. There must be something slightly dismissive about such casual disregard for the popular will, even in the mind of the most resolute Remain campaigner. And, of course, even if the actual legality or legitimacy of the referendum were successfully undermined and overturned in the months to come, the concerns that drove millions of British voters to question the benevolence and effectiveness of Brussels —as I have dutifully outlined in the preceding chapters—would still be there in need of addressing. A second referendum could not simply vote those mounting challenges out of existence.

The actual course that Brexit will cut through Britain and Europe is still being determined. The full consequence of all the various political and diplomatic decisions that have followed the referendum will take decades to emerge. Until then, we must occupy ourselves with a running debate over the mundane details of the Brexit process as it is unfolding before us, including the relative benefits of a "hard Brexit" over a "soft Brexit," as well as how to best adapt to the pound's rapid devaluation after the surprise Leave victory.

Perhaps the most useful thing we could try to do is to undertake a concerted attempt to better understand what drove millions of Britons to actually vote to leave the European Union. Simply assuming they were ignorant or racists—or perhaps ignorant racists!—doesn't do these voters nearly enough justice. Such an inquiry would not only help clarify what the Brexit negotiations should ultimately cover but also provide a glimpse of the possible directions that a post-EU Britain might take in the decades to come. Competitive global economic power? Introverted social democratic oasis?

No one can claim with any certainty to know what the future holds for post-Brexit Britain. Prime Minister Theresa May will have to navigate around dozens of potential hazards (including her own political future), while at the same time maintaining the confidence of both voters and key economic players who will be the drivers of future prosperity. Unfortunately, British politics is now much more chaotic and unpredictable than it has been over the previous generation.

In the fall of 2016, British business leaders were claiming more and more loudly that May's government was freezing them out and refusing to listen to their concerns about the particulars of Brexit's rollout. Will a "soft Brexit" be possible, with Britain retaining access to the single market and existing EU trade deals? Will a "hard Brexit" with London regaining unhampered control over immigration from Brussels at any cost be the preferred option? May set out her position at the dawn of her premiership as "Brexit means Brexit," but such platitudes did not establish what particular form Brexit will take and on what sort of timeline.

The practical challenges are daunting. Britain will need steady flows of international investment to cover its current account deficit. Will international companies and financial institutions still find Britain attractive if access to the single market is cut off? What economic price will the British public ultimately be willing to pay in exchange for border control?

Experts voiced their concerns during the long Brexit campaign, and experts were quick in the days that followed the vote to reiterate their dire predictions of severe economic ramifications. But as then-Justice secretary Michael Gove said in the days leading up to the referendum, "People have had enough of experts." When there was little immediate negative fall-out from the Leave victory, it appeared as if Gove was on to something—namely, that despite the apocalyptic tones taken by economists and academics of all hues, the British voter had been right. Brexit did not appear to mean the end of the world—at least for a while!

* * *

In an age where it has become fashionable to reduce politics to mere contests over economic priorities, the Brexit vote reminds us of the continued importance of non-economic priorities in the day-to-day lives of voters—even where the immediate consequences are severe. The financial markets severely punished the British pound sterling in the months after the Leave victory, and years of economic uncertainty remain on the horizon for Britons. Uncertainty and unconventionality are rarely rewarded in the highly volatile world of global currency trading!

Much was initially made in the press about the weakening pound in the aftermath of the June 23 vote. However, the pain felt by the Newcastle family holidaying in Miami with an extra suitcase to be filled with the latest goodies from Apple, Hermès, Hollister, and Nike will have to be balanced against the benefits enjoyed by British exporters great and small who will now find appetites for their industrial machinery, pharmaceuticals, vehicles, and medical equipment noticeably more robust. In economic shifts, there are always winners and losers. One unfortunate side effect of the decline in the pound since the Brexit referendum was a decline in champagne sales, as British bubbly drinkers balked as paying higher prices!

Many commentators claimed that the pound's exchange rate was a real-time referendum on how severe the economic consequences will be for Britain. In that light, May and her government were getting minute-by-minute feedback on how their policies were being received by the market and how their missteps and gaffes were raising further concerns.

In the immediate aftermath of the Brexit vote, the pound took on the role of "whipping boy" as financial markets attempted to digest the unexpected decision of British voters to rudely disregard the clear and consistent view of financial, political, and social elites that they should—of course!—vote Remain. After the referendum, it appeared as if every pronouncement regarding the implementation of Brexit led to a further drop in the exchange rate.

A little refresher course on markets might be useful now. Simply put, the value of anything—whether baseball cards, comic books, or pounds sterling—tends to decline when the number of sellers exceeds the number of buyers. People who doubted whether the British economy could withstand the Brexit turmoil were less likely to need to continue to hold pounds in substantial quantities.

May's words—including, of course, such chestnuts as "Brexit means Brexit"—were picked over again and again by worried currency traders. However, stock markets at the same time showed a "Brexit bump" that may have been motivated in part by a belief that many British businesses would benefit from a lower pound. A weaker pound makes British exports more affordable to world markets. However, dollar-denominated purchases—whether Miami package holidays or raw materials such as cobalt or nickel—become more expensive.

Critics of Brexit speak frequently of what Britain will be forced to concede in order to gain access to the EU's single market. European politicians have stated repeatedly that the price must be open borders and unrestricted European immigration. It is worth remembering, however, that Britain has a perfectly essential quid pro quo that can be put on the table. In short, Britain can ask for the right to sell goods and services into EU member states in exchange for . . . the rights of EU member states to sell goods and services into Britain. Genius!

* * *

The Brexit referendum was—to the surprise of many—the triumph of political ideals over economic priorities. Questions of accountability and rule of law are worth considering in full. Such debates should not be shunned or shamed. The fundamental political question facing us today may no longer be left versus right, but instead sovereignty and accountability versus unbridled, unquestioning globalization.

Ultimately, many Leave voters felt that the benefits of EU membership accrued primarily to a small number of social, political, and economic elites, while the costs were borne much, much more widely. The party of Davos, which to many critics serves to link up these elites at the expense of working-class men and women around the world, champions the European Union and similar efforts to push the globalization agenda. For example, the siren song of globalization arguably makes any attempts to subject migration policies to political discourse naïve and doomed to failure. Resistance must be futile. But Brexit shows a democratic process resulting in a decision to take the country in a different direction. The continental super-state, unfortunately, continues to suffer in its institutions and attitudes a profound "democratic deficit." To the party of Davos, though, this may not be a serious concern. It is unlikely that even after the Brexit vote anything significant will be done to address this issue.

The Brexit vote was in part a reaction to the erosion of democracy within the European Union. Its leaders are not elected. Its parliament cannot initiate legislation. It is important to bear in mind that a significant part of democracy at the practical level is simply the ability to "vote the bastards out!" However, this is something that is not possible in the current EU structure. Although many elites in Britain and across Europe champion the ideology of managerial Bonapartism that sits at the heart of the European Union, this democratic deficit is real, and the Leave voters recognized its importance.

The Remain camp made the argument that the erosion of British democracy was acceptable since it came along with real economic benefits. Leave voters apparently valued their political rights higher than that. Dictatorships frequently gain and maintain power with promises of economic growth and material benefits. These improvements will come in exchange for a decrease in political liberty that may start small, but then increase over time.

The Leave slogan "Take Back Control" resonated with millions of British voters. For many Britons, the trials and tribulations of the democratic process, even with all of its shortcomings, is worth it as a protector of individual liberty and a barricade against despotism. Still, three national elections in two years may seem to some British voters—including perhaps even Theresa May herself—as too much of a good thing!

Fortunately, the doom-and-gloom crowd who said that a Leave victory would produce chaos and misery of biblical proportions were proven wrong—at least in the short-term. Interestingly, there would have been many Leave voters who no doubt took the dire warnings at face value but ticked the Leave box anyway. They probably agreed with actor and national treasure Sir Michael Caine who when asked about his pro-Brexit sympathies responded, "I would rather be a poor master than a rich servant."

In the nine months between the referendum and May's submission of the Article 50 notice in March 2017, the British economy performed particularly well, especially in light of all the doom-and-gloom being used by Remain campaigners to scare Britons into voting in favor of the European Union. In many respects, May was in a much stronger position in late March 2017 than when she first took office—although this would not last long!

The consequences of the Brexit vote, as well as the link between Remain's surprise defeat and the electoral failure of Hillary Clinton a few months later, are beyond the scope of this book.

Nonetheless, a better understanding of the ideas and imagery that gained momentum in the run up to the June 23 referendum will help better understand the lasting political consequences of the Brexit referendum. For example, will Brexit lead to another Scottish independence vote? While in September 2014, 55 percent voted to stay in the United Kingdom and 45 percent voted to leave, Scots backed Remain in June 2016 by a margin of 62 percent to 38 percent.

Surprisingly, UKIP was one of the most prominent forces in the Leave campaign but found itself in the months following the long-sought-after attainment of their goal—a sovereign Britain independent of Brussels—something of an embarrassment to other Leave voters. Incidents such as an actual "let's step outside" fistfight between senior UKIP members Steven Woolfe and Mike Hookem in the halls of the European parliament in Strasbourg, France, cast an unflattering light on Nigel Farage's party. It seems that you can take the boys out of middle school, but you can't take the middle school out of the boys!

Meanwhile, disgruntled Remainers quickly filed lawsuits and attempted to work out ways to thwart the delivery of the notice required under Article 50 of the Lisbon Treaty. These efforts, though, were unsuccessful as anything more than rallying points for those men and women who had found themselves on the wrong side of the referendum results. In the end, after the Supreme Court ruled that parliamentary assent to the Article 50 notice was required, both the House of Commons and the House of Lords passed the European Union (Notification of Withdrawal) Act, which was promptly signed by Queen Elizabeth and delivered by May in March 2017.

The various legal challenges to the Brexit victory were so essentially British in their tenor and trajectory, even though in the end they failed to derail the Article 50 notice. Eventually each of the judicial, legislative, and executive branches of the British government performed its allocated role, and the choice of more than

17 million Britons was ratified. To the surprise of many Remain voters, survey data in March 2017 showed little change in national sentiment since the referendum. There appeared to be no measureable regret at the original decision, which would have led to a swing over to Remain.

It remained unclear in the months following the referendum whether the reconfiguration of political loyalties witnessed in the surprise Leave win would result in a lasting change of political allegiances to the dominant British parties. Had Britain's electoral landscape radically changed on June 23, 2016? The Labour Party was actually more divided on the Brexit question when the referendum finally came than many observers expected. This division continued into the Article 50 notice process and the June 2017 snap general election, but will it likely continue throughout the entire exit negotiations after Labour's surprisingly strong showing in the June 2017 voting results?

Regarding the Scots, Brexit and Scottish independence are not the same thing, nor are they ultimately driven by the same underlying grievances. Brexit will necessarily raise questions about the role of Westminster and Whitehall in British political life. There is a strong centralizing trend in Britain that might eventually strike similar concerns among former Leave voters. A push for devolution across the country to the regions, counties, and cities may soon follow if the drive for another vote on Scottish independence follows. Brexit opens the door for many opportunities to reexamine government on all levels. For example, even local government in Britain, currently subject to extensive procurement rules by Brussels, could receive substantial benefits from a broad cut in red tape post-Brexit. Community-based businesses and small- to medium-sized companies could benefit significantly, as might local labor.

Perhaps Brexit's ultimate legacy will include a "reformation" of Britain's own domestic constitutional structures. How very British!

★ ✴ ★

In addition to political consequences of Brexit, there will also be significant economic consequences. At the time of the referendum, Britain's economy faced a conundrum. Its largest trading partner was Europe, but four decades of integration and harmonization had not stopped the United States from claiming the top slot as Britain's number one investor, nor Britain from remaining the largest foreign investor in the United States. British companies such as BAE Systems, BP, and Rolls-Royce make significant contributions to the US economy. Why were investing and trading patterns so different? How should this gap be interpreted? What was Britain's proper place in the world?

Without a deal with the European Union in place by March 2019, the terms of Britain's trade with the bloc will be driven primarily by World Trade Organization rules, which govern trade when there are no other treaties in place to supersede them. Of course, it will not be just mundane terms relating to reciprocal quotas and tariffs that will drive the exit discussions—Britain's military and security contributions to the continent will be useful bargaining chips for May in her negotiations with Brussels!

Brexit secretary David Davis voiced his goal for the two-year negotiation process as "a deal that works for every nation and region of the UK." The United Kingdom consists of England, Northern Ireland, Scotland, and Wales, and voting patterns differed significantly by region. But what if there was no deal from Brussels worth signing? According to May, "No deal for Britain is better than a bad deal for Britain."

Let's not forget, Britain has been in this situation before—Henry VIII's break from Rome and the Reformation that followed was the original Brexit. Been there, done that! Regardless of whether a particular British voter supported Leave or Remain on the day of the referendum, all should agree now that Brexit will be transformational and the Britain that ultimately emerges from this process will be very different from the one that existed before votes were cast in June 2016.

While Hollande demanded that Britain "pay a price" for Brexit, National Front leader Marine Le Pen struck a more conciliatory note: "A people decides its own destiny. You cannot force a country to do something that is against its own interests or against the democratic process."

The moral of Brexit may actually be quite modest: National interests evolve over time. Those of neighbors can converge and diverge. We have seen this throughout history. The Leave victory in Britain did not lead to a further wave of European countries running for the exits. In the wake of Brexit, nationalist candidates failed to win at the ballot boxes in Austria, the Netherlands, and France. In the end, the Brexit referendum vote was a particularly British solution to a problem largely derived from uniquely British concerns.

★ ★ ★

After Theresa May took up residence in Number 10 Downing Street and the shell shock related to the unanticipated Leave victory began to wear off, talking heads in the media became utterly consumed with a new debate between "hard Brexit" and "soft Brexit." The referendum itself gave no guide on how Brexit would actually be implemented. This complex and cumbersome task was simply left to May and her cabinet to work through.

The debate between "hard" and "soft" that followed centered on how much access to the EU single market was actually worth to Britain. Enough to entice Britons to give up much of its recently won sovereignty, akin to what Norway and Switzerland had agreed to do in the past? For example, was the single market worth relinquishing newly won control over British borders? Interestingly, although the single market worked quite well for goods, it does not work nearly as well for services—an area in which Britain excels. Is "Brexit at any cost" an effective negotiating stance? Is the scale of actually making Brexit happen too large for either British politicians or Leave voters to fully comprehend?

If Brexit is—as some Remain advocates argue—a practical impossibility given the degree to which EU regulation has become inextricably interwoven into the fabric of British daily life, this raises some important questions. Should prior British governments be held accountable for actively and tacitly allowing the country to proceed down this path of no return without ever telling the British people about the consequences? Perhaps a better Remain slogan might have been something along the lines of "Don't Bother—We Can't Leave Anyway!"

Many hardened Remainers still bristle when discussing the British voters' willingness to incur potential economic costs in exchange for political ideas. It would be hard to imagine, for example, similar arguments getting wide airing if they were being made in the context of countries in other parts of the world breaking up: "Remember to stress to the South Sudanese that they should not vote for independence because their currency will devalue and their GDP growth numbers soften."

In addition to the grand philosophical conundrums, there will be practical problems and annoyances. Remainers fearing the worst from a "hard Brexit" have voiced concerns over whether currently unemployed Britons would even be capable of stepping up to the low-wage service jobs at Starbucks, Nando's, Harvesters, and the like. Having spent thousands of hours watching the current Polish and Romanian and Estonian staff take orders and fill them, I am quietly confident that the complexities of these tasks will not prove too daunting for their British replacements in 2019.

If all goes well for May, on March 29, 2019, London will have treaties in place with Washington, Ottawa, Canberra, and other like-minded capitals that promote free trade and global competitiveness. This will put Britain in a position of strength when it comes to dealing with their EU exit negotiations. If Britain appears weak during the Brexit negotiations, then Brussels may attempt to extract a heavy settlement out of this divorce. If Britain, however, looks strong as it repositions itself to become a global trading and investment power, European negotiators may recognize that losing the British market comes with a steep price for them as well.

Outside of the protectionism and introversion woven into the European Union at every level, Britain may have no choice but to become as nimble and adaptable as it can to succeed on its own in rapidly shifting global markets. This would entail Britain being widely perceived as one of the premier destinations of entrepreneurship and investment.

Britain will succeed outside the European Union if it can be seen, to use May's own words, as "a magnet for international talent." Britain needs to ensure that the best and the brightest innovators move there to start businesses and create jobs and drive economic growth, which will ultimately benefit all Britons. Regardless of how Brexit is finalized, many will still come from Europe, but also from Asia, Russia, the Middle East, and, of course, the United States. Both large FTSE 100 companies and small tech start-ups would benefit from a revised post-Brexit visa system that makes it easier to get high value–added talent into Britain when needed.

May's January 2017 speech at Lancaster House laid out the principles that would govern Brexit and Britain's place in the world once it leaves the continental super-state. According to May, no deal was better than a bad deal. Unfortunately, this ignored how concerned British businesses were about the practicalities of post-Brexit life.

Brexit is not the only item on May's to-do list. She must continue to govern her country day to day and move her economic and social priorities forward at home. Of course, everything is linked. The manner in which the Brexit negotiations are conducted and the final terms agreed could help her achieve her domestic goals. In addition, independent of the negotiation of exit terms with Brussels and new terms of trade between Britain and the European Union, May's government will need to conduct a legislative and regulatory transposition of current EU law and the British law books that will require Herculean efforts.

In the midst of crucial Brexit negotiations, May is also trying to pivot her Conservative Party away from its reputation as the "nasty party" and toward a future where it can be seen as a champion for the working classes against overreaching by both economic and political elites. May must shape British public opinion so that men and women are optimistic about what life will be like in the country post-Brexit. Her setback at the June 2017 general election makes this an even tougher task.

Theresa May was clearly not the second coming of Margaret Thatcher. Did she need to be? In her June 2017 general election campaign, she proclaimed herself the champion of "ordinary working people." However, unlike Thatcher, May believed in a government that was willing to rein in capitalism's excesses and fix broken markets.

The June 2017 snap election started with a focus on only one issue: Brexit. May took a noticeably agnostic view of British business, and as a result, the party of Davos appeared to have abandoned her. As May and the diminished Tory parliamentary party nursed their bruises, awkward questions remained. Was this election about something fundamentally different than the Brexit referendum? Does May's surprise defeat mean that the culture wars that have divided the United States for the last three decades have now crossed the pond to Britain? Can May's weakened Conservative government actually deliver on any promises it makes to its EU counterparts during these contentious Brexit negotiations?

A few old-school observations about partisan politics: First and foremost, Labour is the party of London. Second, it is the party of urban centers up and down the island. Rather than crippling the modern Labour party for a generation, May's electoral gambit pushed her and her Conservatives into a minority government. The consequences of this misstep may be quite profound. Without a clear parliamentary majority, it will become even harder for

May to negotiate the day-to-day complexities of Brexit negotiations, while at the same time wrestling with the same challenges that drove many Leave voters in June 2016 to turn their backs on Europe. Economic pessimism was now growing in prominence with each passing month, but was this actually the delayed results of the Brexit win or the inconclusive results of Theresa May's unfortunate snap election?

★ ★ ★

Concern over migration and terror were front and center in the lead-up to the June 2017 election, just as they were on the day of the Brexit referendum, almost one year earlier—and understandably so.

A post-Brexit Britain will continue to need immigrants. Britons make up just 1 percent of the world's population, but they have a dynamic and entrepreneurial economy that draws to it aspirational men and women from around the world.

Any sensible discussion of migration would begin with establishing what the goal of a migration policy should be. From there we can construct procedures and limits that help meet these goals. Otherwise people risk talking past each other at best or screaming at each other at worst. With this clarified, you can begin to ask some interesting questions. How will this migration policy support or undermine the social safety net? Does this policy harm low-wage workers already in the country? Where will British-born teenagers get their first jobs while Pret a Manger, Costa Coffee, and McDonald's are staffed by Lithuanians and Portuguese?

To the extent that generous migration policies lower wages, these policies shift value from labor to capital. Is the increased value accumulated by capital worth the costs shouldered by the British-born workers unfavored by employers who have access to migrant labor? At the same time, should British taxpayers be asked to subsidize this value transfer by increased funding for safety-net programs that migrants participate in?

Britain must remain an alluring destination for highly skilled migrants who will create jobs through dynamic start-ups that expand the boundaries of the economy. In this contest there are, of course, competitors. The United States, for example, grants approximately 1 million green cards each year. More than 4 million people currently sit on US immigration wait lists.

How big is EU migration into Britain? Official numbers report more than 2 million EU nationals working in the country, with a small drop seen after the Brexit vote. This dip may be the result in part of a weaker pound buying fewer euros to send back home to Bulgaria and Romania!

The debate in Europe on migration differs in important ways from the debate in America. These differences should not be ignored. For example, it is important to remember that in many cases the concern being expressed over unrestricted migration in Europe is voiced by "fringe parties" whose remaining policy platform is indistinguishable from established center-left parties. Geert Wilders's Freedom Party in the Netherlands is a good example. Although non-Western immigrants (including children and grandchildren) make up only 11 percent of the population, they comprise half of Dutch welfare recipients. Open-door immigration policies and gold-plated social welfare schemes appear to such groups to be fundamentally incompatible.

The Dutch, for instance, are genuinely proud that half their income is redistributed by the state away from the original earners in order to create a fairer society for all. Concerns over unassimilated migrants are often directed specifically at the question of whether such policies put the generous safety net at risk. If asked to choose between a welfare state and a sanctuary state, which should generous, open-minded, and tolerant Dutch men and women select?

Going farther north, from 2014 to 2016, Sweden took in more refugees per capita than any other EU member state—almost

300,000 in total. Many were accepted in without passports or other formal documentation. Critics soon argued that the incidents of rioting and social unrest that followed were the direct result of these policies. The Stockholm terror attack in April 2017 was seen by these critics as another reminder of the mounting security threats the country now faces as a result of the national government's refugee policy.

The terror threat, of course, was one all Europe faces to some degree. In 2015 and 2016, however, France was a repeated target of terrorist attacks and quickly became an icon of bloodshed to many around the world.

On January 7, 2015, Chérif and Saïd Kouachi killed twelve people during an attack on the Paris office of the satirical magazine *Charlie Hebdo*. The following day, Amedy Coulibaly also took to the streets of Paris, killing a police office and four persons at a kosher grocery store. On June 26, 2015, Yassine Salhi decapitated his boss and used his van to cause an explosion at a gas factory near Lyon. A dozen people were injured but fortunately none fatally.

In another example of good luck, on August 21, 2015, three Americans on a train heading to Paris from Amsterdam were able to tackle and subdue Ayoub El Khazzani, who had opened fire on their fellow passengers. Despite being heavily armed, the gunman was unable to kill anyone on the train. Unfortunately, good luck has a tendency to run out. On the evening of November 13, 2015, a coordinated series of suicide bombings and shootings in Paris left 130 people dead. Their targets were a soccer stadium, several cafés, and the Bataclan, a famous live music venue.

The following year did not provide much respite for the French from the terrorist violence. On July 14, 2016, Mohamed Lahouaiej Bouhlel drove a truck through a large group of men and women and children celebrating Bastille Day in Nice. He killed eighty people.

Some Leave voters may have thought that Brexit would protect them. Unfortunately, even before the Article 50 notice could be served, the attacks in Britain began. Khalid Masood's attack on parliament in March 2017 was a clear reminder that Brexit was

not a simple, clear-cut, or permanent solution to Britain's problem, as much as it was a shift in how such solutions would need to
be constructed and implemented. The threat of lone-wolf jihadi
terror existed both pre- and post-referendum. The Leave vote did
not in and of itself make such attacks either more or less likely.
Masood's attack—at both the seat of British political power and a
high-density tourist attraction—came just one year after a Brussels attack that left thirty-two people dead.

Then in quick succession came the attack at the Ariana Grande
concert in Manchester and then the London Bridge attacks only
a few days later. After each, news networks managed to find the
usual talking heads across the political spectrum rereading from
their same scripts. Few commentators were entirely wrong in their
concerns—whether about terror itself, individual liberties, or
Islamophobia—but it was difficult to see anyone of their responses
to these attacks as a complete plan of action.

Labour Party leader Jeremy Corbyn even went so far as to argue
that that Britons who support Islamic State were just expressing a
"political point of view"—but how tolerant of intolerance should
tolerant people be?

★ ★ ★

In addition to *jihadi* terror, Europeans are worried about Brexit,
about Trump, about Putin. However, many of Europe's most pressing problems are largely self-inflicted. If this is eventually recognized and accepted in Brussels, at least the solutions to these
problems would also be close at hand. Unfortunately, European
leaders often prefer to sing the union's praises in louder and louder
voices rather than ask awkward questions about unforeseen consequences of harmonization and shared competencies.

At the core of the Treaty of Rome, the "four freedoms" allow
for the movement of goods, services, capital, and people. It was

concern over unlimited legal migration from poorer European countries that drove many Britons to vote Leave. Even some among the remaining EU members diverge in their support of ever closer union. It is worth remembering that not all EU members are fully bought into the Brussels program in its entirety. Several do not use the euro or participate in the Schengen passport-free travel area.

Britain, a member of the European Union and its predecessor organizations for forty-four years, will most likely leave in March 2019. Michel Barnier, the lead negotiator for Brussels, has indicated that he would like to see the negotiations wrapped up by October 2018. In addition to trade and a final accounting of monies due, Northern Ireland and Gibraltar will be hot spots in the Brexit negotiations with Brussels, for which lucrative concessions can be drawn. The Germans will be key to successful negotiations for both sides. Unfortunately, 2016 saw Chancellor Angela Merkel repeatedly alternate between pragmatism and posturing. How vindictive will Brussels be? How much long-term benefit will European leaders be willing to sacrifice in order to score short-term points against bolting Britain?

The British side of Brexit is, of course, only half the story. Competition over who will gain the most from Britain's departure began heating up soon after the referendum. Would Frankfurt usurp London's role as the financial capital of the European Union? What would Paris do to position itself as a viable alternative to UK-based banks and bankers, as well as EU bodies currently located there, such as the European Banking Authority (with its headquarters in London's Canary Wharf)? In addition to tense negotiations with Britain on the terms of its departure, there will also be frantic attempts by the remaining twenty-seven member states to jockey for whatever small relative advantages they can obtain.

Many of the Remainers loudly bemoaned the possibility that Britain might "crash out" of the European Union in March 2019 without a deal of some sort in place with their former trading block. The consequence of this in certain sectors, such as financial services, could be quite horrific. An urgent case was being made in the months after the referendum that London's lucrative role as a global financial center was at risk. A special post-Brexit arrangement might be essential—whether by gaining access to EU member states via passporting or an equivalency regime or even simply a separate deal. Central to these concerns was the quite pragmatic observation that a new trade agreement with the European Union would most likely require not just the sign-off of the European Commission in Brussels but also an affirmative vote of all remaining member states. See, for example, the delays and horse-trading involved in the recent Canadian Free Trade Agreement. Surely such a feat of diplomatic acrobatics could not be achieved in the currently poisonous atmosphere of Brexit!

This raises an interesting point, and one worth bearing in mind as Britons attempt to simultaneously map out a future trajectory of both a post-EU Britain and a post-Britain EU. Brussels has been keen to cut back on unanimous voting as a way to streamline EU decision-making. Interestingly, Britain has been resistant to such changes in fear that it would lose its precious veto of decisions it otherwise found onerous. With Brexit, however, Brussels can now begin crafting the European Union it has always wanted— and which Britain has repeatedly resisted. In fact, the cumbersome realities of wading through two years of contentious Brexit negotiations might serve as an impetus for constitutional reform, which would of course put more power in the hands of Brussels bureaucrats.

There is a distinct and persistent tendency among the well read and the well intentioned to place international multilateral organizations on a lofty pedestal. The weakness of the European Union at its heart is the weakness of all organizations where the linguistic conventions of democracy may be used, but the values of accountability and transparency are missing. For example, the soccer governing body FIFA again easily springs to mind!

The current European configuration has proved unable to deal with the great challenges facing the continent: economic competition, a mounting refugee crisis, and Russian adventurism. Is the answer to these challenges the same answer that Brussels has advocated for the past six decades—namely, evermore integration and shared sovereignty? Will a post-Brexit Britain be better able to evolve and adapt to such challenges?

However, for the past decade, the European Union has failed to deliver the jobs and the economic growth that Europeans require. A constant critique of Brussels has been that it was, in short, "too European"—a phrase that implies it is bureaucratic, secretive, distant, protectionist, unresponsive, and statist. As a result of this managerial Bonapartism, Brussels and its apologists regularly came across to Britons as arrogant and indifferent to public opinions.

Simply put, Europe faces a moral and ideological crisis that Brexit compounds but did not cause. The June 2016 Leave victory was a result of a failure of European leaders to put individual rights and political liberty at the center of their vision for a united Europe. The most important questions still remain unanswered—what values are Brussels actually promoting? Are they in line with the values held by most Europeans?

*　*　*

The French presidential election in April and May 2017 provided an effective contrast to the 2016 Brexit referendum. Emmanuel Macron, a fresh-faced, reform-minded ex-banker, became the youngest French leader since Bonaparte. In Macron, the French chose a centrist and would-be reformer over the nationalist Le Pen. The political center held, but France's traditional political party system demonstrated on April 23, 2017, that it was no longer fit for purpose. Was Macron's victory an endorsement of his vision or simply a rejection of Le Pen's? Echoes of the Hollande victory over Sarkozy could be heard by some observers. Would France be so lucky in the next presidential election in 2022?

Like her father Jean-Marie, Marine Le Pen was denied the presidency despite populist appeal, although she did double the size of her father's 2002 vote total, showing significant progress. By contrast, Macron was unashamedly pro-EU. His victory, therefore, was seen as an endorsement of Brussels and the European Union as a whole. French voters had demonstrated their renewed commitment to the EU project. To see Macron's victory as a guarantee of the European Union's future, though, would be overly optimistic. Brussels must demonstrate to its remaining citizens that it respects their priorities and their concerns. To ignore them risks forcing them to vote with their feet.

For example, a very large number of talented French men and women have left their country—having first benefited from expensive educations at their most elite institutions—to seek their fortunes in London, New York, and Silicon Valley. A frequently noted statistic is that 250,000 French citizens currently live in London. What has been the impact of this emigration on French political and economic life? Interestingly, Macron stayed at home. Now he has the keys to the Élysée Palace as his reward! But what of the other French who have stayed home? Will Macron be able to tell the French people the deep and abiding truths they may not be ready to hear? Perhaps. But perhaps it is also useful to reflect on a key element of Bonaparte's beloved legal codes. Under French law, a defendant is not obliged to tell the truth. Witnesses must, but not the accused. This may go some way toward explaining French political practices over the past two centuries.

★ ★ ★

London is a great city in which to be very, very, very rich. Anyone who has strolled through Mayfair or walked down Knightsbridge will realize this quite quickly. However, the deeper impact of this important fact on post-Brexit Britain is worth special consideration.

To take just one pragmatic example, Britain has some of the finest private secondary schools in the world, with sufficient spare capacity to digest wave after wave of Russian oligarchs, Saudi and Emirati minor royals, American lawyers and bankers, and however many French and German derivatives traders and fund managers care to cross the Channel. An opportunity to move to London is much more easily explained to your fretful "plus one" concerned about the children's educational accomplishment than a corresponding move to Frankfurt, Paris, Luxembourg, or Dublin.

Contrary to the claims of many Remain voters, London's ascendency to being a rival to New York as an international financial capital, however, was not initially driven by the benefits of EU harmonization. Instead, London thrives in good measure because of the ease with which it welcomed new arrivals to its financial services industry.

The risks to the City of London's stature as a global financial center post-Brexit are essentially twofold. First, Brexit may result in British-based banks being unable to sell their services easily and efficiently into the European Union. Second, there may be difficulties in being able to hire and retain talented EU financial professionals.

London's future prospects will be tested repeatedly during the two-year negotiating period. Its near-term prospects in Europe could be limited if they are unable to retain the passporting rights they currently enjoy under various EU directives, but its long-term prospects are where the meaningful costs and benefits will be seen.

The importance of financial services and the City are clear, as their mention in May's Article 50 notice reaffirmed. Equally true is the fact that Europe needs the City for access to capital from around the world. Some critics fear that 75,000 finance jobs could be lost in London as a result of Brexit. However, moving London-based jobs to other EU countries will not be a simple, straightforward decision. The big banks and other financial services firms have invested so heavily in the British capital over the past thirty years. Such moves will be costly if companies are willing to pay out generous severance packages to individuals willing to accept redundancies, or engage in costly litigation if they are not. British law on constructive dismissal will be easily invoked if employees are given a choice between relocation on the one hand and loss of a job on the other.

To adequately measure the long-term effects of Brexit, we must have a clear sense of where Britain currently stands economically. Unfortunately, economists debate exactly how strong the underlying British economy actually is. By some measures, it is indistinguishable from its European neighbors, which can be awkward for Leave supporters committed to a narrative in which Brussels is holding back Britain's potential tiger economy. Outside of London and the home counties, many Britons could appear envious of their continental counterparts. The practical challenges that British workers face include lack of relevant skills, limited housing options, and underinvestment in infrastructure, such as roads and airports.

The European Union has historically frowned on tax competition, but a Trump tax reform that lowers US rates could make it harder for Brussels to maintain that line. Britain may be poised post-Brexit to take the lead in cutting corporate and personal rates in an effort to boost economic growth. Without growth, the social safety net established after World War II across the continent and in Britain risks becoming unsustainable. Britons face scores of tough choices that have the potential to transform the country as they disengage from Brussels and once again set their own course. These choices will determine the type of country that Britain will eventually become.

Is the point of Brexit to simply let Britain be Britain? Or is Brexit a unique opportunity for Britain to reassess and reposition itself, charting a course for the future rather than being constrained by a worldview from the past? Was the referendum as much a choice between two pasts as between two futures? Europe—home of Dante, Monet, and Bach. Britain—home of Shakespeare, Wren, and Turner.

Democracy actually means something quite important to Britons. They have been electing mayors of the City of London since 1189, and their Magna Carta was signed by King John in 1215 at Runnymede, near Windsor. Britain is a nation with a distinct history, culture, and reason for being. Britain can at times appear to be very polarized. The same, however, can be said recently of the United States and many other countries around the world.

Of course, there will be serious challenges in the short-, medium-, and long-term. Those challenges will need to be addressed. For now, though, we are left with perhaps the most difficult question to consider: Will history ultimately judge Brexit as an ending or a beginning?

Epilogue

*Nothing except a battle lost can be half
so melancholy as a battle won.*

—FIELD MARSHAL ARTHUR WELLESLEY,
FIRST DUKE OF WELLINGTON

The Fourth of July is not typically celebrated in Britain. Unsurprising, really. However, in July 2011, grand festive celebrations were held outside the US Embassy in London to commemorate the 235th anniversary of the signing of the Declaration of Independence. The focus was not only on traditional Independence Day activities, but also on the unveiling of a statute to honor former US president Ronald Reagan.

The statute was placed alongside statues of Franklin Delano Roosevelt and Dwight Eisenhower in Grosvenor Square, the leafy English garden located in front of the US Embassy, which, with its brutalist modern architecture and constant armed security, stood in stark contrast to its tranquil Edwardian surroundings. Grosvenor Square had long held strong American historical associations, as the original home for the first US ambassador to London, future president John Adams, as well as where the plans for the D-Day invasions of Normandy were first devised during World War II.

An impressive list of speakers and guests attended the unveiling ceremony. Joining the current US ambassador to Britain and his predecessor on center stage were Condoleezza Rice, former secretary of state, and a senior British government minister, Foreign Secretary William Hague. Unfortunately, neither Reagan's stalwart ally, Margaret Thatcher, nor his own wife, Nancy, could attend in person.

Upon entering Grosvenor Square for the ceremonies, all guests were generously given both American flags and Union Jacks to waive at opportune moments. A video loop of Reagan's funniest anecdotes, stories, and jokes was playing on a large screen. Groups of local English schoolchildren, dressed in their red and gray uniforms, lined up along the garden wall to witness the day's events. In the background, a brass band played reassuring renditions of classic American tunes from the nineteenth century. And there were mimes passing out complimentary bags of jelly beans, so pretty much everything was covered!

The English love outdoor activities during those long summer days that they enjoy due to their island's high latitude. The Wimbledon tennis tournament and the three-day rock festival at Glastonbury are just two of the most well-known examples. As a result, the unveiling of the Reagan statute in Grosvenor Square felt as much like an English village summer fete as it did a traditional American barbeque.

This particular year was the centenary of Reagan's birth, and ceremonies were also being conducted across Eastern Europe, commemorating the life and achievements of a man who saw as a central theme to his presidency the need to bring freedom to millions. It would be interesting to have known his opinion on this day of the Arab Spring then unfolding across the Middle East and North Africa, as well as what his views would be on the demands for greater transparency and accountability building in China.

As our present leaders alternately wrestle with and then ignore the knotty problems that they face, we may be tempted to compare them to a famous past leader, such as Reagan. However, with the passage of time and the safe distance from the cut-and-thrust of current events, such comparisons are usually unkind to contemporary politicians.

Reagan was a politician led by principles, who directly engaged in the political and philosophical challenges that faced the world he lived in. On this basis, he sought to share with the world his personal commitment to freedom at home and abroad, which has been the foundation of both America and Britain over the last two centuries. Together with Margaret Thatcher, Reagan stood up to the leaders of the Soviet Union and directly confronted their totalitarian regime. Using the power of political rhetoric and diplomacy, the Berlin Wall eventually fell without a shot being fired. Imagine how a leader of this caliber would have supported the Arab Spring and sought to quench the thirst for democracy in China. Such a leader would recognize that freedom is vulnerable, but with optimism and diligence it can survive and grow.

In an age of increasingly bitter partisan politics on each side of the Atlantic, it is interesting to note Reagan was an active Democrat for many, many years. It is difficult to imagine someone with such political inconsistencies making it through a modern primary campaign to win his party's nomination. The young Reagan voted for FDR four times before casting his first Republican vote for Eisenhower in 1952. Fittingly, statues of both leaders will be his neighbors in Grosvenor Square for many warm English summers to come.

★ ★ ★

During World War II, FDR—so admired by Reagan at the time—positioned the United States as a steadfast ally of Britain during its darkest hour. Afterward, the United States laid the foundation of European security and prosperity (and integration) with the Marshall Plan and NATO, rather than simply reverting to its pre-war isolation. To this day, the US–Britain military alliance is uniquely—and perhaps purposefully—underappreciated. In fact, NATO's continuing mission was famously doubted by no less than current US president Donald Trump.

At the heart of the NATO military alliance is Article 5, the treaty provisions that establish the binding commitment that an attack on one is an attack on all. It has been invoked only once—in response to the September 11, 2001, attacks on the United States. A memorial to that decision was recently unveiled at NATO headquarters in Brussels. Despite Trump's doubts on the campaign trail, NATO still has a vital ongoing role in addressing threats on Europe's eastern flank, as well as in combating terrorism and dealing with large-scale illegal migration. Operation Atlantic Resolve was the United States' response to Russia's Bonapartist adventurism in Ukraine and entailed the US Army sending the Second Armored Brigade of the First Infantry Division to Europe in autumn 2017 to expand its NATO commitments.

In addition to the special relationship between the United States and Britain, there is also a unique bond between North America and Europe. NATO reflects this bond in both its composition and its dedication to shared values. NATO and the European Union should strengthen their ties in the years to come, and Brexit could be a convenient context through which that cooperation and coordination can be discussed. Britain—together with the United States and Canada—complements and supplements the ability of Europeans to address the security challenges that they face, even though if we are being honest, France has always had an awkward relationship with NATO!

Many difficult questions remain when considering how best to provide security to Europe. What role should European countries play in their own defense? If there is to be such a role, are the Europeans willing to provide the equipment, personnel, and funding required?

As a creation of the postwar settlement seventy years ago, NATO can often appear ill-equipped to deal with the challenges it faces today, which include at the top of the list terrorism and Russian adventurism. There is, however, much scope to improve and update the NATO structure. Prime Minister Theresa May and her cabinet clearly feel that a reinvigorated NATO adapted and improved to fit its members' needs in the twenty-first century could be an excellent platform on which Britain can make its international presence felt in the coming years.

Completely separate from Brexit is Britain's ongoing role guaranteeing peace and security on the continent through its membership in NATO, but these two conversations will necessarily influence each other. When May met with Trump after his inauguration, she made her support clear in a joint statement: "We're 100 percent behind NATO." The Trump administration's financial concerns about the defense pact were well known. Trump called NATO "obsolete" on the campaign trail and early signals from Secretary of State Rex Tillerson about the mutual defense pact were mixed, but these criticisms should be put into context. Importantly, the United States accounts for two-thirds of NATO expenditures. As a result, in parallel with the Brexit negotiations will need to be a comprehensive rethink on the proper role and priorities of NATO in the twenty-first century. Much of that rethink will be driven at least in part by Britain's leadership on these issues.

In looking for European members of the alliance to pay their fair share, Trump is merely echoing points raised again and again by former secretary of defense Robert Gates, who served under both George W. Bush and Barack Obama. Trump's Anglophilia clearly doesn't extend to any sort of rose-tinted affection for the continent, at least when it comes to dollars-and-cents issues!

Trump has not been shy about proclaiming his fondness for Britain. Like Churchill himself, Trump is half American and half British. Whether in gestures (such as returning a bust of Winston Churchill to the Oval Office) or in words ("My mother loved the queen; she was so proud of the queen"), Trump's Anglophilia represents a significant shift from the previous eight years.

By contrast, Obama was a reflexive, uncritical Europhile, who saw the accomplishments of the European Union as one of the greatest achievements of the last century, despite its democratic deficit and unrelenting Bonapartist tendencies. His passion for Brussels was so intense and one-eyed that he boldly inserted himself into the domestic British debate over Brexit. Embarrassingly, he was unable to swing the vote to the Remain camp despite well-crafted threats of US retribution in trade negotiations should Britons vote Leave.

It is in the United States' interest that Europe be democratic and prosperous. To the extent that the European Union is the continent's principal means of achieving those goals, then Washington must accept this and support Brussels when necessary—but that support shouldn't detract from the United States' special relationship with Britain. Brexit raises a number of regional security concerns outside the borders of the European Union. Will the loss of Britain make Brussels more amenable to a deal with Turkey, admitting them as a full EU member? Will Putin be able to take advantage of Brexit-related chaos and Trump's America First rhetoric to maximize Russia's advantages across Europe? Washington will look to London to help navigate these obtacles and countless others.

The bonds between Britain and the United States were forged and fastened over a long history interspersed with short, bloody periods of great sacrifice. More than treaties and proclamations, more than speeches and summit meetings—the special relationship is not special simply because of the history between the two countries. It is special because this history is vibrant and ongoing.

Of course, history can take many forms. History can be an old document that describes how a military decision was made. It can be a diary of a mother and housewife describing in detail the trials and tribulations of daily life while her husband was away fighting in a distant country. It can be a place, like a battlefield or a birthplace. It can be an object that was held in the hand of a famous leader or a brave soldier. Or it can be a person—a person whose life or death (or both) symbolized an important event in the lives of his fellow countrymen.

When Harry Patch (age 111), the last surviving British soldier from World War I, passed away on July 25, 2009, the people of Britain were again reminded in a real and meaningful way of the sacrifices made by their country and their countrymen in that horrendous bloodletting a century ago. Then prime minister Gordon Brown announced that a public memorial service would be held in his honor, with more than 1,000 people attending and paying tribute to him. The Queen joined in the tributes made on his behalf.

Patch was the last surviving "Tommy" to have seen action on the Western Front. He fought at the infamously bloody Battle of Passchendaele, at which more than 300,000 British soldiers died. In addition to the personal example of sacrifice, dedication, and bravery, Patch's passing also provided his fellow Britons with the opportunity to reflect on a generation that engaged in an epic struggle, on a scale never before seen on this planet, to fight for concepts of freedom and democracy that have in recent decades been bandied about in a more casual and callow manner.

The world we are confronted with—and confounded by— today was born in the trenches of the Western and Eastern Fronts of World War I. Although many of the post-1945 certainties have fallen away in recent years, the challenges that remain were present in the mud and stench and unforgiving damp of those trenches. Democracy or dictatorship. Empire or nation-state. The role of the state and the military in the lives of citizens. Patriotism and the proper role of internal dissent. The realities of a "single Europe." The place of the Arab world in modern life.

Both individual and national psyches were scarred by the events that unfolded during the "Great War" of 1914–1918. Revolutions and repercussions followed the fighting, and generations later they are still seeking their final resolutions. Those nations that fought the war for its full duration—including Britain, Germany, and Russia—were significantly changed as a result. The United States' role—being much more limited—left this country more removed from the war's longer-term impact on our domestic institutions and philosophies.

There was a time when many of the nations of Europe saw themselves as "exceptional," but the "mud, mud, mud" of battlefields like Passchendaele made those feelings impossible for many people to maintain. Perhaps the fact that America retained its "exceptionalist" philosophy for so much of this country might be due in part to our more abbreviated role in this punishing, brutal conflict. We were spared being prolonged witnesses to these horrors, and as a result, the siren songs of pacifism, socialism, and nationalized health care were less seductive to us as a result.

Gratitude is owed to every soldier who serves his or her country. Regardless of the suitability and merit of their political masters, these men and women who serve—like Harry Patch—put their lives at risk over and over, as their families wait at home to see what sacrifices they in the end will be required to make. Ultimately, Patch and his fellow soldiers did not succeed in preventing further wars. Bravery on the field was followed, as it is too often, by cowardice and venality elsewhere. We continue to face wars and the prospects of wars—Iraq and Afghanistan being only the most recent examples.

To understand the "Great War" and what it meant, we are now consigned to the pages of books—whether historical or literature—rather than eyewitnesses. But a small measure of this history can be seen in each new soldier—whether from Norfolk or Hull, Grand Rapids or Anaheim—who still goes off, at the request of his or her country, to engage a different enemy in a different war fought on a different field of battle.

Unfortunately, the need for individuals with courage to overcome cynicism and aggression remains as pressing—and as unrelenting—as in the days when Harry Patch, born in Somerset, England, fought on the muddy fields of Passchendaele.

★ ⋆ ★

War memorials, of course, are established for the survivors. They are objects made tangible in known locations, where we can go and assemble and remember an event or a person or a sacrifice. We can construct these memorials from marble, stone, or metal, if we wish. We can make them as representative or as abstract, as individualistic or as egalitarian, as current artistic fashion dictates.

From 2007 to 2011, a small market town in rural England established itself as a living memorial for those lives lost in the wars in Iraq and Afghanistan. Royal Wootton Bassett, with a population of around 11,000, sits near RAF Lyneham, an airbase for the Royal Air Force until its closure in September 2011.

The collection of locals and visitors, family and guests, who regularly lined the streets of this town to mourn the passing dead began originally as a spontaneous and respectful assembly, bearing witness to the bodies of deceased soldiers that were being driven down the Wootton Bassett High Street, in transit from RAF Lyneham, where they were repatriated, to the nearby mortuary. Around this simple transit route for coffins and their contents grew the most direct and unmediated expressions of public grief addressing the recent wars and the mounting deaths in recent memory.

In a quintessentially English way, the public processions grew incrementally, without centralized control or top-down orchestration. People assembled along the streets. Bells tolled at the local church, St. Bartholomew's and All Saints, in honor of each procession. In other parts of the England, there were marches, protests, and rallies against the wars and the elected leaders (and unelected bureaucrats) who made the decision to wage them. In Wootton

Bassett, however, there was grief for loved ones lost and many fellow citizens seeking some physical way to show their respect for the heart-rending sacrifices that have been made for them and on their behalf.

As the Wootton Bassett commemorations gained in prominence and become part of the nation's consciousness, increased media coverage has also led to political gestures and attention seekers. In 2009, the leader of the far-right British National Party attended the processions, alongside an assortment of television vans and news reporters. In 2010, an extremist Islamist group in Britain announced publicly its intention to conduct its own march down these streets, carrying empty coffins, to draw attention to the lives of Muslims who have also died as a result of the fighting in Afghanistan. The question of whether a political protest should be conducted on the same streets on which many family members grieve the loss of their loved ones is a difficult one. Despite however objectionable some may find the thought of these protests, the fact that an open and liberal society such as Britain values free speech and public discourse means that space needs to be made for these opposing views to be expressed. The country for which these soldiers died showed its respect for their sacrifices by remembering this fundamental commitment.

More recently, the Christopher Nolan film *Dunkirk* was released around the world to sterling reviews during the summer of 2017. Nolan paints a picture of Britain during the early weeks of World War II that both confirms and challenges present-day notions of Britishness. Although complaints over the absence in the film of Prime Minister Winston Churchill were raised in certain quarters—fans no doubt of the more-obvious-the-better school of film making!—audiences were still drawn to a meticulous portrayal of individual courage and sacrifice on an epic scale.

The lines of Rupert Brooke's 1920 poem "The Soldier," commemorating the sacrifices of his countrymen in World War I, still carries weight to many Englishman today: "If I should die, think only this of me; that there's some corner of a foreign field that is forever England." In Wootton Bassett, perhaps, there is now some corner of England that is forever Basra and Amarah, Kandahar and Helmand.

* * *

As we contemplate the centennial of the "war to end all wars," its repercussions still influence European thinking to this day. Jean-Claude Juncker, former Luxembourg prime minister and currently president of the European Commission, made news in March 2013 when he warned that the rise of nationalism across the continent was threatening peace and stability in much the same way as was originally seen in the years leading to the outbreak of the Great War in 1914. "I am chilled by the realization of how similar circumstances in Europe in 2013 are to those of one hundred years ago," remarked Juncker.

Animosity between European countries about the allocation of blame for the causes and responsibility for the consequences of the global financial crisis stirred up deep-seated resentments. As Greece teetered on the edge of economic oblivion, highly emotive accusations were being angrily lobbed at Germans, who were critical of the role the Greeks allegedly played in their own downfall. Italian elections had also just featured a full portion of German bashing, among other theatrics. With the economic turmoil in Europe the worst in more than sixty years, tempers were frayed on all sides.

Juncker argued that there were many Europeans in 1913 who believed there could never be another war on the continent—surprising, considering the massive loss of life that was only months away. They based this excessively optimistic belief on the false sense of security created by high levels of economic integration across the continent. To these men and women, war was inconceivable. This belief that naked economic self-interest would forever preserve the peace was labeled by Juncker as simply "complacency." He feared his fellow Europeans were not taking the recent upsurge in nationalism seriously for similar reasons.

At its heart, a federal European Union offers the promise of institutions that can defuse tension and avoid the outbreak of war on a continent that has suffered greatly in the past. To see the European Union potentially undermined by in-fighting and bickering was disheartening to its more fervent supporters. Germany has always been at the heart of European integration, both before and after 1951, when the Treaty of Paris was signed, launching what is today the European Union. Interestingly, even many German men and women are now expressing doubts about the euro currency and the mutual benefits of union. Past polls indicate that a quarter of Germans support pulling out of the single currency.

As continued austerity takes a toll on many across Europe and anxiety over Brexit runs high, it is uncomfortable to recall that these same concerns underlined the tense state of affairs that existed in 1914 when Archduke Franz Ferdinand was assassinated. Some will claim that the world is a much different place today than it was then, but it is important to remember that even a place as civilized and prosperous as modern Europe can see the fog of war readily descend. Bosnia and Kosovo are two clear examples of how superficially small conflicts can still lead to large-scale bloodshed and atrocities.

Downgraded to "World War I" after the outbreak of hostilities in Europe again in 1939, the Great War of 1914–1918 is still largely ignored in America. Fair enough, perhaps, since America joined the festivities quite late and, as a result, was spared the jaw-dropping casualties that accrued to all of the other participants. But America's walk-on role in this great calamity has meant that its perspective on subsequent events has always remained slightly out of tune with the perspective of those countries that suffered immensely as a result of the fighting. America prefers Manichean conflicts, where good and evil are clearly on display. In that regard, Americans prefer the sequel, World War II, to the original, in much the same way as the bombastic *Rambo: First Blood Part II* has proven more appealing to moviegoers than the ambivalent morality at the heart of *First Blood*.

The horrors of trench warfare and the sufferings shouldered by enlisted men on the field, as well as their families back at home, set the stage for more social-oriented public policy across Europe in the interwar years, as well as the failures in continental diplomacy that allowed war to break out again in 1939. While Americans enjoyed a straightforward narrative during World War II of the hero riding to the rescue of those in need, as well as an unprecedented economic boom in the years that followed, Europeans saw the return of war through the lens of the tremendous sufferings that were endured only twenty years earlier. When peace came in 1945, instead of an American boom time, Europeans were left with broken economies and the bitter realities of austerity.

When Juncker remarked that "the demons have not gone away—they're only sleeping," he was intentional striking at a nerve that remains raw in the minds of many Europeans to this day. Of course, after the immense violence and bloodshed of the Great War, the demons were awakened again just a few years later. Today, the future stability and security of the European continent is being ensured by both the European Union and NATO, two different organizations with different goals but sharing certain core values and many—but not all!—of the same participants. Should these demons awake again, both alliances will have roles to play in order to resecure the peace.

* * *

The history of Britain and the European Union is a history of missed opportunities. Before Britain succeeded in joining the European Communities in 1973, it faced rejection twice before, each time to French smirks—in 1963 and again in 1967. It took monumental efforts by Conservative prime minister Ted Heath to get Britain accepted into the continental club in 1973, but there remained such domestic resistance to the tie-up, especially on the radical left, that when Harold Wilson won power the following year, his Labour cabinet called for a referendum to give greater domestic legitimacy to Britain's membership. Socialist poster boy Tony Benn's adamant opposition to joining Europe would be echoed forty years later in a somewhat diluted and banal form by Labour leader Jeremy Corbyn's own studied indifference to the Remain campaign.

The 1975 photo of Margaret Thatcher wearing a sweater emblazoned with the flags of the various members of the European Community seems jarring and awkward when viewed today, especially in the aftermath of the 2016 Brexit referendum. In this earlier referendum, two-thirds of Britons voted to remain in an organization that they referred to colloquially as the "common market." Four decades later, after an expanded and empowered European Union had replaced the much more modest goals of a mere continental trading bloc with ever-loftier aspirations, Britons ultimately decided that their future lay elsewhere. Once you had removed the threat of possible Soviet invasions and the ever-present risk of nuclear holocaust, the value of remaining in the European Union had become a decision that in June 2016 voters could make simply on its own merits.

Voting in favor of Europe in 1975 was for many Britons a way of putting two fingers up to the French. In 2016, voting against Europe gave many Britons the chance to spite the French once again. At least the two referenda had that much in common!

No less a British patriot than Winston Churchill once championed a "United States of Europe," but this would necessarily have been a Europe with which Britain could partner—and importantly not a Europe that Churchill felt his country should actually join. To Churchill and Thatcher, the special relationship with the United States would always be paramount. However, for many other British politicians in the postwar era, their country needed a counterweight to prevent their postcolonial country degenerating into a mere vassal state of their American cousins. For them, European engagement and integration were the answer.

The European Union began modestly with the 1951 treaty between France and Germany to establish the Coal and Steel Community, but behind this bureaucratic exercise was a Bonapartesque vision of a reestablishment of the emperor's Continental System. By 1957, the European Economic Community was established by the Treaty of Rome. In between, an initial attempt at postwar European federalism, signed in March 1953, foundered when France's legislature refused to approve it, fearing it went too far. Four years later they took another crack at it, opting then for a watered-down version. The European Union—as it was eventually rebranded after years of geographic and aspirational expansion—was born.

At its founding, the European Union recognized the nation-state as the indispensable building block of its current and future endeavors. After the end of the Cold War, this swiftly changed. The nation-state was shoved aside in favor of a continental superstate. The adoption of the euro, for example, was a significant shift away from democratically elected national governments and a move toward unelected and unaccountable committees.

When the Berlin Wall eventual fell and the Soviet Union disbanded, Brussels declared victory and promptly expanded to include several countries previously in Moscow's orbit. Did the European Union really keep the Soviet Union at bay? Or did perhaps the US military commitment to NATO play some role?

Today the future of the European Union remains in the hands of Europeans. Days before May submitted the Article 50 notice to European Council president Donald Tusk, the remaining twenty-seven members states of the European Union celebrated the sixtieth anniversary of the foundation of the European Union with the Treaty of Rome, which was signed on March 25, 1957. Onward!

Just as Obama was ineffective in influencing the Brexit referendum, Trump will have little impact on where the European

Union goes next. Britain's departure will release the hand brake that has been limiting further European integration for the past two decades. Simply put, a European Union without Britain will be more European. Many Europeans may even eventually come to see Brexit as a positive step. As German chancellor Konrad Adenauer once remarked to French prime minister Guy Mollet during the 1956 Suez Crisis, "Europe will be your revenge." This mantra—which would have rung particularly sweet in the ears of Bonaparte himself—has remained forefront in the minds of the most committed Europhiles for the past sixty years.

A melancholy observation—it is worth remembering that Britain was intentionally excluded from the establishment of the original European Economic Community when it was formed in Rome on March 25, 1957. Instead, Britain would have to wait sixteen years to gain admission to an expanding club. By then, much of the EU's DNA had been set. Perhaps that DNA would have been significantly different if Britain had been on board since day one. Conversely, if Britain had not joined in 1973, it is easily conceivable that it would have developed a positive, mutually beneficial relationship with the European Union that would have been far better than the deal May's government, wounded and staggering from this mistimed June 2017 snap election, eventually strikes during the acrimonious Brexit negotiations.

This divorce has already forced one British prime minister to take the painful drive to Buckingham Palace to tender a resignation. More may well follow before May 2019, but such is the nature of the British constitutional arrangements.

★ ★ ★

In September 2015, Queen Elizabeth became the longest reigning monarch in British history, edging out the previous record holder, Queen Victoria. It took more than 23,000 days on the throne to outlast her great-great-grandmother, and arguments can be made that Elizabeth has witnessed as much—if not more—change in her beloved Britain than Victoria did a century ago.

Officially, Buckingham Palace did little to overtly celebrate the Queen's achievement, although the media refused to let the occurrence go by unremarked. In official bodies such as the House of Commons, time was also set aside to lay down appropriate tributes to her long reign. Then-prime minister David Cameron celebrated her "unerring grace, dignity, and decency." These expressions of thanks and support, however, did not impede her duties, and she was reliably in action on Wednesday—the record-breaking day—opening a new railway in Scotland. "Business as usual" was the Queen's preferred theme for this occasion, rather than indulging in festivities and pageant.

One reason suggested for the lack of public celebrations is that her achievement is an inevitable reminder of the premature death of her own father, King George VI, who passed away at the relatively youthful age of fifty-six. As a result, young Elizabeth was thrust into the spotlight decades before she had any reason to expect to.

Her life unfolded through the key events that have shaped Britain, Europe, and the world. From World War II and its austere aftermath, the loss of Britain's empire, the rise of the Iron Curtain and the fall of the Berlin Wall, joining the nascent European Union and then leaving the Bonapartesque continental system, Queen Elizabeth has had an important role to play in helping steer her country through many rough seas.

During her six decades on the throne, she has been served by a dozen prime ministers of strong opinions and various political stripes. Although she is said to be happiest at her Scottish retreat, Balmoral, she has witnessed increasingly independent thinking in Scotland and Wales, which, with the much larger England, share the small island over which she reigns. Perhaps more easily observed from vantage points outside of Britain, Elizabeth has seen her country exchange military and colonial power for a leading role in the creation of a popular culture juggernaut that has ensured her subjects a recurring place on the global stage.

Although official events commemorating her record-breaking reign were limited and restrained, the creative juices of many Britons were stirred up by the Queen's record-breaking reign. One artist made a portrait of her out of 1,952 pennies—a reference to the year she first ascended to the throne. Another artist used several hundred coffee cups to construct a unique rendition of her. Even famous street artist Pegasus joined in the fun, with a classic pin-up representation of a young and vivacious Elizabeth, which borders on the tasteless but still seems to be enthusiastically patriotic and even curiously supportive of the royal institution that the Queen has served so many years.

Of course, there are always naysayers who champion the deeper and more authentic values of republics. These men and women relish any good opportunity to voice their displeasure in the overt and covert messages sent by hereditary monarchies. And the usual suspects were out and about making their case again to a British public that seems largely indifferent to their claims. To these erstwhile republicans, the Queen is a representation of privilege who—despite whatever positive traits she possesses—has watched her country become less egalitarian. In essence, she has served as a cloak behind which archaic British institutions and practices have been allowed to survive long past their sell-by date.

The answer for these antimonarchists is simple—do away with the monarchy and make way for the British republic that would take its place as liberal, progressive, and most likely neo-socialist utopia.

However, this vision fails to resonate with many Britons for two key reasons. First, a quick survey reveals that the most generous social safety nets are provided by such fellow constitutional monarchies as Sweden, Norway, and the Netherlands. Second, Britain is fundamentally a conservative country, both in actions and in thoughts. Of her seven decades in office, almost two-thirds of those years have seen Tory governments in place at 10 Downing

Street rather than Labour governments. The resounding 2015 parliamentary victory by Cameron displayed once again that pundits and columnists discount the conservative sentiments of Britons at their peril. Even as Cameron whistled his way into the sunset after the unforeseen failure of his Remain camp to win the Brexit referendum, the Queen enjoyed the second female prime minister of her reign, Theresa May.

Regardless of partisan political squabbles and ideological bunfights, regardless of how the minutiae of Brexit is negotiated and implemented over the next few years, Queen Elizabeth has demonstrated the no-fuss, get-on-with-work attitude that has endeared her to so many for so long. The Royal Family and their standing abroad will be crucial to the many bilateral negotiations that will follow Britain's tumultuous withdrawal from the European Union. As a source of soft power that can be used to help the British government achieve its political aims, the Royal Family is indeed a national resource of significant value. Since Queen Elizabeth no longer travels abroad, it now falls on Prince Charles and his children and grandchildren to fly the flag abroad in the years ahead. She must be content for now to be the symbol of her country in moments of great celebration—such as the 2012 Summer Olympics Games—and in moments of great despair—such as the Grenfell Tower fire in west London in June 2017, when a blaze overcame a 24-story public-housing towerblock and an entire nation witnessed scenes of lives needlessly lost in front of their own eyes.

Perhaps part of Brexit was simply to let Britain be Britain, and hopefully the best Britain that it can be. A noble goal in many respects. Britain works as a country, perhaps as much by accident as design. Central to the country's new journey will be more than a millennium of British history and British values, both of which no doubt remain close to the Queen's very British heart to this very day.

Index

Index

Index

secularism in, 194–195
soccer scandal, xvi–xviii
strikes (October, 2010), 3–5
terrorism in, 217
Toulouse terror attacks (2012),
9–12
and Turkish–Russian relations,
179
Francis, Pope, 91
Franz Ferdinand, Archduke of
Austria, 58, 238
Free Syrian Army, 107
French National Assembly, 191
French Suicide, The, 88

G

Gaddafi, Muammar, 129
Gagrin, Yuri, 122
Galletti, Gina Luca, 190
Garcia, Michael, xiv
Gates, Robert, 231
Gay rights, 174–176
George VI, king of England, 243
Germany. *See also* Merkel, Angela,
and administration
anti-immigration sentiment,
87–89, 157–158
bond ratings, 37
and Brexit negotiations, 219
debate on immigration and
social safety net, 146
and EU debt crisis, 38
and French 2012 presidential
election, 62
and Greek debt crisis, 35, 65
immigration and crime, 158–160
immigration crisis, 95–97
labor market, 156
Look Who's Back, 157
opposition to Merkel's
migration policies, 96
and origins of EU, 238
origins of Merkel's migration
policies, 156

sexual assaults by migrants,
162–163
and soccer, xiii
and Ukraine, 119
Gibraltar, 219
Global financial crisis (2008), xxv
and 2015 EU elections, 167
Britain and, 15–18, 28
and intra-EU resentments, 237
Globalization, 189, 206
Golodets, Olga, 176
Gorbachev, Mikhail, 51, 116, 144
Gove, Michael, 203–204
Grain exports, 117
Grande, Ariana, 218
Gravoin, Anne, 187
Greece
debt crisis (2010), 32, 34–36,
65, 237
Kos migrant camps, 93
as part of migrants' land route,
96
refugees in, 164
Grosvenor Square, London,
227–229
Gypsies (Roma), 5–6, 130–132

H

Hague, William, 228
Hamburg, Germany, 159
"Hard" Brexit, 211–212
Harvard University, 77
Heath, Ted, 143, 240
Hénin-Beaumont, France, 66
Henry VIII, king of England, 210
Hitler, Adolf, 157
Hollande, François
anti-terrorism initiatives,
195–197
and antimigrant movements in
France, 89
approval ratings, 127
and austerity, 69–70
beginning of presidency, 68

Index

Index

Union of European Football
Associations (UEFA)
championships, xx–xxii
United Nations, 119, 163
United Russia Party, 50
United States
balancing of British and EU
interests, 232
British investment relations
with, 210
class in, 22
and Crimean crisis, 56
and exceptionalism, 234
and federalism, 32
immigration debate, 2
and Kurds, 110–111
national character, 16–17
political discourse in, 67
and post-WWII Europe,
229–230
2008 presidential election,
173
2016 presidential election, viii,
24, 90
race in, xvi
religion in public sphere, 194
and Russian Arctic seabed
claims, 170
social class in, 24
space exploration, 121–122
"special relationship" with
Britain, 230, 232, 240
and Ukraine, 119
views of British class system,
76–77
and WWI, 238–239
United States Institute of Peace, 39

V
Valls, Manuel
"Français de souche"
controversy, 187
labor reforms, 197–199

Jean-Marie Le Pen's comments
on, 188
and Roma, 131–132
Values, European, 101, 221
Veils, 7–9
Victoria, queen of England, 242–243
Vodka, 116

W
Wages, migrants' influence, 44,
215–216
War memorials, 235–237
War on Terror, 53, 197
Warsaw Pact, 56
Waterloo, Battle of, vii, 13, 191
We Are Stockholm festival, 161
Wealth, British class system and, 23
Welfare, 216
Wellesley, Arthur, first Duke of
Wellington, vii, 227
West Bromwich Albion, 135–136
Westminster School, 76
WikiLeaks, xv
Wilders, Geert, 43, 133, 216
Wilson, Harold, 240
Woolfe, Steven, 208
World Cup, xii, xv, xx, 48, 57, 180
World Economic Forum, 40
World Trade Organization, 210
World War I
Britain and, 236–237
Europe and, 233–234, 237–239
US and, 238–239
World War II, 157, 227, 229–230, 239

Y
Yanukovych, Viktor, 115, 120
Yiannopoulos, Milo, 4
Youth crime, British, 19–21
YouTube, 173

Z
Zoopla, 136

From the
American Bar Association

ABA Publishing

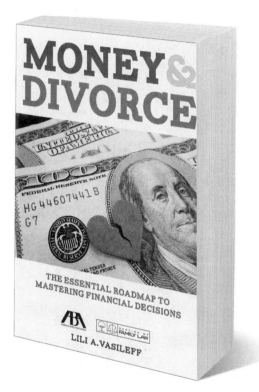

Money and Divorce:
The Essential Roadmap to
Mastering Financial Decisions

Lili A. Vasileff

To order 🌐 visit **www.ShopABA.org**
or call 📞 **(800) 285-2221.**

From the
American Bar Association

 ABA Publishing

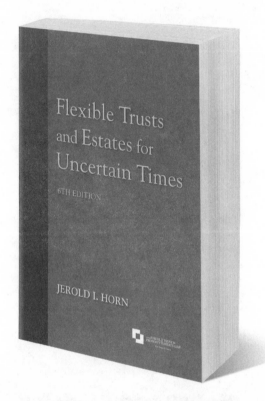

Flexible Trusts and Estates for Uncertain Times, 6th Edition
Jerold I. Horn

To order 🌐 visit **www.ShopABA.org**
or call 📞 **(800) 285-2221.**

From the
American Bar Association

 ABA Publishing

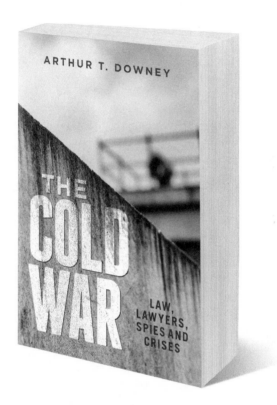

The Cold War:
Law, Lawyers, Spies and Crises
Arthur T. Downey

To order 🌐 visit **www.ShopABA.org**
or call 📞 **(800) 285-2221.**

From the Solo, Small Firm and General Practice Division

ABA GPSOLO
Solo, Small Firm and General Practice Division
YOUR SUCCESS, OUR MISSION™

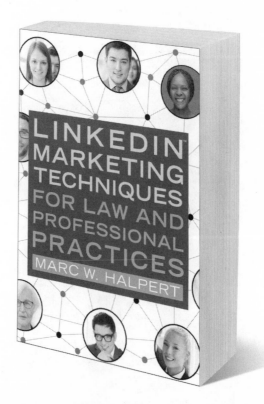

LinkedIn™ Marketing Techniques for Law and Professional Practices
Marc W. Halpert

To order 🌐 visit www.ShopABA.org
or call 📞 (800) 285-2221.

AMERICAN BAR ASSOCIATION
ABA Publishing